Roland® VS Recorder®

P O W E R !

THE COMPREHENSIVE GUIDE

Chris Skelnik, Vince Gibbs, and Karl Frick

THOMSON

™

COURSE TECHNOLOGY

Professional ■ Technical ■ Reference

ISBN: 1-59200-836-4

Library of Congress Catalog Card Number: 2005924927

Printed in Canada

05 06 07 08 09 WC 10 9 8 7 6 5 4 3 2 1

Professional ■ Technical ■ Reference

Thomson Course Technology PTR, a division of Thomson Course Technology
25 Thomson Place
Boston, MA 02210
http://www.courseptr.com

Publisher and General Manager, Thomson Course Technology PTR:
Stacy L. Hiquet

Associate Director of Marketing:
Sarah O'Donnell

Manager of Editorial Services:
Heather Talbot

Marketing Manager:
Kristin Eisenzopf

Senior Editor and Acquisitions Editor:
Mark Garvey

Marketing Coordinator:
Jordan Casey

Developmental Editor:
Orren Merton

Project Editors:
Rodney Wilson and Brian Proffitt

Technical Reviewer:
Michael Barrett, Roland US

Thomson Course Technology PTR Editorial Services Coordinator:
Elizabeth Furbish

Copyeditor:
Rodney Wilson

Interior Layout Tech:
Digital Publishing Solutions

Cover Designer:
Mike Tanamachi and Nancy Goulet

Indexer:
Sharon Shock

Proofreader:
Gene Redding

Chris Skelnik: "To my wife, Cristine, who completes me, and to my two little angels, Cora Beth and Catherine, who sustain me. You are a blessing from Him, and I cherish your love, support, and patience when I throw myself into a project such as this one."

Vince Gibbs: "To my parents, Theodore and Willia Gibbs, for putting up with all the noise I made in the basement while I was discovering the art of making music in the 70s. You all never complained and always encouraged me to be the best I could be. Because of you, I am who I am today. Thank you for nurturing me, loving me and allowing me to be me."

Karl Frick: "To my honey, Dot, without whose encouragement I would not have had the opportunity to get to know the VS-2480, and to our children, Brian, Shane, and Kelsey, whose dad spends way too much time in the studio."

Foreword

It's a great time to be a musician. The Internet has opened up new and exciting ways to market all kinds of music. You no longer have to be signed to a "major label" to have some good options for letting people hear your music and even for selling your songs.

But more importantly, very high-quality tools for recording, mixing and mastering all of this music have become incredibly affordable. It really wasn't that long ago that it could easily cost $10,000 *per song* to get professional recordings of a band. And when you were in the studio, the pressure was on... not exactly the easiest atmosphere for artistic exploration. Today you can spend a fraction of that and have what you need to make high-quality recordings of as many songs as your creativity and time will allow!

The VS recorder series was one of the first, and it was certainly the most successful, pioneers of this new wave of affordable, high quality workstations. With hundreds of thousands of units sold, the VS series is arguably one of the primary forces in giving musicians a way to take their music as far as they can. From award-winning records done all or in part on a VS, to (no doubt sometimes great, sometimes painful) family Christmas CDs, the VS series has been used by many musicians and artists to bring their creativity to fruition.

All along its path of development, much thought and many engineering resources have been brought to bear for the VS, so that it could have new and innovative ways to help this creative process. The VS-880, in its seminal form, had many brand new, ground-breaking features designed to help musicians make better-sounding music. A great example of Roland's innovation for the 880 is virtual tracks. Although the VS-880 only had 8 primary playback tracks, the addition of Virtual Tracks greatly expanded the choices that songwriters had at their disposal. In traditional studios, many tracks were often used to record multiple takes of an important lead vocal or guitar solo. Using Virtual Tracks, VS users could also have access to many different choices in their search for the "best of the best" takes, but in an affordable format. Who knew whether the guitarist was a "one beer" or "three beer" player? Instead of throwing away early takes, part or all of which might turn out to be the best ones for the song, the VS owner could store them all on Virtual Tracks, and then later decide what to use, with lots of choices. This was impossible to do with traditional 8 or even higher count tape-based recorders. Virtual Tracks greatly increased the VS-880 owner's ability to experiment.

Another enabling benefit of Virtual Tracks was storage of the sources for bounced tracks. How often did even large studios bounce their drum parts to free up tracks only to find out later that the snare level wasn't quite right once they began mixing the whole song? With the VS's Virtual

Tracks, the original tracks could be recalled and re-bounced easily; and the song's mix would end up much better for it. Or guitarists could store their "dry" guitar part on a V Track in case during mixdown it became evident that a different processed sound would be better for the song.

The VS studio was also designed to include lots of effects processing. The idea behind this was that implementing effects, especially for the less technical musician, was one of the more difficult parts of the recording and mixing process. Not only were external effects processors expensive, but they were also fraught with potential difficulties, including possible ground-hums, and cabling and routing problems. In addition, the VS development team knew that many VS users were musicians who only had a limited amount of time to spend making their music. If the VS could instantly recreate the last state of their song, including the effects, this would greatly increase the amount of time available to users for actually "making music," as opposed to tracking down the processor that had been moved to the closet, to say nothing of hunting down the cables.

The Scenes feature is another tool that the VS development team spent a lot of resources developing. Another industry "first" for the VS series, Scenes are probably one of the most useful features of the VS series. They are a great learning tool, and are great for enhancing your creativity. How many times have musicians and producers, sitting at a traditional console, given up on what might have been a great direction for a song, because they didn't dare risk losing their current mixer settings? Scenes, at a touch of one button, by storing all of the mixer, FX, and Virtual Tracks settings, allow musicians and producers to quickly and easily try many different ideas. From a new approach to vocal FX, to differing amounts of drum processing, to comparing song arrangements, Scenes make it very easy to store and compare mixing and processing approaches. What a great way to learn! Not sure about how much reverb to use on the snare? Do several mixes with varying amounts, store the new versions as Scenes, and then compare them quickly and easily. Scenes are also useful for improving your bounces. If that drum submix isn't right, recall the stored scene from the bouncing process, push the snare level up a bit and hit record. Another Scene button press will put the newly bounced track right where it needs to be, so you can immediately continue the mixing process.

Roland also pioneered 999 levels of undo stored with the song. This "no fault" capability of the VS-880 was a real anxiety remover! Users could try different versions of their song, maybe by doubling the chorus or shortening the intro, without fear of erasing or destroying any tracks. More than any feature, the stored Undos helped VS owners proceed with abandon, trying anything they could imagine, knowing that they wouldn't ever cause any permanent damage to their tracks. This is a very enabling feature of the VS!

Virtual tracks, built-in FX, Scenes: All of these powerful features were developed for the first time by Roland for the VS series. This is an incredible legacy. The VS series was also the first affordable digital workstation to have a built-in CD burner, Mastering Tools, VGA output, mouse-based graphical editing, and a well-supported third-party plug-in program. This plug-in program is very important for the VS series, supports even the legacy VS products back to the VS-1680, and bring to VS owners the rich resources of third party processing algorithms from Antares Auto-tune© to Universal Audio's vintage dynamics processors to IK Multimedia's T-RackS vintage mastering suite.

The book you hold in your hands can aid you in opening the doors to your VS workstation's great features. It can help you find, and encourage you to explore, the many diverse VS features that have been designed to enhance your music-making experience. The VS series offers many different ways to process, edit, automate, mix and master your music. The better you understand all of your VS's features, the more options you will have to experiment with, and the more tools you'll have on hand to help you to improve the sound and quality of your music. Read, enjoy, and experiment with your VS. Only the sky and your creativity are the limits!

Tom Stephenson
Manager of Recording and Mixing Technology
Roland

} Acknowledgments

Chris acknowledges and thanks: Paul Olito, for his friendship, guidance, and encouragement; the management and members of VS-Planet, past and present, from whom I have learned more than I could ever share; Tim, Kirk, and Ray, whom I consider true friends and comrades in the VS; Mighty Joe, KJ, Greg, John, and Casey, for letting me experiment on you; to my father-in-law, Dan, for your insight and daily encouragement; and to my big brother, Phig, and to my little brother, Danny P, I love you guys! Finally, to my mother, Judy: without your wisdom, knowledge, care and love, I never would have become the person I am today. I love you more than you can imagine.

Vince would like to acknowledge all his friends at VS Planet, but especially the ones in the 1680 forum who have helped him learn the nuts and bolts of the machine. A special acknowledgement goes out to Paul Olito (Walrus44), Tom Duval (flatcat), Michael Megadanz (Darth VSer) and Andy McClellan (Silversmith) from VS Planet for their wonderful support and friendship at VS Planet over the years.

Karl would like to acknowledge Ritchie DeCarlo for introducing him to the VS-2480, and also give a tip of the old fedora to the various bands and local singers who have allowed me to hone my skills with their fine music. A special nod goes out to Jack Murray, my Lodge Brother, for sharing his consistently refreshing view of music, recording, and the world in general.

Collectively, the authors wish to thank: Orren, Rodney, Mark, and the rest of the Thomson Course Technology publishing team for seeing this project to fruition; Tom, Laura, Dan, Michael, Kellie, Stacy, and the rest of the team at Roland US for your help, guidance, and support.

About the Authors

Chris "Hook" Skelnik has been playing drums for over 20 years. He has played hundreds of live gigs throughout the Midwest, and his drumming can be heard on various independent releases. He has been a Roland VS user since 1999, and uses various VS workstations at C4 Studios, his small project studio, specializing in solo artists, small band projects, and on-location recording. Skelnik is also an administrator and moderator for VSPlanet.com, the world's largest online community for VS users. He has written various technical documents and FAQs related to the VS workstations, and is the Editor of the VSPlanet Newsletter.

Vince Gibbs has been a home recording enthusiast since purchasing his first multi-track recorder in 1983. He has developed training curricula for such companies as DirecTV, Cricket Wireless, and AOL to name a few. He has performed throughout Asia with top-40 bands as a singer, drummer, and bass player and has released his own independent CDs. Gibbs' passion is music, home recording and getting the best out of the gear he owns. He can also be found helping VS users at VSPlanet, the largest online community of VS users.

Karl Frick has been an electronics aficionado since the early 1960s, and has been a part-time working musician since 1970. He started tinkering with multi-track recording in 1974, bouncing tracks back and forth between two stereo reel-to-reel decks. He worked as a musician, engineer, and equipment technician at a 24-track facility from 1978 to 1984. During a stint as a design engineer, Frick was awarded a patent for an electronic bell-playing system that was installed in dozens of churches and other facilities worldwide from 1988 to 1995. He loves to play bass guitar and Hammond organ, and has performed in bands that have opened for such diverse artists as B.B. King, John Hammond, and America.

TABLE OF } Contents

CHAPTER 1   **History of the VS Workstations** 1

1996: The VS-880 1
   Highlights of the VS-880 1
   Software Upgrades 2

1998: The VS-1680 3
   Highlights of the VS-1680 3
   Software Upgrades 4

1999: The VS-880EX 4
   Highlights of the VS-880EX 5
   Software Upgrades 5

1999: The VSR-880 6
   Highlights of the VSR-880 6
   Software Upgrades 6

2000: The VS-1880 7
   Highlights of the VS-1880 7
   Software Upgrades 7

2000: The VS-890 8
   Highlights of the VS-890 8
   Software Upgrades 9

2001: The VS-2480 9
   Highlights of the VS-2480 10
   Software Upgrades 10

2002: The VS-1824CD 10
   Highlights of the VS-1824CD 10
   Software Upgrades 11

2002: The VS-2480CD 11

Highlights of the VS-2480CD 11

Software Upgrades 11

2003: The VS-2400CD 12

Highlights of the VS-2400CD 12

Software Upgrades 13

2004: The VS-2000CD 13

Highlights of the VS-2000CD 14

Software Upgrades 15

2004: The VS-2480DVD 15

Highlights of the VS-2480DVD 15

Software Upgrades 15

CHAPTER 2   Overview of the VS Workstation Architecture 17

Input/Output 18

Analog Connections 18

Digital Connections 18

Peripheral Connections 19

Mixing Console 19

Channel Strips 19

Transport Controls 19

Display Screen 19

Time/Value Dial 20

Dedicated Function Buttons 20

Internal Effects 20

Hard Disk Recorder 22

Disk Partitioning 22

Recording Time 23

Recording Modes 23

Sample Rates 25

Common Concepts 25

Mixer Modes 25

The Input Mixer 26

The Track Mixer 27

The Effects Return Mixer 27

Routing 28

Virtual Tracks 29

Editing 31

Copy 31

Move 31

Erase 31

Cut 31

Insert 32

Compression/Expansion 32

Using Internal Effects 32

Algorithms and Effect Blocks 32

Types of Effects 32

Scenes, Locators, and Markers 34

Automix 35

CHAPTER 3   **Introduction to the VS-880/890 Series** 37

Connecting Your Inputs and Outputs 39

Analog Inputs 39

Analog Outputs 39

Digital Inputs 40

Digital Outputs 40

SCSI Port 40

MIDI Connections 41

Front Panel Layout 41

Mixer Section 42

Recorder Section 42

Display Section 44

Mixer Modes Redux 48

A Few Important Tips 49

Re-Initializing the Hard Drive 49

Splitting and Merging Songs 49

Transferring Individual Tracks to a Computer 50

Backups Are in a Proprietary Format 50

Save, Save, Save 50

Rome Wasn't Built in a Day 50

CHAPTER 4 **Basic Recording on the VS-880/890 Series** 51

Creating a New Song 51

Naming the Song 52

3-Band EQ 52

Routing Your Inputs to Recording Tracks 53

    The Input Mixer 53

    The Concept of Routing 54

    The Routing Display 54

    Creating Your Routings 57

    Routing Stereo Tracks 58

Setting Input Levels 62

Recording the Tracks 62

Advanced Recording on the VS-880/890 Series 62

    Overdubbing Tracks 62

    Punch-In Recording 63

    Track Sheets 64

Exploiting V-Tracks 65

Recording Dry, Listening Wet 66

Recording Wet 67

Additional Recording Topics for the VS-880/890 Series ...68

    Song Templates 68

    EZ Routing 69

    STATUS Button Indicators 70

    Recording from the Digital Inputs 70

    Using the Internal Compressor Effect While Recording ...71

CHAPTER 5   **Editing on the VS-880/890 Series** 73

Locators 73

Markers 74

Editing Tracks 75

     Setting Your Edit Location Points 76

     Selecting the V-Tracks to Edit 77

     The Track-Editing Functions 78

Undo 83

Song Optimize 84

CHAPTER 6   **Mixing on the VS-880/890 Series** 85

Planning Your Mixing Strategy 85

Track Parameters 87

Scenes 88

Automix 89

     Enabling Automix 91

     Realtime Automix 91

     Snapshot Automix 93

     Gradation 94

     Automix Considerations 95

Bouncing Tracks 96

     Mono and Stereo Bouncing 96

     Creating Your Routings 97

     Previewing the Bounce 99

     Performing the Bounce 99

     Bouncing Using the Internal Effects 101

     Bouncing Using External Effects 105

Putting It All Together 106

     Step 1–Bounce the Drum Tracks with Effects 107

     Step 2–Bounce the Rhythm Tracks with Effects 107

     Step 3–Perform Final Bounce with Automix 108

CHAPTER 7   **Finishing Your Project on the VS-880/890 Series** 111

Mastering Your Song 111

    Using Internal Effects 111

    Using the Mastering Tool Kit 112

    Mixing to an External Source 113

Burning Your Song to a CD via the SCSI Burner 114

    SCSI CD Burner Limitations 114

    Preparing to Burn 115

    Performing the Burn to CD 117

Backing Up Songs to CD 118

Recovering Songs from CD 120

Updating Your Operating System 121

Interfacing the VS Workstation with a Computer 122

    Analog and Digital Transfers 122

    SCSI Transfers 123

Syncing Multiple VS Workstations 124

Miscellaneous Utilities, Functions, and Parameters 124

    Drive Check 124

    System-Level Parameters 125

    Mute and Solo 125

    Vari Pitch 125

CHAPTER 8   **Introduction to the VS-1680/1880 Series** 127

Larger LCD for Easier Viewing 127

Recording Modes 128

Two Fully Independent Mixers 129

    Input Mixer 130

    Track Mixer 130

    Master Block 131

Ten Inputs 133

Two Effects Cards at Once 133

Phantom Power 134

Markers and Locators 134

Undo and Redo 135

Dedicated Mastering Room 136

Differences Between the VS-1680, VS-1880, and VS-1824 137

    VS-1880 Upgrades 137

    VS-1824 Upgrades 139

CHAPTER 9   **Advances in Recording with the VS-1680/1880** 141

Creating a New Song 141

Setting Up a Track for Recording 142

Setting the Recording Level 142

Recording a Vocal Track 144

    Using an External Preamp 144

    Using an External A/D (Analog to Digital) Converter 144

Compressing a Track While Recording 146

Adding Effects to a Track During Playback 147

Using Virtual Tracks 148

Using the Digital Inputs to Record a Track 148

Punch In/Out 150

    Manual Punch 150

    Auto Punch 152

Bouncing 153

Recording with MIDI 154

    Recording a MIDI Drum Track 155

    Recording with a Sequencer 156

Song Templates 157

CHAPTER 10   **Advances in Editing with the VS-1680/1880** 159

Track Editing Versus Phrase Editing 159

Basic Steps for Track Editing 161

    Setting the Edit Points 162

    Perform the Steps for the Desired Track Edit Function 162

Creating a Seamless Loop Using Track Copy 163

Phrase Editing Features 165

Selecting the Phrase for Editing 165

Song Editing 167

    Song Arrange 167

    Song Split 169

    Song Combine 171

CHAPTER 11   **Advances in Mixing with the VS-1680/1880** 175

Channel Edit Screen 176

Channel Link 177

    Unlinking the Defaulted Linked Channels 177

    Adjusting the Volume Levels of Linked Channels 178

    Adjusting the Panning of Linked Channels 179

Attenuation 180

Phase 180

Grouped Faders 181

Signal Buses 181

    Recording Bus 181

    Mix Bus 181

    Effects Bus 181

    Aux Bus 181

Mixing with Effects 182

    Assigning a Loop Effect 183

    Assigning an Insert Effect 183

User Effects 185

    Creating a User Effect 185

    Saving a User Effect 185

Important Reminders About Using Effects 186

Using EQ 186

Scenes 188

    Saving a Mixer Scene 188

Recalling a Mixer Scene 188

Deleting a Mixer Scene 188

Updating a Mixer Scene 188

Vari Pitch 189

Automix 189

Adjusting the Automix Display 191

Realtime 192

Snapshot 193

Gradation 195

Micro Edit 197

Adding an External Mixer 198

Initializing the Mixer Settings 199

CHAPTER 12   Advances in Mastering with the VS-1680/1880 201

Mastering Room 202

Mixing Down to the Master Tracks 202

Playing Back the Master Tracks 203

Understanding the MTK 204

Tone-Shaping Processors 204

Dynamic Processors 205

Mixing Down with the MTK 206

Getting the Best from the MTK Presets 208

Recording Your Mastered Tracks 209

CHAPTER 13   Roland VS-2480 211

Hooking Up 211

ANALOG I/O 211

DIGITAL I/O 212

Other Connections 214

Inside the Box 214

Sixteen Faders in Four Groups 214

Input Channels 215

Track Channels 215

AUX MSTR Channels 215

FX RTN Channels 215

Routing 215

Patch Bay 215

Track Assign 216

Output Assign 217

Loop Effects Assignment 217

FKey Options 218

Making Connections 218

Tracks, V-Tracks, and Master Tracks 219

CHAPTER 14   The Channel Strip 221

Changing Data 221

With the Mouse 221

With the Cursor Buttons and Time/Value Dial 222

Track Selection and Control 223

Patch Bay (Input Mixer Channels Only) 223

Phantom Power (Analog Input Channels 1–8 Only) 223

Status (Track Mixer Channels Only) 223

V-Track (Track Mixer Channels Only) 223

Phase 223

Channel Group 223

Channel Link and Fader Link 223

Phrase Pads 224

Dynamics 224

Compression 224

Expander 225

Combined Compressor and Expander 225

Dynamics Key Source 226

Dynamics Metering 226

Effects Inserts 226

Attenuator 226

EQ 227

    Filter 227

    4-Band EQ 229

    EQ with Your Mouse 229

AUX Sends and DIR Assignments 229

    Mono versus Linked AUX Operation 229

    PRE/POST Sends 229

    DIR Sends 229

Mix, Mute, and Solo Buttons 230

CHAPTER 15   **Project Basics** **231**

Project Management 231

    The Project List Dialog 231

    Creating a New Project 232

    Saving and Protecting Projects 233

    Copying and Backing Up Projects 233

    Sharing Data 234

Moving Around Within Your Project 234

    Cursor Buttons and Time/Value Dial 234

    Shuttle Ring 236

    Previous and Next 236

    Locators 236

    Markers 237

    Jump Button 237

Viewing Your Project 237

    Home Screen View 238

    Mixer Views 241

CHAPTER 16   **Tracking** **243**

Input Monitoring 243

Input Mixer Monitoring 244

Recording Dry 244

Recording with Effects 244

Have It Both Ways 245

Recording FX Separately 247

Name Your Tracks 247

CHAPTER 17   Track Editing **249**

Phrases and Regions 249

    Regions 249

    Phrases 249

    Phrase Parameter Editing 249

    Take Manager 251

    Moving Regions and Phrases 251

Nondestructive Editing and Pointer-Based Playback 252

    Phrase Trim Demo 253

Setting Edit Points 257

    The Preview Controls 257

    .WAV View 257

    Working with Measures and the Grid 258

CHAPTER 18   Mixes, Scenes, and Automix **261**

Record Monitor Selection 261

Submixes 261

    Submixes on the AUX Busses 262

    Submixes via Routing 262

    Submixes via Mastering 263

Using Printed Effects 264

Linked Track Tricks 265

Using Scenes 267

Automix 269

    Automix Controls and Setup 269

    Viewing Automix Data 270

Automix Record Mode 271

Automix Snapshots 271

Automix After Punch Out Operation 272

Automix Editing 273

Automix Edit Target Section 277

Automix Pattern Save and Load 278

Automix Micro Edit 278

Using Scenes and Automix Together 280

Individual Track Adjustments 280

EQ Before Dynamics 280

Kicking a Hole in the Bass 282

Adding External Sources at Mix Time 283

CHAPTER 19   Tempo Map, Metronome, Sync, and MIDI 285

Metronome 285

Printing the Metronome 288

Tempo Map 288

Implementing Gradual Tempo Changes 290

Synchronization 292

Recording a Sync Track from an External Source 293

Creating a Sync Track from Time Points 294

Creating a Tempo Map from Tap Points 295

MIDI 295

SETUP 295

SysEx. (System Exclusive) 296

MMC (MIDI Machine Code) 296

BlkDmp (Bulk Dump) 296

APPENDIX   The VS-2000CD Workstation 299

INDEX 307

Introduction

In 1996, Roland introduced the VS-880 Digital Studio Workstation. The VS-880 brought together all the tools needed to make a finished song in a small form-factor at a very inexpensive price. The VS-880 combined digital recording, digital mixing, effects processing, and mastering—putting all the power of a recording studio in a small, powerful, and portable box. This new digital recording machine had many advantages over the tape-based recording systems, including the ability to store and recall settings, recording in a non-linear fashion, non-destructive editing and bouncing of tracks, and the concept of virtual tracks.

Suddenly, musicians could record what they wanted, when they wanted, and how they wanted, without spending a small fortune or having to leave the comforts of their own home. Soon home recording hobbyists and even commercial studios were harnessing the power and flexibility of the Roland V-Studios. Within three short years, Roland had sold over 100,000 VS-880 workstations. The digital revolution had begun.

Since 1996, Roland continued to improve the V-Studios, adding more features and functions in each subsequent model. Today the flagship VS-2480 workstation can be found in professional recording studios across the world. Given the power and performance of the VS-2480, you may be wondering why we've chosen to include the older VS workstations in this book. The reality is there are thousands of musicians around the globe who are using these older workstations with much success. And, with the advent of online auction services such as eBay, older VS workstations can be purchased for a few hundred dollars, bringing the power of digital recording to a whole new group of consumers. The revolution continues.

In the chapters that follow, we'll take a look at the history of the VS series, from the revolutionary VS-880 to Roland's flagship VS-2480, highlighting the features of each VS model. Regardless of which VS model you use, they all share some things in common, so we'll explore the functions, features, and methodologies that are consistent across the VS product line. Finally, we'll take a more in-depth look at the VS-880/890 series, the VS-1680/1880 series, and the VS-2400/2480 series, providing details on recording, editing, and mixing on each series. Along the way, we'll also provide tips, tricks, and techniques to help you get the most out of your VS recorder.

History of the VS Workstations

In 1996, the VS-880 brought the power of a recording studio to the masses. Since then, Roland has continued to be the leader in powerful, portable, and affordable digital workstations. Let's take a look back at the last 10 years and see how the VS workstations have evolved.

1996: The VS-880

In January 1996, Roland introduced its breakthrough VS-880 Digital Studio Workstation, shown in Figure 1.1. Digital recorders had existed since the 1980s, and the first half of the '90s gave birth to digital tape-based systems like the ADAT and DA-88. Roland's VS-880 provided an affordable, all-in-one recording device, the likes of which had never been seen before.

Highlights of the VS-880

Since the VS-880 really was revolutionary, all of its features could not be listed here. When comparing it to other affordable recording solutions available at the time, the following items stand out as things that made the VS-880 unique.

* Non-linear digital recording
* Non-destructive digital editing
* Eight 'Virtual Tracks' per physical track
* Four simultaneous recording tracks, eight simultaneous playback tracks
* Mixer snapshots via scenes
* Internal hard drive
* Optional effect processor board
* Familiar tape-based Transport Control (FF, RW, Play, Stop, Record)
* 18-bit A/D and D/A converters

Figure 1.1
Roland VS-880 Digital
Studio Workstation.

> ※ **ALL THAT JAZ**
>
> The VS-880 was sold as three different models: the VS-880 (without an internal hard drive), the VS-880-HD (with an internal 540MB hard drive), and the VS-880-J (with an internal 1GB Iomega Jaz drive). Although the Jaz drive received accolades when it first appeared, VS-880 users began encountering problems with the Jaz drive and its cartridges. Roland discontinued the VS-880-J model in late 1996, but offered existing VS-880-J customers the option to replace the Jaz drive with an internal 1GB hard drive.

Software Upgrades

In 1997, Roland introduced a major software upgrade for the VS-880. This upgrade turned an existing VS-880 into a VS-880 V-Xpanded unit. Roland also began shipping VS-880 workstations labeled as V-Xpanded units. The V-Xpanded upgrade offered a number of new features to the base VS-880, including:

※ Increased number of playback tracks in linear mode (from 4 to 6)

※ Onboard Automix function

❅ Ability to change Scene and Effects settings via MIDI

❅ Ten new effect algorithms with 100 additional presets

In 1998, Roland provided another major software upgrade for the VS-880, dubbed the S2 upgrade. This new software allowed users to create audio CDs via an external SCSI CD writer. With the S2 upgrade, the VS-880 became a truly self-contained production recording system, allowing users to record, mix, master, and now create CDs.

1998: The VS-1680

In January of 1998, Roland announced the VS-1680, a 16-track Digital Studio Workstation, shown in Figure 1.2. The VS-1680 was a new generation of VS workstation, providing many new features and overcoming some of the limitations of the original VS-880.

Figure 1.2
Roland VS-1680 Digital
Studio Workstation.

Highlights of the VS-1680

The VS-1680 offered 16 tracks of 24-bit audio, which was a major improvement over the VS-880. The VS-1680 also shipped with two important features: an internal 2.5GB hard drive and one of the new 24-bit VS8F-2 effect expansion boards already installed (with the option of installing a second effect board). Other highlights of the VS-1680 included:

❅ Eight simultaneous recording tracks, 16 simultaneous playback tracks

❅ Sixteen virtual tracks per physical track

❅ EZ-Routing templates

❅ Two balanced XLR inputs

❅ Dedicated Hi-Z guitar input

* Phantom power
* Dedicated display navigation buttons
* Hard drive usability: 8 partitions, 2GB per partition
* 20-bit A/D and D/A converters

Software Upgrades

In 1999, Roland introduced the V-Xpanded software upgrade for the VS-1680. The biggest feature in this V-Xpanded upgrade was the ability to do 18-track playback. This feature meant that users could now mix down all 16 tracks to two additional tracks for mastering—a feature not found on any previous VS workstation. This upgrade also included Roland's new Mastering Tool Kit effects algorithm, as well as new COSM Speaker Modeling for use with Roland's new DS-90 powered monitors.

1999: The VS-880EX

A few months after the announcement of the VS-1680, Roland announced the VS-880EX Digital Studio Workstation, shown in Figure 1.3. The VS-880EX was a replacement for the original VS-880, and it was built on the architecture of the VS-1680. The VS-880EX was an eight-track workstation and was an affordable solution for users who didn't need 16 tracks.

Figure 1.3
Roland VS-880EX Digital
Studio Workstation.

Highlights of the VS-880EX

The VS-880EX implemented a number of features found on the VS-1680, including a backlit display, EZ Routing templates, and the ability to record eight simultaneous tracks. The VS-880EX also included the following features not found on the VS-880:

❋ Internal 2GB hard drive

❋ Six balanced analog inputs

❋ Optical S/PDIF digital I/O

❋ VS8F-2 effects board pre-installed

❋ 20-bit A/D and D/A converters

❋ **EX MARKS THE SPOT**

There is often a good deal of confusion regarding the VS-880 V-Xpanded and the VS-880EX workstations. The term "expanded" gets incorrectly attached to both of these models. The V-Xpanded version of the VS-880 was really just a software upgrade, and it did indeed "expand" the functionality of the base VS-880. The VS-880EX was a completely new workstation and was physically different than the VS-880, both in terms of its appearance and its operating system. If you are in the market for one of the VS-880 series of workstations, beware of the "EX" terminology that is often used. Since the VS-880EX has more features than the V-Xpanded version of the VS-880, some sellers will incorrectly advertise the V-Xpanded workstation as an "EX" workstation.

VS workstations are bought and sold on auction sites such as eBay every day. If you are looking at one of the VS-880 models, there are a couple of ways to make sure you are getting the one you want. The most obvious way is to look at the area where the actual model number is listed just above the display screen. There should also be a label on the bottom of the unit that shows the model number as well. Another way to check is to look at the digital connectors, as the VS-880EX has both digital coax and optical S/PDIF connectors. Also, the VS-880EX has six ¼" analog inputs on the back of the unit, whereas the VS-880 only has four. Finally, the effect expansion board is not removable on the VS-880EX, so if someone is selling one without an effects board, it's not a VS-880EX.

Software Upgrades

In 1999, Roland introduced the Version 2.0 operating system software upgrade for the VS-880EX. This upgrade allowed the VS-880EX to create audio CDs via an external SCSI CD writer. In addition, this upgrade included Roland's new "Mastering Tool Kit" effects algorithm, as well as new COSM Speaker Modeling for use with Roland's new DS-90 powered monitors.

1999: The VSR-880

In mid-1999, Roland released the VSR-880 (see Figure 1.4), a rack-mount workstation based upon the VS-880EX. This workstation could be connected to any analog mixer, but the real benefit was for users of the new Roland VM-7000 and VM-3100Pro digital mixers. The VSR-880 was the first Roland VS workstation to feature R-BUS. R-BUS is Roland's proprietary 8-in/8-out 24-bit audio transfer protocol, and it can communicate with the ADAT and T-DIF digital protocols via Roland R-BUS interface boxes. The VSR-880 was also the first Roland workstation to include 24-bit A/D converters.

Figure 1.4
Roland VSR-880 Digital
Studio Workstation.

Highlights of the VSR-880

Although the physical appearances of the two workstations were very different, the VSR-880 contained practically the same feature set as the VS-880EX. However, since the VSR-880 was a rack-mount unit, it did not have any faders, as it was meant to be the back-end recording device for Roland's front-end digital mixers. Also important to note is that while the VSR-880 could use the VS8F-2 effect boards, none were factory installed. In addition to R-BUS, the VSR-880 also had different analog inputs: 8 RCA inputs and 2 ¼" balanced inputs. The VSR-880 also contained the following features:

- ❋ 24-bit recording mode
- ❋ Internal 6GB hard drive
- ❋ Hard drive usability: 10 partitions, 1GB per partition
- ❋ Eight simultaneous recording tracks in linear mode
- ❋ Dedicated CD Mastering function
- ❋ Faster CD burning format
- ❋ 24-bit A/D and D/A converters

Software Upgrades

There were various operating system upgrades available for the VSR-880, but no major functionality was ever added to the VSR-880.

2000: The VS-1880

In January 2000, Roland announced its new 18-track workstation, the VS-1880, shown in Figure 1.5. The VS-1880 capitalized on the success of the VS-1680, while adding the features introduced in other recent VS models.

Figure 1.5
Roland VS-1880 Digital Studio Workstation.

Highlights of the VS-1880

The VS-1880 looked a lot like the VS-1680, but it was housed in a black case instead of a grey case. The VS-1880 included a dedicated CD Mastering button, and since the VS-1880 can play back 18 tracks, faders 7 and 8 now pull double duty via the SHIFT key in order to manage the two additional tracks. All of the features of the VS-1680 V-Xpanded upgrade were implemented in the VS-1880, as well as the following:

❅ 24-bit recording mode

❅ Faster CD burning format

❅ 24-bit A/D and D/A converters

Software Upgrades

There were various operating system upgrades available for the VS-1880, but no major functionality was ever added to the VS-1880.

2000: The VS-890

In July 2000, Roland announced its latest eight-track workstation, the VS-890, shown in Figure 1.6. Even though the VS-880EX had only been on the market for about a year, there were new developments in technology that Roland felt would be selling points for this new workstation.

Figure 1.6
Roland VS-890 Digital
Studio Workstation.

Highlights of the VS-890

Apart from using a black case instead of a grey case, the VS-890 is almost identical in appearance to the VS-880EX. Like the VS-880EX, the VS-890 had a VS8F-2 effect board factory-installed. The VS-890 combined the best features of the VS-880EX desktop workstation with the advanced features found in the VSR-880. The VS-890 had the following improvements over the VS-880EX:

* 24-bit recording mode
* Internal 10GB hard drive
* Hard drive usability: 10 partitions, 1GB per partition
* Eight simultaneous recording tracks in linear mode
* Dedicated CD Mastering function

❈ Faster CD burning format

❈ 24-bit A/D and D/A converters

Software Upgrades

There were various operating system upgrades available for the VS-890, but no major functionality was ever added to the VS-890.

2001: The VS-2480

In January 2000, Roland again broke new ground when it announced the VS-2480 Digital Audio Workstation, shown in Figure 1.7. The VS-2480 was the first self-contained hard disk desktop recording workstation to offer 24-track/24-bit digital recording. The VS-2480 incorporated a long list of new features, as well as conveniences such as motorized faders and "drag and drop" editing, and wrapped the package in a very affordable price.

Figure 1.7
Roland VS-2480 Digital
Studio Workstation.

Highlights of the VS-2480

The VS-2480 brought so many great new features to the VS series, it's impossible to list them all in this section. Here are some brief highlights of the VS-2480:

* Sample rates up to 96kHz
* 64-channel digital mixer with motorized faders
* 56-bit internal mixing bus
* Sixteen simultaneous recording tracks, 24 simultaneous playback tracks
* Up to eight onboard stereo effect processors, 2 pre-installed
* Sixteen analog ¼" balanced inputs and 8 XLR inputs with phantom power
* Hard drive usability: 13 partitions, 10GB per partition
* Dynamic processing and 5-band EQ on every channel
* 24-voice Phase Sample Pads for triggering and arranging samples directly from disk
* VGA monitor output and mouse-based waveform editing and control

Software Upgrades

There have been a number of operating system upgrades for the VS-2480, many of which introduced even more features. These new features included the ability to split and combine projects, full import and export capabilities for all previous VS workstations, .WAV file export, Automix enhancements, and more. Perhaps the biggest upgrade was in January 2002, which implemented full support for an external VGA monitor. In 2004, a new operating system upgrade was announced, which allowed the VS-2480 to use the new VS8F-3 Plug-in effects board.

2002: The VS-1824CD

In January 2002, Roland announced its newest 18-track workstation, the VS-1824CD, shown in Figure 1.8. The VS-1824CD was targeted as a replacement for the VS-1680 and the VS-1880.

Highlights of the VS-1824CD

The VS-1824CD had all the same features of the VS-1880, but it included components that were optional on the VS-1880. The VS-1824CD was the first VS workstation to include a built-in high-speed CD-R/RW drive for easy data backup and creation of audio CDs. The built-in CD drive could also import audio, such as drum loops, directly from a CD. The VS-1824CD shipped with a 10GB hard drive and also came with one VS8F-2 effect board factory installed, with the option of installing a second board. The VS-1824CD also shipped with a 10GB hard drive.

Figure 1.8
Roland VS-1824CD Digital
Studio Workstation.

Software Upgrades

There were various operating system upgrades available for the VS-1824CD, but no major functionality was ever added to the VS-1824CD.

2002: The VS-2480CD

Along with the announcement of the VS-1824CD, Roland also announced the new VS-2480CD (see Figure 1.9) in 2002. The VS-2480CD added a handful of features to the already popular VS-2480.

Highlights of the VS-2480CD

Like the VS-1824CD, the VS-2480CD added a built-in high-speed CD-R/RW drive for easy data backup and creation of audio CDs. The VS-2480CD also shipped with a massive 80GB hard drive, which provided more recording space than any other workstation on the market. The Version 2.0 operating system upgrade, which allowed for full support for external VGA monitor operations, was pre-installed on the VS-2480CD.

Software Upgrades

The VS-2480 and the VS-2480CD use the exact same operating system code. Since the introduction of the VS-2480CD, there have been a few operating system upgrades for the VS-2480.

Figure 1.9
Roland VS-2480CD Digital
Studio Workstation.

In 2004, a new operating system upgrade was announced, which allowed the VS-2480 to use the new VS8F-3 Plug-in effects board.

2003: The VS-2400CD

In January 2003, Roland announced a new 24-track workstation, the VS-2400CD, shown in Figure 1.10. The VS-2400CD inherited many of the features found in the flagship VS-2480CD, but it was priced at approximately 30 percent less.

Highlights of the VS-2400CD

Like the VS-2480CD, the VS-2400CD was a 24-track/24-bit workstation capable of sample rates up to 96kHz. The VS-2400CD also provided a VGA monitor output and mouse-based waveform editing and control and, like the VS-2480CD, included a VS8F-2 effect board pre-installed. The

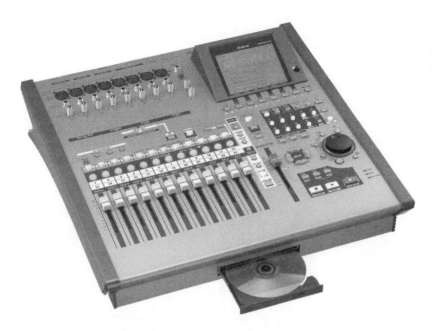

Figure 1.10
Roland VS-2400CD digital studio workstation.

VS-2400CD also included features not found on the VS-2480CD, such as RSS 3-D panning and V-LINK for integrating Edirol video products. Here is a list of the highlights of the VS-2400CD:

- ❄ 48-channel digital mixer with motorized faders
- ❄ 56-bit internal mixing bus
- ❄ Sixteen simultaneous recording tracks, 24 simultaneous playback tracks
- ❄ Up to 4 onboard stereo effect processors, two pre-installed
- ❄ Eight analog ¼" balanced inputs and 8 XLR inputs with phantom power
- ❄ Internal 40GB hard drive
- ❄ Hard drive usability: four partitions, 10GB per partition
- ❄ Dynamic processing and 4-band EQ on every channel

Software Upgrades

In 2004, a new operating system upgrade was announced, which allowed the VS-2400CD to use the new VS8F-3 Plug-in effects board.

2004: The VS-2000CD

In January 2004, Roland announced a new 20-track/24-bit workstation, the VS-2000CD, shown in Figure 1.11. This was the first VS workstation to support the new VS8F-3 Plug-in effects expansion board, and it included a number of features not found on any other VS workstation.

Figure 1.11
Roland VS-2000CD Digital
Studio Workstation.

Highlights of the VS-2000CD

One of the new features found on the VS-2000CD was a USB 2.0 port, allowing users to transfer data quickly and easily between the VS-2000CD and a computer. Another new feature was the Harmony Sequence function, allowing vocalists to add instant harmonies. The VS-2000CD also included a built-in chromatic tuner, and the Rhythm Track feature included onboard drum sounds to allow users to create their own drum tracks. Other features included:

* Eight simultaneous recording tracks, 18 simultaneous playback tracks
* Up to 4 onboard stereo effect processors, two pre-installed
* Eight analog ¼" balanced inputs and 8 XLR inputs with phantom power
* Internal 40GB hard drive
* Hard drive usability: four partitions, 10GB per partition
* Dynamic processing and 4-band EQ on every channel

Software Upgrades

In 2004, Roland released the V2.0 software upgrade for the VS-2000CD. This software upgrade, in conjunction with the optional VS20-VGA Output Board, allowed for full VGA editing and control.

❄ **WHAT THE VS-2000CD DIDN'T HAVE**

While the VS-2000CD introduced a number of new features, there were a number of things Roland chose to omit on this particular VS workstation. The most notable missing item on the VS-200CD was Roland's R-DAC compression scheme. Given today's low cost of hard disk storage, R-DAC certainly isn't necessary anymore, but its exclusion from the VS-2000CD does limit its ability to import data from older VS workstations. The VS-2000CD also lacks the ability to record at sample rates other than 44.1kHz. Since audio must be at 44.1kHz in order to create an audio CD, this isn't necessarily bad, but it is the first VS workstation to limit the sample rate to 44.1kHz. Also missing are optical S/PDIF digital connectors and a SCSI port, which have been standard on every VS workstation since 1998.

2004: The VS-2480DVD

In January 2004, Roland announced its latest model in the 2480 series, the VS-2480DVD, shown in Figure 1.12.

Highlights of the VS-2480DVD

The new VS-2480DVD was identical to the VS-2480CD, but now included is an internal DVD-RW drive instead of a CD-RW drive. The DVD-RW drive allowed users to burn up to 4.7GB of song data to a single DVD-R or DVD-RW disc. The VS-2480DVD also supported the new VS8F-3 Plug-in effects expansion board.

Software Upgrades

Like the VS-2480CD, the VS-2480DVD and the VS-2480 use the exact same operating system code. Since the introduction of the VS-2480DVD, there have been only minor operating system upgrades.

Figure 1.12
Roland VS-2480 DVD
Digital Studio Workstation.

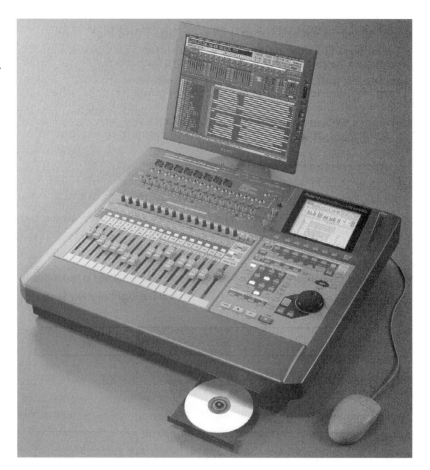

2} Overview of the VS Workstation Architecture

Each VS workstation is a stand-alone, all-in-one digital audio workstation (DAW). Consider a conventional multitrack recording studio. In its simplest form, that studio would have a mixing console, some sort of recording medium, effects processors, and a patch bay to connect inputs and outputs as necessary. The Roland VS workstations bundle all of these components (and more) into one physical workstation.

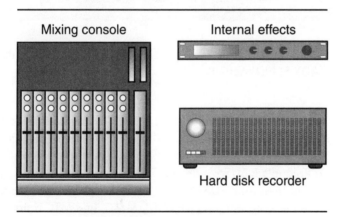

Input jacks and connectors

Mixing console   Internal effects

Hard disk recorder

Output jacks and connectors

Figure 2.1
Anatomy of the
VS workstation.

As you can see in Figure 2.1, the VS workstations pack a number of components into a single box. Let's take a more in-depth look at each of these components.

Input/Output

The VS workstations provide multiple input and output connections for connecting microphones, instruments, monitors, outboard processors, and more. Every VS workstation provides analog, digital, and peripheral connections.

Analog Connections

All VS workstations have a set of ¼" balanced TRS analog inputs. The VS-880 and the VSR-880 workstations also included a set of RCA analog inputs. All of the VS workstations that have 16 tracks or more include XLR inputs, a dedicated Hi-Z guitar ¼" input, and phantom power. Figure 2.2 shows the input section of the VS-2480. There is also a footswitch ¼" input jack on each VS workstation, which allows you to connect any standard momentary-type foot switch to control certain operations on the VS.

Figure 2.2

Analog inputs on the VS-2480CD workstation.

All VS workstations contain various analog outputs, including main outputs, monitor outputs, headphone outputs, and auxiliary (AUX SEND) outputs.

Digital Connections

All VS workstations contain one or more digital input and output connectors. The VS-880 and the VS-2000CD contain S/PDIF digital coaxial connectors, while all other VS workstations include both S/PDIF digital coax and S/PDIF optical connectors. Figure 2.3 shows the digital connections available on the VS-2400, including Roland's R-BUS connector. R-BUS connectors can also be found on the VSR-880 and VS-2480 workstations. R-BUS can transmit and receive eight separate digital audio signals; it can also be used to send and receive MIDI, MMC, and MTC data.

Speaking of MIDI, each VS workstation also contains two standard MIDI connectors: IN and OUT/THRU. You can use these MIDI connectors to synchronize multiple VS workstations, synchronize the VS with external MIDI devices like keyboards and drum machines, and control certain functions of the VS workstation from an external device. Certain VS workstations also include a Word Clock input connector, allowing you to synchronize the VS to an external word clock source.

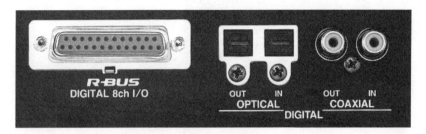

Figure 2.3
Digital connections on the
VS-2400CD workstation.

Peripheral Connections

Many of the VS workstations have SCSI connectors, allowing you to connect items such as external SCSI CD burners, external SCSI hard drives, and external SCSI ZIP drives. Some VS workstations have USB connectors, which can be used to transfer .WAV files between the VS and a computer. In addition, external keyboard, mouse, and VGA-display connectors can be found on certain VS workstations.

Mixing Console

Although each VS workstation has unique features and functions, the layout of the mixing console is fairly consistent across all VS workstations.

Channel Strips

Each VS workstation has a series of channel strips. The channel strips of a VS-890 are shown in Figure 2.4. Each channel strip consists of a fader, a status indicator light, a channel select button, a Pan knob, and a Sensitivity knob. To the right of the channel strips, you will find the Master fader.

Transport Controls

Each VS workstation contains Transport Control buttons—Play, Stop, Record, and Zero-Return—located at the bottom right of the front panel. Most of the VS workstations also have dedicated buttons for fast forward and rewind, but some implement the Fast Forward and Rewind controls via the Time/Value dial. Each of the dedicated Transport Control buttons can be used with the SHIFT key to provide additional functions such as shut down, store, restart, and enable Automix record.

Display Screen

The display screen is found at the upper right of each VS workstation. This screen is your window to the inner controls of the VS workstation. Every function you perform on the VS will be shown on the display screen. Some VS workstations allow you to connect an external VGA monitor to view an enhanced version of the display screen.

Figure 2.4
Channel strips on the
VS-890 workstation.

Time/Value Dial

This dial serves multiple purposes on the VS workstations. It can be used to move position within a song and can also be used to change the values and settings when performing certain functions.

Dedicated Function Buttons

Each VS workstation includes a number of buttons that perform specific functions. These buttons are arranged into groups based on their function. These functions include setting and recalling location points within a song, setting and recalling mixer snapshots, setting punch-in and punch-out locations, and more.

Internal Effects

All VS workstations have the ability to use a wide variety of internal effects. These effects are contained on a Roland Effect Expansion Board. These effect boards contain two internal stereo effects processors. Each stereo effects processor can also be used as two mono effects processors.

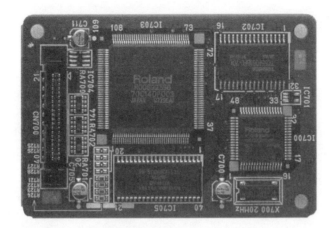

Figure 2.5
The VS8F-2 Effect
Expansion Board.

The first version of these effect boards was the VS8F-1. This effect board can only be used in a VS-880. All other VS workstations use the VS8F-2 effect board, shown in Figure 2.5. Both the VS8F-1 and VS8F-2 include a wide variety of effects, including reverbs, delays, choruses, flangers, phasers, filters, compressors, limiters, gates, and Roland's COSM (Composite Object Sound Modeling) modeling effects. The 16-bit VS8F-1 effect board provides 200 effect presets and the ability to save 100 user-customized effects. The 24-bit VS8F-2 effect board can hold up to 250 effect presets and 200 user-customized effects. The VS8F-2 also includes Roland's MTK (Mastering Tool Kit) effects, which provide mastering effects such as multi-band expansion and compression.

Some of the first VS workstations that were produced, such as the VS-880 and VS-1680, were shipped without any effect boards installed. More recently, VS workstations were shipped with one effect board pre-installed by Roland. Table 2.1 lists the effect processor configurations for each VS workstation.

In 2004, Roland introduced the VS8F-3 Plug-In Effect Expansion Board. This new effect board, which is compatible with all VS-1xxx and VS-2xxx workstations, uses 56-bit internal processing and works with sample rates up to 96kHz. Roland opened up its architecture with this new effect board, allowing various third-party vendors to write VS plug-in software. The VS8F-3 card comes bundled with five plug-in effects from Roland, including Stereo Reverb, Tempo Mapping, Pre-Amp Modeling, Vocal Channel Strip, and an enhanced version of the Mastering Tool Kit. Plug-ins from various third-party vendors, such as Antares, IK Multimedia, Universal Audio, and Massenburg DesignWorks, are now available.

Table 2.1   Stereo Effect Processor Configuration

VS Workstation	Onboard Stereo Effect Processors	Optional Stereo Effect Processors
VS-880	0	2*
VS-880EX	2**	0
VS-890	2**	0
VSR-880	0	2
VS-1680	0	4
VS-1880	0	4
VS-1824CD	2	2
VS-2000CD	2	2
VS-2400CD	2	2
VS-2480CD	2	6

*The VS-880 can only use the VS8F-1 effect board.

**The VS-880EX and VS-890 have one VS8F-2 effect board permanently installed.

Hard Disk Recorder

The heart of every VS workstation is the hard disk recorder, which stores data on a hard drive. The VS workstations use standard internal IDE hard drives. However, the disk drives need to conform to certain specifications in order to work with the VS workstations. For best results, consult Roland's VS-Series Digital Studio Workstation Compatible Media Guide.

Disk Partitioning

The VS architecture requires that the hard drive be partitioned into multiple logical drives. Each VS workstation limits the maximum size of a partition and the number of partitions that can be used, as shown in Table 2.2. The maximum usable size of a hard drive is calculated by multiplying the maximum partition size by the maximum number of partitions.

Table 2.2   Hard Drive Partition Limits

VS Workstation	Max Partition Size	Max Number of Partitions
VS-880	1GB	4
VS-880EX	1GB	4
VSR-880	1GB	10
VS-890	1GB	10
VS-1680	2GB	8
VS-1880	2GB	8

VS Workstation	Max Partition Size	Max Number of Partitions
VS-1824CD	2GB	8
VS-2000CD	10GB	4
VS-2400CD	10GB	4
VS-2480CD	10GB	13

One thing to keep in mind about this calculation: The resulting size of the hard drive is the maximum that the VS workstation will recognize. In other words, you can install hard drives that are larger than the maximum, but some of the hard drive will end up being wasted. For example, the VS-880EX will only use a maximum of 4GB on a hard drive. If you installed a Roland-approved 8GB hard drive in a VS-880EX, it will work, but 4GB of the hard drive would not be accessible by the VS-880EX.

Recording Time

A common question for new VS users is "How many songs can I record?" Technically, the answer is "unlimited," since you can always back up your songs, delete them, and record new songs. What new users really want to know is how many tracks they can record. When we look at recording in the digital realm, we need to think in terms of available track minutes. The available number of track minutes depends on the size of the hard drive, the size of the partition, the sample rate you record at, and the recording mode you choose. We've already looked at the hard drives and partitions, so now we'll take a look at the recording modes and sample rates available on the VS workstations.

Recording Modes

All VS workstations, other than the VS-2000CD, provide the ability to record data in either linear or compressed mode. Table 2.3 shows a list of the various recording modes. Linear recording modes can record 16-bit audio or 24-bit audio, depending on the VS workstation. The compressed recording modes use Roland's proprietary R-DAC compression scheme. The original version of R-DAC found on the VS-880 was a 16-bit routine. When Roland introduced the VS-1680, it included a new version of R-DAC written as a 24-bit routine.

Table 2.3   Recording Modes

Recording	Mode Description
M24 (Mastering 24-bit)	24-bit linear
MTP (Multi Track Pro)	24-bit RDAC with an average 3:1 compression ratio (also called VSR mode on older workstations)
CDR (CD-R Writing)	16-bit linear non-separable stereo

Recording	Mode Description
M16 (Mastering 16-bit)	16-bit linear (also called MAS mode on older workstations)
MT1 (Multi Track 1)	16-bit R-DAC with an average 2:1 compression ratio
MT2 (Multi Track 2)	16-bit R-DAC with an average 3:1 compression ratio
LIV (Live Recording 1)	16-bit R-DAC with an extreme compression ratio
LV2 (Live Recording 2)	16-bit R-DAC with a very extreme compression ratio

Today, Roland's flagship VS-2480DVD workstation supports both 24-bit and 16-bit linear recording modes, as well as both 24-bit R-DAC and 16-bit R-DAC recording modes. Roland continues to supply the older 16-bit R-DAC recording modes in order to support import and export functionality between older and newer models of VS workstations. Table 2.4 shows the available recording modes for each VS workstation.

> ❄ **R-DAC**
>
> One of the things that made the original VS-880 revolutionary in 1996 was R-DAC (Roland Digital Audio Coding). According to Roland, R-DAC was a completely new compression technique, optimized for professional music recording, which was developed to reduce the amount of digital data needed to record an audio waveform. Unlike compression schemes that function in the "frequency domain," such as those used by MiniDisc and MPEG, R-DAC processes audio in the "time domain," where no frequencies are singled out or thrown away. The end result of using R-DAC is a doubling or tripling of recording time available. Remember, back in 1996, hard drives were much more expensive than they are today, and a 2GB hard drive was considered big.

Table 2.4   Available Recording Modes

VS Workstation	M24	MTP/VSR	CDR	M16/MAS	MT1	MT2	LIV	LV2
VS-880		X	X	X	X			
VS-880EX			X	X	X	X	X	
VSR-880		X	X	X	X	X	X	
VS-890	X	X	X	X	X	X		
VS-1680		X	X	X	X	X	X	X
VS-1880		X	X	X	X	X	X	X
VS-1824CD		X	X	X	X	X	X	X
VS-2000CD	X			X				
VS-2400CD	X	X	X	X	X	X	X	X
VS-2480CD	X	X	X	X	X	X	X	X

Sample Rates

The original VS-880 supported three sample rates: 48kHz, 44.1kHz, and 32kHz. All subsequent VS workstations also supported these three sample rates, except for the VS-2000CD, which only supports 44.1kHz. With the introduction of the VS-2480, Roland provided three additional sample rates: 64kHz, 88.2kHz, and 96kHz. The VS-2400 also provides these three additional sample rates.

Now let's get back to the question of how many track minutes can be recorded on a VS workstation. Table 2.5 shows the amount of track minutes available on a 1GB partition for the various recording modes. If you are using a different partition size and/or sample rate, you can easily calculate the appropriate track minutes based on the values shown in Table 2.5.

Table 2.5   Available Track Minutes Per 1GB @ 44.1kHz Sample Rate

Recording Mode Available	Track Minutes
M24	144
MTP/VSR	404
CDR/M16/MAS	202
MT1	404
MT2	539
LIV	646
LV2	808

Note: For VS workstations that support 10GB partitions, the available track minutes may be slightly more than calculated.

Common Concepts

There are a number of concepts and functions that are common across the entire VS series. Understanding these common concepts and functions makes the transition to a different VS workstation much easier.

Mixer Modes

One of the unique aspects of the VS workstations is the concept of mixer modes. Each VS workstation contains multiple digital mixers in one physical box. Each of these mixers is active and available at all times. If we laid all these mixers out end to end, the physical box would be pretty big!

To keep the VS workstations small and truly portable, the VS provides a way to toggle between the different mixers with the press of a button. When you activate one the various mixers, the channel strips are used to adjust the channels specific to that particular mixer. Once you've configured the channels for one mixer and toggled to another mixer, the VS remembers (and keeps active) the settings for the previous mixer. You can now adjust the channel strips to suit your requirements for this mixer without disturbing the settings you made in the previous mixer.

THE MIXED UP MODES OF THE VS-880

The VS-880 was revolutionary, but its implementation of mixer modes was based on the popular tape-based multitrackers of that time. The VS-880 contained two mixer modes: Input → Track and Input Mix/Track Mix. The Input → Track mode does not have any mixer between the physical inputs and the recording tracks, and it allows you to route an input directly to a recording track. The Input Mix/Track Mix mode contains an Input Mixer and a Track Mixer and uses shared-track busses. For example, if you want to record to track 5, you would need to route the input to the 5-6 bus and pan the input hard left. Shared-track bussing was also used with effects routing.

The architecture of these two mixer modes can be confusing, even for experienced VS-880 users. It seems that Roland also found this confusing, as all subsequent VS workstations featured independent Input, Track, and Effects Return Mixers.

This concept can be confusing for new users, so let's see a few examples. In Figure 2.4, we saw the channel strips for the VS-890. The VS-890 contains an eight-channel Input Mixer, an eight-channel Track Mixer, and a two-channel Effects Return Mixer. If we add these all up, we see that the VS-890 is an 18-channel digital mixer, but there are only eight physical channel faders. The concept of mixer modes allows us to toggle between these various mixers and configure them appropriately.

Here is another example. The VS-2480DVD is a 64-channel digital mixer, but there are only 16 physical channel faders. Figure 2.6 shows the conceptual layout of the various mixers for the VS-2480DVD.

Figure 2.6
The 64 channels of the
VS-2480DVD.

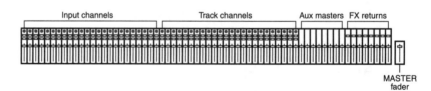

Input channels   Track channels   Aux masters FX returns

MASTER
fader

Let's take a closer look at the three common mixer modes found on VS workstations.

The Input Mixer

The Input Mixer is where you assign inputs—things plugged into the VS—to recording tracks. You can route a single input to one or more recording tracks. Normally you'll use the Input Mixer to assign your microphone and line inputs to recording tracks. One or more physical input devices will be the source, and one or more tracks will be in the record condition, and these will be the destination tracks. Any signal processing changes that you make while in the Input Mixer will be recorded on the destination tracks. For example, if you use the channel strip to change some EQ settings on Input 1, then the recorded track will contain the signal after it has passed through the EQ. When you apply changes in the Input Mixer, you are recording the affected signal. You can think of the Input Mixer as a set of devices that sit between your physical input devices and the hard disk recorder, and any changes made within these devices affect what is actually recorded on the hard disk.

The Track Mixer

The Track Mixer is where you listen to tracks that have already been recorded or are in the process of being recorded. The Track Mixer is also used when you want to mix down or bounce tracks. Any signal processing changes you make while in the Track Mixer do not affect your original source material. For example, you might want to apply some reverb to the lead vocal track that you've already recorded. You can apply a particular reverb, adjust some of the reverb parameters, or change to a different type of reverb. You will be able to hear the reverb, but the source material is not changed.

When bouncing tracks, one or more tracks will be your source tracks, and one or more tracks will be your destination tracks. With some of the VS workstations, bouncing all tracks down to two tracks isn't possible. For example, on the VS-880EX, you cannot bounce all eight tracks down to two tracks in a single step. Roland addressed this issue in a feature called the mastering room, which is now available on most VS workstations. The mastering room provides a way to bounce all tracks down to two tracks, allowing you to more efficiently use all the tracks available on the VS workstation.

The Effects Return Mixer

The Effects Return Mixer is where you'll assign the output of any send/return effects. When you use insert effects, the effects are applied directly to the track, and no routing is necessary. By default, the returns from any send/return effects are routed to the Master bus. In order to better understand the Effects Return Mixer, let's look at using effects in the Input Mixer and in the Track Mixer.

When working in the Input Mixer, you are assigning inputs to recording tracks. Suppose you are recording an electric guitar, and you would like to hear a bit of chorus effect added to the sound of the guitar. To do this, you would choose a chorus effect and assign that effect to the guitar input channel in a send/return configuration. When you play the guitar, you'll hear the chorus effect. Now you have a decision to make: record the guitar track with the chorus effect or without the chorus effect. If you want to hear the chorus effect when you play the guitar but do not want to record the chorus effect, you don't have to do anything. But, if you do want to record the chorus effect, you will need to assign the output of the effect to the destination track in the Effects Return Mixer.

In addition, since you can route a single input source to multiple destination tracks, you could route the guitar input to two different recording tracks. One of those tracks (destination track 1) can be recorded dry and the other track (destination track 2) can be recorded wet by assigning the output of the chorus effect to destination track 2.

In the discussion of the Track Mixer, we looked at applying a reverb effect to a lead vocal track. Suppose you want to bounce the lead vocal track and the reverb to another track. In this case, the original lead vocal track is your source, and the new track is your destination. In order to have the reverb applied to the destination track, you would need to assign the output of the reverb effect to the destination track as well. To do this, use the Effects Return Mixer to assign the output of the reverb effect to the destination track.

Remember, if you want to print any send/return effect, you must specifically assign the output of the effect to a track. If you do not assign the output of the effect to a track, you will be able to hear the effect, but it will not be recorded.

Routing

Now that we've seen the various mixer modes, we need to know how to route signals in and out of them. In an analog environment, you'd use a number of patch cables to connect your mixing console, effects, and recording medium. With the VS workstations, the connections between the mixers, internal effect processors, and hard disk recorder can be done internally. The internal routing capabilities of the VS workstations eliminate the need for external patch cables and provide flexible routing scenarios while keeping your signals in the digital domain. Many of the VS workstations include a feature called "EZ Routing." EZ Routing contains a set of routing templates designed for most common tasks, including recording, bouncing, and mastering. Some of the VS models also include a graphical patch bay within the display, allowing you to drag and drop connections.

All the VS workstations allow you to manually configure your routings by pushing a few buttons. Some routing functions are specific to the VS model you are working with and will be covered in the workstation-specific chapters of this book. However, there is a common routing methodology used by all VS workstations. When routing signals, there will always be one or more source signals and one or more destination tracks. When routing within the VS, you first indicate your destination track(s) and then assign your source signal(s) to that track(s). For example, to route a guitar plugged into physical Input #1 (the source signal) to recording track #3 (the destination track), you would first identify recording track #3, and then route Input #1 to it. Again, we'll see specific routing examples in the chapters that follow.

Virtual Tracks

Each recording track on a VS workstation has a set of 16 virtual tracks, or V-Tracks, associated with it. On some VS workstations, the V-Tracks are separated into two banks, with only one bank available at any particular time. To better explain how V-Tracks are used, I like to use the analogy of a tip-proof filing cabinet. Figure 2.7 shows all the V-Tracks (drawers) for a given recording track (file cabinet). Since these filing cabinets are tip proof, you can only have one drawer open at a time. When one drawer is open, the others will not open.

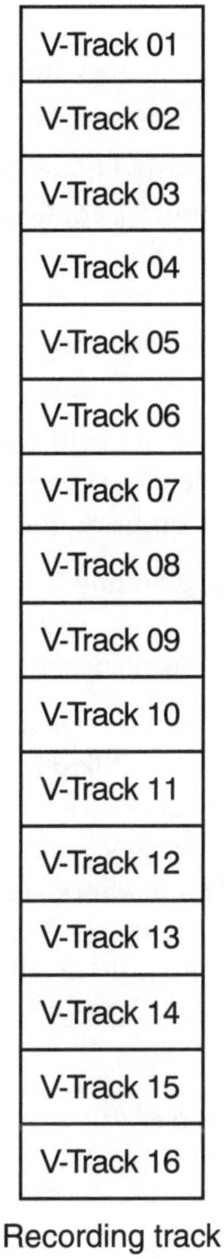

V-Track 01
V-Track 02
V-Track 03
V-Track 04
V-Track 05
V-Track 06
V-Track 07
V-Track 08
V-Track 09
V-Track 10
V-Track 11
V-Track 12
V-Track 13
V-Track 14
V-Track 15
V-Track 16

Recording track

Figure 2.7
Sixteen V-Tracks per recording track.

Likewise, when we are working with a recording track, we can access only one of its V-Tracks at a time. If we want to access a different V-Track, we must stop working with the current V-Track (close the drawer) in order to work with a different V-Track (open a different drawer). You cannot switch V-Tracks on the fly while the VS is playing or recording.

When you create a new song, each recording track defaults to using V-Track 1. The combination of recording track and V-Track is usually expressed as 1-1 or 1.1, where the recording track is always first and the V-Track is always second. So, track 5-2 refers to V-Track 2 on recording track 5.

I've heard people say, "I never use V-Tracks." That is a false statement. Look at our filing cabinet in Figure 2.7. There isn't any drawer for "non-V-Track," is there? The reason they think they are not using V-Tracks is because they never change from the default of V-Track 1.

Another misconception people have is thinking that they need to erase a track so that they can record something else on that track. For example, I've heard people state, "I recorded on tracks one through six, bounced them to tracks seven and eight, then erased tracks one through six so that I could record more instruments." By simply selecting a different V-Track for tracks 1 through 6, you can record additional material without deleting the six original tracks.

V-Tracks are useful for recording multiple takes of an instrument or vocal. For example, you could use four V-Tracks to record four takes of the lead vocal. You could then piece together the best parts of these takes into a single track, which would reside on yet another V-Track. All the original takes still remain on their V-Tracks, so you could always go back and use them again.

It's important to understand that you can record anything on any V-Track. You can have a vocal track on 1-1, a guitar track on 1-2, and a bass track on 1-3. The key concept with V-Tracks is that only one V-Track per recording track can be active during recording and/or playback.

To manage V-Tracks, you can use the Track Exchange function. Track Exchange allows you to swap any two V-Tracks. Let's go back to the example of recording four takes of the lead vocal track. We've recorded all four of these to different V-Tracks on recording track 1, resulting in vocal tracks on 1-1, 1-2, 1-3, and 1-4. Because all four of these V-Tracks are on the same recording track, we cannot play back all four at the same time. This is where we use the Track Exchange function. We can swap three of these V-Tracks on recording track 1 with any other V-Tracks. So, in this example, we could swap 1-2 with 2-8, 1-3 with 3-8, and 1-4 with 4-8. Now, our four takes of the lead vocal exist on 1-1, 2-8, 3-8, and 4-8. We can now play back all four versions at the same time.

Whether you use Track Exchange or not, it is a good idea to use a track sheet to document what material exists across the matrix of recording tracks and V-Tracks.

Editing

All VS workstations include a set of track editing functions. On some machines, these editing functions are referred to as region editing functions. For now, we'll just refer to them as track editing functions. Some workstations also have a set of phrase editing functions, and those details will be covered in the appropriate workstation-specific chapters.

When you edit audio on the VS, you're actually just editing sets of pointers that tell the VS how to play the data. This is referred to as non-destructive editing. The benefit of non-destructive editing is that you are not editing the actual audio, just the pointers. This means you can perform an edit, and if you don't like it, you can undo it. This also means that you can be creative and experiment with different edits, knowing that you can always get back to where you started.

All track editing functions require you to specify starting points and ending points. These starting and ending points are called IN and OUT points, or START and END points, depending on the VS model you are working with. Some functions also allow you to set FROM points and TO points. Using a FROM point allows you to set a reference point within the source section of data to be moved or copied and allows you to place that reference point in a particular location (TO point) in the target data.

Let's take a look at some of these track editing functions. Depending on which VS model you have, there may be additional parameters and controls within these functions, and some functions may have limited use.

Copy

This will copy a section of audio to another location. You can copy audio within the existing V-Track, to a different V-Track within the same recording track, or to a V-Track on a different recording track. If audio already exists at the destination, it will be overwritten, although some VS models give you the option to insert within the existing audio. You can also have multiple copies of the data placed in the destination V-Track.

Move

Move is similar to Copy, except the section of audio on the source V-Track will be replaced with silence. Like the Copy function, if audio already exists at the destination, it will be overwritten, although some VS models give you the option to insert within the existing audio.

Erase

Use Erase to remove a section of audio from a V-Track. After the Erase, that section of audio will be silent.

Cut

Similar to Erase, Cut removes a section of audio from a V-Track. However, all data that occurs after the cut section is shifted forward in time so that there is no gap of silence.

Insert

Insert is the opposite of Cut. It will insert blank space into a V-Track at a given point. All data after that point is shifted backward in time.

Compression/Expansion

This function allows you to time-shrink or time-stretch a section of audio and select whether the pitch should be changed or kept. This function is good for small sections of audio, but it may not provide satisfactory results for large sections of audio.

Using Internal Effects

Roland provides a wide range of effects via its VS8F-1 and VS8F-2 Effect Expansion Boards. The ways in which you use effects is up to you. However, when you use any of the internal effects on a VS workstation, it is important to understand how they work within the VS architecture.

Algorithms and Effect Blocks

Roland provides 36 unique effects processing routines, called algorithms. Each algorithm contains one or more effect blocks. For example, there is an algorithm called Delay, and it contains two effect blocks: Delay and EQ. Each effect block contains one or more settings. The Delay effect block has 12 settings, and the EQ effect block has 13 settings. The combination of an algorithm, effect blocks, and effect block settings is called an effect patch. Roland provides over 200 preset effect patches, and you can create and save your own custom effect patches.

The relationship between algorithms and effect blocks is fixed. You cannot change the order of effect blocks within an algorithm. In the Delay algorithm, the Delay effect block is first, and the EQ effect block is second. There is no option to have the EQ effect block first, followed by the "Delay" effect block. Likewise, you cannot change the order of individual settings within an effect block.

Types of Effects

Effects can be configured as either send/return effects or insert effects. There are a number of differences between these two types of effects, so let's look at each in detail.

Send/Return Effects

You typically use effects in a send/return setup when you want the effect blended with the original signal. These types of effects are also called loop effects, as the effected signal is looped back in with the original signal. Effects commonly used in a send/return setup are effects like reverb, echo, delay, chorus, and so forth.

When you configure an effect as a send/return effect, it will use one stereo effect processor. A send/return effect can be used by one or more tracks, and it can be applied in the Input Mixer and/or the Track Mixer. When you route a track to a send/return effect, you designate where in the signal path the routing occurs. When you route the signal PreFader, the level of the signal sent to the effect is not affected by the track fader. If you route the signal PostFader, then the level of the signal sent to the effect is determined by the position of the track fader. However, since the fader is the last component within a channel strip, the signal sent to the effect will have already passed through all the other components of the channel strip, regardless of whether it is sent PreFader or PostFader.

Insert Effects

You typically use effects in an insert setup when you want only the processed signal and none of the original signal. These types of effects are also known as processors, as they process the entire signal. Effects commonly used in an insert setup are effects like compression, EQ, microphone simulators, amplifier simulators, and so on.

❄ **TWO SIMPLE RULES**

People will ask me, "What are the rules for determining whether an effect is an insert effect or a send/return effect?" I have two simple rules:

Rule #1: There are no rules.

Rule #2: There are no rules other than Rule #1.

There are certainly recommendations on how to use effects, but there are no hard and fast rules. Many people have gotten interesting results by using effects in a non-conventional manner. Experiment, and if you like it, use it.

Insert effects also use one stereo effect processor, but they work differently than send/return effects. Insert effects can be used on tracks in the Input Mixer, Track Mixer, or across the entire mix. Once you insert the effect into a given track or across the entire mix, that effect cannot be used on any other tracks. However, most algorithms designed to work as insert effects can run in a mono mode, thereby allowing the insert effect to be used on two different tracks. When you use an insert effect on a track, you have four different insert options. Let's look at an example of these four options when using the four-band graphic equalizer effect.

Insert

The Insert setting routes the signal to both sides of the stereo effect. If you use this setting on a single track, you get a single four-band equalizer. If you use this setting on a stereo track or across the entire mix, the four-band equalizer is applied to both signals, but the same EQ settings apply to both signals.

Insert-L/Insert-R

Use Insert-L and Insert-R when you are using the insert on two different tracks and want to have different EQ settings for each signal. The effect acts as a dual-mono effect, and you would set one track for Insert-L (left) and the other for Insert-R (right). Each track now has its own four-band equalizer with its own EQ settings.

Insert-S

This setting configures the effect as a dual-mono effect, and it allows a single track to run through both mono effects serially. Using Insert-S allows a single track to use the four-band equalizer as an eight-band equalizer.

Scenes, Locators, and Markers

Scenes provide a way to save a variety of mixer settings, including fader levels, panning, routings, effect settings, and more. Scenes are stored within a song, and the number of scenes available ranges from eight to 100, depending on the VS workstation you have. Some VS workstations allow you to name scenes as well. One important thing to note about scenes is that they cannot be recalled while a song is playing back. Locators and markers can be recalled while a song is in playback mode.

Here is one way I use scenes. Let's say I'm recording a band, and all the instruments have been recorded. Now it's time to record the lead vocal. When the vocalist wants to record his part, he only wants to hear the drums and rhythm guitar. I can create scene #1 so that the vocal track is in record mode, the bass and lead guitar tracks are muted, and the levels of the drums, rhythm guitar, and vocal tracks are adjusted to his liking. Once he records his track, I can then create scene #2 that has all the instruments un-muted and has his vocal level adjusted to fit in the mix. After listening to the playback, the vocalist decides he wants to re-record the vocal. I can simply recall scene #1, and all the settings are back to my record-ready mode. After recording the vocal again, I can now recall scene #2, which contains my playback mode.

You can set various location points within a song by using locators. These locations are set and recalled using the dedicated LOCATOR buttons on the VS workstation, allowing you to quickly and easily jump to a specific location within a song. The number of locator points available ranges from 32 to 100, depending on the VS workstation you have.

I commonly use locators to mark the beginning of verses and choruses within a song. By doing this, I can quickly jump to these parts of the song.

Markers are similar to locators, except that you can't directly jump to a particular marker by pushing a button. The TAP button is used to place a marker within a song. There are dedicated buttons that allow you to move to the previous or next marker, and some VS workstations allow you to bring up a list of all markers and select the specific marker to move to. Each VS workstation allows you to have 1,000 markers per song.

I typically use markers to set specific points of interest within a song. For example, when listening back to a vocal track, I might drop in markers when I hear a bit of sibilance, or when I hear some unwanted noise during parts where the vocalist is not singing. I can then cursor through each marker and decide what action I want to take to fix these problems.

Automix

Automix is a function that allows you to create automated mixes. By using Automix, you can have the mixers change settings while a song is playing. When you create an Automix, the VS stores the changes you make to a variety of mixer settings. When you recall an Automix, all the changes are performed during playback, allowing you to listen to the mix exactly as you created it. Most VS workstations only allow you to save one Automix per song, but some allow multiple Automix versions per song.

Automix data can be created two different ways. The first is called Realtime Automix. As the name suggests, Realtime Automix records changes you make to the track faders and the track settings while the song plays. All your fader and parameter changes are recorded as Automix data. When you finish recording your Automix data, you can play back the song, and the VS will re-create all the fader and parameter changes you performed.

Another way to create Automix data is via snapshots. With Snapshot Automix, you can capture all your fader and parameter settings for a point in time. To do this, move to the point where you want to change your settings, make those changes, and then record those settings into Automix. Then move to the next point in time, make the appropriate changes, and record those settings into Automix. When you finish recording your Automix data, you can play back the song, and the VS will recall the appropriate settings at the appropriate point in time.

When using Snapshot Automix, you can also use gradation. Gradation allows you to create a smooth transition between 2 consecutive snapshots. For example, if you wanted to sweep a guitar from hard left to hard right, you could use gradation to perform a smooth sweep. Gradation can also be used for fade-ins and fade-outs.

The exact procedures for recording and playing back Automix data are workstation dependent. Additionally, some VS workstations allow you to edit, copy, move, and perform realtime punch-ins of your Automix data.

3 } Introduction to the VS-880/890 Series

In the first two chapters, we looked at the entire VS series. Now it's time to dig a bit deeper into the VS-880/890 series. In Chapter 2, we covered a number of concepts that are common across the entire line of VS workstations, such as V-Tracks and mixer modes. If you haven't yet read the previous chapters, I'd recommend you do so before continuing.

Between 1996 and 2000, Roland produced four different eight-track VS workstations: VS-880, VS-880EX, VSR-880, and VS-890. Table 3.1 recaps some of the differences between these workstations that were mentioned in the previous chapters.

Table 3.1   The VS-880/890 Series Differences

VS Workstation	A/D Converters	V-Tracks	Effect Boards	Analog Inputs	Digital I/O
VS-880	18-bit	64	Optional	4(RCA & ¼")	Coaxial
VS-880EX	20-bit	128	Built In	6(¼")	Coaxial, Optical
VS-890	24-bit	128	Built In	6(¼")	Coaxial, Optical
VSR-880	24-bit	128	Optional	8(RCA) & 2 ¼"	Coaxial, Optical

So why devote a section of this book to seemingly old technology? The fact is, the VS-880/890 workstations are still immensely popular, and hundreds of thousands of these workstations are being used in home studios around the world. These workstations are frequently sold on auction sites such as eBay for a few hundred dollars, making them an affordable solution for musicians looking to purchase their first digital workstation.

❀ SAME AS IT EVER WAS

In 1997, Roland provided a software upgrade for VS-880 users, turning the workstation
into a VS-880 V-Xpanded unit. Roland also began shipping VS-880 workstations labeled as
V-Xpanded units, which were simply the base VS-880 workstations with the V-Xpanded software upgrade
already installed. All software upgrades for the VS-880 since 1997 were considered V-Xpanded upgrades. It's safe to say that most VS-880 users are running on the V-Xpanded version of the software.
However, in 1999, Roland also produced the VS-880EX, which is a completely different machine. In
order to avoid confusion with the VS-880EX, I'll refer to the to VS-880 and VS-880 V-Xpanded models
as simply the VS-880 workstation.

❀ POINT OF VIEW

Before we continue, I need to point out that any functions, features, and examples will be presented using
the VS-880EX. That is the VS workstation I cut my teeth on, and it is the only eight-track VS workstation
I've ever used. And while many of the functions and features are consistent across the entire VS-880/890
series, there are some notable differences.

Aside from some of the technical specs, the VS-880EX and VS-890 are almost identical in appearance and function. Since the VS-890 was the successor to the VS-880EX, all the functions
and features found on the VS-880EX are found on the VS-890.

The VS-880 has a similar layout to the VS-880EX, but it uses mixer modes and routing concepts
that are not found on any other VS workstation. The VS-880 is limited to recording only four
simultaneous tracks, and some of the functions on the VS-880 are accessed via different buttons
compared to the VS-880EX.

The VSR-880 is the wild-child of the VS-880/890 series, if not the entire VS line. First of all, it's a
rack-mount workstation, whereas all the other VS workstations are desktop models. Because it's
a rack-mount unit, the VSR-880 has no faders. While it is possible to record directly to the VSR-880,
it is typically paired with a Roland VM-7000 or VM-3100Pro digital mixer. The VSR-880 is also
commonly found synced up with a VS-2480 via R-BUS.

If you are using a VS-880 or VS-890, I'll do my best to note where things might be different on
your machine. VSR-880 users will find that the concepts and functions presented will certainly
apply to their workstation. However, due to the numerous physical differences between the
VS-880EX and VSR-880, VSR-880 users will need to translate fader references and function
invocations into the proper button-pushing sequences as necessary.

The goal in writing these chapters is not to simply regurgitate the manuals. Rather, it is to show
you how to utilize your VS workstation to its fullest potential and your fullest potential, using

practical examples and techniques. Once you understand how to quickly perform common tasks, you'll be able to spend less time pushing buttons and more time being creative.

Before we get into the practical, I want to spend a little time reviewing the technical aspects of these workstations.

Connecting Your Inputs and Outputs

There are a number of connectors on the back on the VS workstation, so let's review them.

Analog Inputs

The analog inputs are used to connect external inputs to your VS workstation. The VS-880 has four RCA inputs and four ¼" inputs, labeled Input A and Input B, respectively. Input A takes precedence over Input B in cases where both inputs are connected. The VS-880EX and VS-890 have six ¼" inputs, and the VSR-880 has eight RCA and two ¼" inputs.

You can connect microphones and instruments directly to these inputs. The Input Sensitivity knobs on the front panel control the amount of gain applied to the input signal. If you are using condenser microphones, you'll need to connect them to an external device that can provide phantom power, as none of the VS-880/890 workstations provide phantom power. Many people also use external microphone pre-amps, instrument pre-amps, and/or mixing boards, connecting the outputs of those devices to the inputs on the VS.

Analog Outputs

There are various analog outputs on your VS workstation. The Master Outputs are normally connected to your monitors. There are also Auxiliary Outputs, which can be used to route one or more tracks to external devices. Finally, there is a standard Headphone Output jack.

By default, the audio going though the Mix bus is sent to the Master Outs, but you can have the audio on the Aux Bus, Effect Bus, or Recording Bus sent to the Master Outs. This can be useful for diagnosing routing or signal overloading problems.

The Headphone Out carries the same signal as the Master Outs. This cannot be changed. If you want to send one signal to the headphones and another signal to your monitors, you could connect your monitors to the Aux Outs and adjust the Aux settings on each track accordingly.

The Aux Outs can also be used when you want to use external effects processors. You can route one or more tracks to the Aux Outs and then to the external device and bring the outputs of the external device back into the analog inputs on the VS.

You can also configure the Master Outs and the Aux Outs as Direct Outs. This allows you to output four tracks at a time via these outputs.

Digital Inputs

The digital inputs allow you to bring signals from external digital devices into the VS. The VS-880 has a coaxial digital input, whereas the rest of the VS-880/890 workstations have both coaxial and optical digital inputs. The VSR-880 includes an R-BUS connector, which can transmit and receive eight separate digital audio signals. See the chapter on the VS-2480 for more information on using R-BUS.

When connecting digital inputs to the VS, the VS will need to "clock" to the external digital device. By default, the VS uses its internal clock. You can change the setting of the VS Master Clock in the SYSTEM settings. When changing the Master Clock, be sure to pull the Master fader all the way down, as a loud click occurs when changing the clock.

Bringing signals into the VS digitally is the only way to bypass the internal VS pre-amps. I've used a number of external devices connected to the digital input on my VS, including pre-amps that provide a digital output, stand-alone analog to digital converter boxes, and CD players equipped with a digital output.

Digital Outputs

The digital inputs allow you to send digital signals from the VS to external devices. The VS-880 has a coaxial digital output, whereas the rest of the VS-880/890 workstations have both coaxial and optical digital outputs.

If you have monitors with digital inputs, you can connect them to the digital outputs on the VS. You can also use the digital outputs on the VS to send signals to devices such as stand-alone audio CD recorders and effect devices with digital inputs. If you want to use an external digital effect device and bring the signal back into the VS digitally, make sure the external device can be configured as the Master Clock.

SCSI Port

The SCSI port allows you to connect devices such as a SCSI CD burner, SCSI hard drives, and SCSI ZIP or Jaz drives. You can connect up to seven external SCSI devices to the VS. The SCSI device most commonly used with a VS workstation is a SCSI CD burner, allowing you to create CD backups and audio CDs. We'll cover the details of these operations a bit later.

Since the VS-880 and VS-880EX can only use 4GB of space on the internal hard drive, external SCSI hard drives are a great way to expand your storage options. If you use a SCSI CD burner as well as external SCSI hard drives, ZIP drives, or Jaz drives, be aware that you cannot back up to the CD burner from these devices. Backups can only be done from the internal hard drive.

You can also exchange song data between different models of VS workstations by using the Song Export and Song Import functions. In general, you can export data from one model via a SCSI device and then connect that SCSI device or medium to the other model and perform the import.

There are some limitations when using Song Import and Song Export, so it's best to refer to the appropriate owners manuals for any compatibility issues.

MIDI Connections

Each VS workstation also contains two standard MIDI connectors: IN and OUT/THRU. You can use these MIDI connectors to synchronize multiple VS workstations, synchronize the VS with external MIDI devices such as keyboards and drum machines, and control certain functions of the VS workstation from an external device.

The chapters on the 1680/1880 workstations will provide details on connecting external MIDI devices with a VS workstation.

Front Panel Layout

The front panel layout is fairly consistent between the VS-880, VS-880EX, and VS-890. The front panel layout of the VSR-880 is completely different, but it does contain many of the same buttons found in the other workstations. Figure 3.1 shows the front panel of the VS-880EX, which consists of the mixer section, the recorder section, and the display section.

DISPLAY SECTION

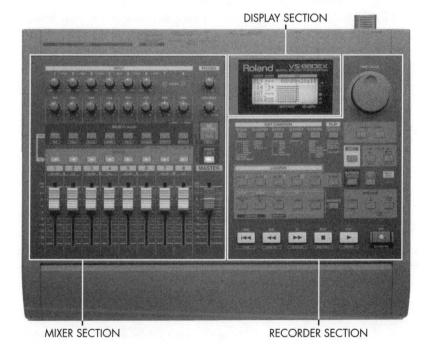

Figure 3.1
The mixer, recorder, and display sections of the VS-880EX.

MIXER SECTION   RECORDER SECTION

Mixer Section

The mixer section contains a series of faders, knobs, and buttons, which are used in conjunction with the various mixer modes. The mixer section is also used to configure your signal routings. The way in which these faders, knobs, and buttons work is dependent upon which mixer mode you are working in; therefore, we'll cover the details in the sections that discuss recording and mixing.

Recorder Section

The recorder section contains various groupings of buttons, the Time/Value dial (which I call the jogwheel), and the Transport Controls. At first glance, the number of buttons may seem overwhelming, but they are grouped into subsections on the front panel. Some of these buttons are used for recording, others are used when editing, and some can be used for multiple purposes. We'll cover many of these buttons in detail when we discuss recording and mixing, but let's take a quick look at some of them now.

SHIFT Button

The SHIFT button is used to invoke secondary button functions. The secondary button functions are imbedded within a rectangle, as shown in Figure 3.2. On the VSR-880, the secondary button functions are in blue text. The SHIFT button can also be used in conjunction with the jogwheel, allowing various settings to be changed in increments of 1 or 10.

Figure 3.2
Holding the SHIFT button and pressing the ZERO button invokes the STORE function.

PLAY/DISPLAY

Pressing the PLAY button returns you to a home state, also known as the Play Condition. If you get buried in a menu and want to escape, press the PLAY button. When used in conjunction with the SHIFT button, the display will toggle through the four display modes.

> ❊ **LIGHT ME UP**
>
> To quickly adjust the contrast of the display on the VS-880EX or VS-890, hold down the PLAY/DISPLAY button and turn the jogwheel. The contrast of the display can also be changed on all VS-880/890 models via SYSTEM → SYS System PRM? → SYS LCD Contrast.

Transport Controls

The Transport Controls, from left to right, are

- ❄ ZERO: Return to 00:00:00:00.
- ❄ RW: Press once to move back one second, hold for true rewind.
- ❄ FF: Press once to move forward one second, hold for true fast forward.
- ❄ STOP: Stop playback or recording.
- ❄ PLAY: Begin playback or recording.
- ❄ REC: Enable/disable record mode.

You'll also notice that there are additional functions listed above or below each Transport button. Holding the SHIFT button and pressing the Transport button performs the following functions:

- ❄ STORE: Save the current song.
- ❄ SONG TOP: Move to the first location in the song that contains recorded material.
- ❄ SONG END: Move to the last location in the song that contains recorded material.
- ❄ SHUT/EJECT: Shut down the VS workstation.
- ❄ RESTART: Restart the VS workstation after it has been shut down.

Edit Condition Buttons

There are five Edit Condition buttons:

- ❄ SONG: Perform song-related functions, such as Select, Create, Copy, and Delete.
- ❄ LOCATOR: Edit locator, loop, and Auto Punch data.
- ❄ TRACK: Perform track-related functions, such as Copy, Move, Insert, and Erase.
- ❄ EFFECT: Select and edit effects used by the effects processors.
- ❄ SYSTEM: View and change system-level or global settings.

Repeatedly pressing an Edit Condition button cycles though its available menu choices. The menu choices are listed below the Edit Condition button, as shown in Figure 3.3.

LOCATOR Buttons

These is a series of buttons related to setting and recalling locators, markers, scenes, loop points, and Auto Punch points.

Preview Buttons

These buttons allow you to preview a small section of audio either before or after the current point in time. The SCRUB button allows you to see a representation of the waveform for a given track, and it can be used in conjunction with the preview buttons.

Figure 3.3

The menu choices for each Edit Condition button are listed below the button.

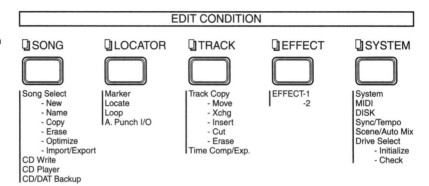

Parameter Buttons and Cursor Buttons

These buttons are used to change settings in the various display screens and to confirm or deny changes.

Display Section

The display screen, as shown in Figure 3.4, is your window to the inner controls of the VS workstation. Every function you perform on the VS will be shown on the display screen. Since it's important to understand what is on the display and, more importantly, what it means, we'll spend a bit of time exploring the various components of the display.

Figure 3.4

The display screen on the VS-880EX.

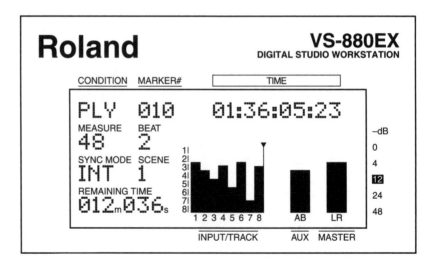

Current Condition

The current condition is shown in the upper-left corner of the display. These conditions describe where you have navigated within the mixer modes or functions.

- ❋ PLY: Home state/normal condition
- ❋ INN: Editing parameters for a track in the Input Mixer
- ❋ TRN: Editing parameters for a track in the Track Mixer
- ❋ RTN: Editing parameters within the Effects Return Mixer
- ❋ SNG: Working in the Song Edit Condition
- ❋ LOC: Working in the Locator Edit Condition
- ❋ TRK: Working in the Track Edit Condition
- ❋ SNG: Working in the Song Edit Condition
- ❋ FX: Working in the Effect Edit Condition (N/A on VS-880)
- ❋ SYS: Working in the System Edit Condition
- ❋ CDR: Working in the CD-RW mastering room (VS-890 only)

PLAYING WITH CASE

If the current condition is Ply instead of PLY, then the song is protected. When a song is protected, the song cannot be changed or edited.

When the current condition is anything other than the Play Condition, the display will correspond to the particular parameters of the function or mixer mode you are working in.

Current Marker

The current marker number is shown just to the right of the current condition. You can have up to 1,000 markers per song. If there is an asterisk (*) after the marker number, it means that the current marker is also an Automix marker. If you haven't placed any markers in the song, the display will show three dashes.

NAVIGATING MARKERS

When in the Play Condition, pressing the PREVIOUS button will jump to the previous marker, and pressing the NEXT button will jump to the next marker.

Current Measure and Beat

The current measure and beat are shown below the current condition and current marker. A plus sign (+) next to the beat indicates that you are past the beginning of the beat but have not reached the next beat. By default, the current measure and beat are always displayed. You can change the display so that this information only shows when the metronome is playing. To do this, go to SYSTEM → SYSTEM PRM? → SYS MeasurDsp= and use the jogwheel to set the value to Auto.

Sync Mode

The sync mode is shown below the current measure. If you have configured the VS to synchronize with external devices via MIDI, the display will show EXT (external sync). Otherwise, it will show INT (internal). To quickly toggle between INT and EXT sync modes, hold SHIFT and press the SYSTEM button.

❋ FLASHING PLAY BUTTON

If you press PLAY and the button flashes and nothing else happens, you might have accidentally changed the sync mode to EXT. This can happen when you attempt to change the display mode but press the wrong button. To change the display mode, hold SHIFT and press the DISPLAY button. To change the sync mode, hold SHIFT and press the SYSTEM button. Since the DISPLAY and SYSTEM buttons are next to each other, it's easy to press the wrong button. If the PLAY button flashes and the sync mode is EXT, simply toggle the sync mode back to INT.

Current Scene

The current scene number is displayed below the current beat. An asterisk (*) preceding the scene number means one or more mixer settings have been changed since the scene was recalled. If you haven't created any scenes in the song, the display will show three dashes.

Remaining Time

The amount of remaining recording time is displayed in the lower left-hand corner of the display. The remaining time depends on the size of the partition, the recording mode and sample rate of the song, and how many tracks are armed for recording. The display defaults to showing the remaining time in minutes and seconds. By navigating to SYSTEM → SYSTEM PRM? → SYS RemainDsp=, you can use the jogwheel to change how the remaining time is displayed:

❋ TIME: Remaining minutes and seconds

❋ CapaMB: Remaining megabytes in the partition

❋ Capa %: Remaining space as a percentage of total space in the partition

❋ Event: Remaining events for the song

> ❄ **EVENTS**
>
> The VS workstations use a pointer-based recording architecture, and they use events to store information related to the pointers. For example, when you record on a single track, the start time and end time of that recorded segment are stored as two events. Each song can contain approximately 12,800 events. If you do an extreme number of overdubs or punch-ins, or you create a lot of Automix data, it is possible to run out of events. Once you run out of events in a song, you will not be able to do any further recording in the song.

Current Time

The upper right of the display shows the current time within the song. The time is shown in SMPTE time code, which translates to hours:minutes:seconds:frames. The VS defaults to having 30 frames per second, and each frame can have 100 sub-frames. If you are mathematically-challenged, that means you can edit down to ⅓ of a millisecond in time.

You can change the current time when the VS is in the Play Condition by using the jogwheel. By pressing the ← and → CURSOR buttons, you can change the point of reference relative to how the current time changes. Let's run though how all this works.

When the current time is displayed in standard SMPTE format, turning the jogwheel will change the time in one frame increments. Holding down the SHIFT button and turning the jogwheel will change the time in 10-frame increments.

If you press the CURSOR → button, the current time is displayed in sub-frames. Turning the jogwheel will change the time in 10-subframe increments. Holding down the SHIFT button and turning the jogwheel will move the time in one-subframe increments.

If you press the CURSOR ← button, the current marker number will flash. Turning the jogwheel will now change the marker, and the current time will get moved to the marker location you select. You could also do this type of operation by pressing the PREVIOUS or NEXT marker button. If you hold down the SHIFT button and turn the jogwheel, the change will be in 10-marker increments.

If you press the CURSOR ← button again, the current beat will flash. Turning the jogwheel will now change the beat, and the current time will get moved to the beat you select. If you hold down the SHIFT button and turn the jogwheel, the change will be in 10-beat increments.

If you press the CURSOR ← button once again, the current measure will flash. Turning the jogwheel will now change the measure, and the current time will get moved to the measure you select. If you hold down the SHIFT button and turn the jogwheel, the change will be in 10-measure increments.

NUMERICS

When changing the current time or the point of reference relative to the current time, you can directly enter numeric data by pressing the NUMERICS button. Then, use the numbers listed below the LOCATOR buttons to enter the values. You can use the ←← and →→ parameter buttons to move around within the data. When done, press the YES/ENTER button. This technique can also be used when editing locator and punch-in data.

Bar Display

The lower-right section of the display normally shows the levels of the tracks, Aux Sends, and Master fader. By holding SHIFT and pressing the PLAY/DISPLAY button, you can toggle the display through four different display modes.

The PRE LEVEL display mode shows the levels of the tracks PreFader. When you are in the Input Mixer, you can use this display mode to view the levels of the signals coming into the Input Mixer. When you are bouncing tracks in the Track Mixer, you can use this display mode to view the level at which the destination tracks are being recorded.

The POST LEVEL display mode shows the levels of the tracks PostFader. When you are in the Input Mixer, you can use this display mode to view the levels of the signals as they are being recorded. When you are in the Track Mixer, you can use this display mode to view a graphical representation of the actual fader positions of the tracks.

The PLAY LIST display mode shows where recorded material exists for the currently selected track/V-Track. The vertical line in the display is in reference to the current time, and the display shows approximately 16 seconds of time before and after the current time. You can use this display mode to see where within a track you have recorded material.

The FADER/PAN display mode shows the relative positions of the track faders, Pan knobs, and the Master fader. When switching mixer modes or when recalling scenes, these fader and pan settings may not match the current position of the faders and Pan knobs. When the current position is different than the actual setting within the mixer or scene, the current position will show as a blinking bar.

In both the PRE LEVEL and POST LEVEL display modes, the levels of the Aux Master and Master fader are always shown as PostFader.

Mixer Modes Redux

In the previous chapter, I introduced the concept of mixer modes. I can't stress enough how important it is to understand the function of each of these mixer modes. In case there is still any confusion, let me give you a few scenarios.

❋ To assign physical inputs to recording tracks, use the Input Mixer

❋ To listen to tracks being recorded or tracks already recorded, use the Track Mixer

❋ To bounce existing tracks to new recording tracks, use the Track Mixer

❋ To have send/return effects recorded as part of recording from physical inputs, use the Input Mixer and the Effects Return Mixer

❋ To bounce existing tracks to new tracks and to have any send/return effects currently applied to those existing tracks also recorded to the new tracks, use the Track Mixer and the Effects Return Mixer

To toggle between the various mixer modes, press the FADER[EDIT] button. This button should always be lit, and the color of the button determines which mixer mode you are in. Each time you press the button, the mixer mode toggles between:

❋ Input Mixer: FADER[EDIT] button is orange.

❋ Track Mixer: FADER[EDIT] button is green.

❋ Effects Return Mixer: FADER[EDIT] button is red.

Just to reiterate what was mentioned in the previous chapter, the VS-880 has different mixer modes from the rest of the VS-880/890 workstations. On the VS-880, each of the mixer modes is listed toward the top of the recorder section, along with a light next to the mixer mode name. Pressing SHIFT and the SELECT button toggles between them.

A Few Important Tips

"Persistent people begin their success where others end in failure." —author Edgar Eggleston

Before we dive headfirst into putting the VS to use, there are few key concepts, features, and functions that are important to understand. In fact, I think they are important enough that I've grouped them all together in one spot.

Re-Initializing the Hard Drive

The internal hard drive on the VS is divided into multiple partitions. The partitions are named IDE0, IDE1, IDE2, and so on. When you execute the Drive Init function to re-initialize your hard drive, the display allows you to select which partition you want to re-initialize. The problem is that the re-initialization process works on the entire drive, not just on a single partition. In other words, it doesn't matter which partition you select, the entire drive will be re-initialized. All data will be erased, and this process cannot be undone with the UNDO button.

Splitting and Merging Songs

The VS-880/890 workstations do not have any function to split one song into multiple songs. For example, let's say you are recording a live performance. You create a song on the VS and hit record, the band plays 10 songs, and then you hit Stop. You now have one long song on the VS. Unfortunately, there isn't an easy way to split this one long song into 10 songs. The only way to accomplish this within the VS would be to make a copy of the long song and delete everything except the first song the band played. Now you'll have to make another copy of the long song and delete everything except the second song the band played. Tedious work, but it can be done.

Also, these workstations do not have the ability to merge songs or tracks from different songs together. If you want to do this, you'll need to play the tracks of one song out to an external storage medium (like a DAT or stand-alone audio CD burner) and then record them back into the other song.

Transferring Individual Tracks to a Computer

Is it possible to transfer individual tracks from the VS to a computer? Yes. Is it easy to do? No. These VS workstations don't have any easy way to export .WAV files. The VSR-880 can transfer eight tracks at a time via R-BUS, but you'll need the appropriate PCI card installed on the computer and the appropriate cable. For all other workstations in the VS-880/890 series, it's a bit more complicated. We'll explore some of the ways to do this a bit later, but they require either a bunch of extra work or a combination of external SCSI devices and a SCSI card on the computer. Believe me, once you understand how to mix on the VS, you'll probably find it much simpler to do all your work within the VS.

Backups Are in a Proprietary Format

It's been asked and answered to death: You cannot extract .WAV files from a Roland backup. The backup file is in a proprietary format, and it includes all your audio as well as all the pointer files and other information necessary in a non-destructive, pointer-based recording system. Spend your time recording instead of trying to figure out how to get .WAV files extracted from a backup CD.

Save, Save, Save

Get in the habit of saving after every important operation. Hold SHIFT and press the ZERO transport button. You should be so used to doing this that you could do it with your eyes closed. On second thought, keep at least one eye open when saving, just to make sure you did it correctly.

Rome Wasn't Built in a Day

Learning how to use these workstations takes time, practice, and patience. These workstations may look simple, but there are a lot of powerful features and functions inside. Some of these things may be easy to grasp and understand; others may be more difficult. Sometimes the best way to learn how and when to use these features and functions is to just do it. If you're in a "just do it" mood, be sure to work on a test song or a copy of a song. In fact, if you're new to the VS series, I'd suggest you create a test song and practice the basics of recording, bouncing, and mixing.

Basic Recording on the VS-880/890 Series

Recording tracks on the VS-880/890 series is a pretty simple process. We'll start by creating a new song, and then we'll record song tracks within that new song.

Creating a New Song

To create a new song, press the SONG button multiple times until you see "SNG Song New?" on the display, then press the YES button. The display will show the default sample rate and recording mode, with the first prompt at the sample rate. You can change the sample rate by using the jogwheel. If you eventually want to create this song on an audio CD, I'd suggest you use 44.1kHz, as audio must exist in a 44.1kHz format before it can be burned to an audio CD. To change the recording mode, press the →→ parameter button, and then use the jogwheel to change the selection. I recommend using either MAS or MT1, so let's choose MT1 for our new song. When you have finished, press YES. The VS will prompt you with "SNG Create NewSong ?" Press YES if you want the new song created. The VS will prompt you again, this time with "SNG Create New-Sure?" Press YES again, and the new song will be created.

Once you create a song, you cannot change the sample rate or the recording mode for that song.

> ❄ **NEW SONG DEFAULTS**
>
> The first time you create a new song on your VS, the default sample rate is set to 44.1kHz, and the default recording mode is set to MT2. Each time you create a new song, the sample rate and recording mode you selected for that song now become the defaults for any subsequent new songs created within that partition.
>
> If you ever re-initialize your hard drive, the first song you create will default back to using 44.1kHz and MT2.

Naming the Song

You cannot name a song when you create it. New songs are automatically named "Init Song xxx," where "xxx" is a sequentially assigned number. Before you begin recording, I'd recommend that you rename the song to something more meaningful. To rename the song, press the SONG button multiple times until you see "SNG Song Name/Prtct?" and then press the YES button. This song option allows you to rename songs and to protect/unprotect songs. The display will show the current song name. Use the ← and → CURSOR buttons to move the cursor, and use the jogwheel to change the characters. When using the jogwheel, holding down the SHIFT button will allow you to move in 10-character increments.

When you are done renaming the song, simply press the PLAYDISPLAY per convention button and then manually save the song (SHIFT + ZERO). If you instead press the →→ parameter button, the VS assumes you want to toggle the protection mode of the song. Since this song is brand new and unprotected, the display will show "SNG ChangePrtct→On?" If you don't want to protect the song, press the NO button. If you really do want to protect the song, press the YES button. The VS will save the song and mark it as protected, and you won't be able to record or edit any tracks. If you accidentally protected a song, just repeat the above process to unprotect the song.

> ❊ **DEMO SONGS**
>
> New VS workstations are shipped with pre-recorded demo songs. If you want to delete the demo songs, you'll have to unprotect them before you can delete them.

3-Band EQ

When you create a new song, each channel in the Input Mixer and the Track Mixer (or Input Mix/Track Mix on the VS-880) has a 2-band EQ. The 2-band EQ contains a low shelf and high shelf EQ. I'd suggest you change the song to use the 3-band EQ, which adds a mid-band parametric EQ. To do this, hold down SHIFT and press FADER/EDIT and use the ←← and →→ parameter buttons until the display shows EQ Sel=2BandEQ, then use the jogwheel to set it to EQ Sel=3BandEQ. On the VS-880, you must be in the Input Mix/Track Mix mixer mode, then press the EDIT/SOLO button repeatedly until you see "EQ Sel=2BandEQ," and then use the jogwheel to set it to "EQ Sel=3BandEQ."

When you change to the 3-band EQ, the EQ for any channel can be activated in either the Input Mixer or the Track Mixer, but not both. On the VS-880, you can have the 3-band EQ available for any eight channels in the Input Mix/Track Mix mode.

Unfortunately, there isn't any way to automatically create new songs with the 3-band EQ option.

❄ **MASTER BLOCK**

Holding SHIFT and pressing the FADER/EDIT button brings up the Master Block settings. These settings include levels and pans for the Master fader, Aux Sends, and effects. The Master Block is also where you can change Direct Out and channel EQ settings. You can also insert effects into the Master Block, such as a compressor, which are applied across the entire mix. On the VS-880, press the EDIT/SOLO button to access the Master Block settings.

Routing Your Inputs to Recording Tracks

Now it's time to get your inputs routed to recording tracks. This is done in the Input Mixer. To bring up the Input Mixer, press the FADER/EDIT button repeatedly until the button is orange.

❄ **ROUTING ON THE VS-880**

The VS-880 has mixer modes and routing techniques that are not found on any other VS workstation. In the sections that follow, references to the Input Mixer and Track Mixer will mostly equate to using the Input Mix and Track Mix mixer modes on the VS-880, but some recording functions can also be performed when using the Input → Track Mixer mode. When it comes to routing, the concepts discussed in the following sections are applicable to the VS-880, but the actual routing techniques may be different, depending on the mixer mode being used.

The Input Mixer

Think of the Input Mixer as a mixing console that sits between your physical inputs and the hard disk recorder. In most cases, you will use the Input Mixer to do one simple task: route a physical input to a recording track. Since the Input Mixer is placed before the hard disk recorder, all the track faders and the Master fader should be set to 0dB, or unity gain, in this mixer. If you adjust the faders, you are directly affecting the amount of signal recorded on the hard disk. Instead, you should control the amount of signal coming into the VS via the Input knob that corresponds to the physical input. When you route a physical input to a recording track in the Input Mixer, you don't have to worry about adjusting the Pan knob. In fact, changing the panning in the Input Mixer can cause problems when recording stereo tracks, so it's best to leave the panning alone.

❄ **INPUT MIXER TECHNIQUES**

If you plug a device into an input jack on the VS but do not route it to a recording track, the signal is passed directly to the Mix bus. This technique is commonly used when syncing to external MIDI devices, such as a drum machine. By using the Input Mixer in a pass-through mode, you don't have to actually record the drum machine tracks, leaving you more options for your recording tracks.

When doing this, you may want to adjust some of the track parameter settings to manipulate the signal, such as panning.

If you change any of the track parameters within the Input Mixer, such as EQ settings, you will be changing the signal that gets recorded. In other words, any signal-processing adjustments you make in the Input Mixer will be reflected in what actually gets recorded. Most people like to record "dry," meaning they don't make any changes to the signal in the Input Mixer. We'll look at recording wet and dry a bit later on.

The important thing to understand when using the Input Mixer is that the track faders and track parameters correspond to the physical inputs. If you plug something into physical Input 1 and want to alter the signal that gets recorded, you would use track 1's faders and track parameters, independent of which track the signal will be recorded on.

The Concept of Routing

When you create a new song, the VS defaults to having Input 1 recorded on track 1, Input 2 recorded on track 2, and so on. This default routing makes it easy to get started, but to exploit the flexibility of the VS, you need to know how to change the routing to suit your needs.

The concept behind routing is that you are always routing a signal "from" somewhere "to" somewhere else. On the VS workstations, the "to" is always a recording track. Regardless of what mixer mode you are in, the goal in routing within that mixer mode is to get a signal "to" a recording track. Now, that signal could be a physical input such as a mic, guitar, or a synth; it could be an existing recording track; or it could be the output of one of the internal effect processors. It doesn't matter what that signal is or where it comes from; what does matter is that the destination in routing is always a recording track. When routing signals on the VS, you'll always begin with the recording track, and then you'll route signals to it.

The Routing Display

To see the Routing display, make sure you are in the Play Condition and then hold down the STATUS button on any track. The display will flash * * * Assign * * * at the top, and the rest of the display will show a matrix of which signals are routed to which recording tracks. This display isn't the most intuitive, so let's take a detailed look at it.

Figure 4.1 shows an example of the Routing display. The vertical bar in the middle of the Routing display divides the display into two sections: the Input Mixer and Track Mixer matrix and the Effects Return Mixer matrix.

To the left of the vertical bar, all Input Mixer and Track Mixer routings are displayed. The numbers at the bottom refer to the recording track, and the numbers along the left-hand side refer to both the physical input jack and the existing recorded tracks. The display has room to show two bars for each number along the left-hand side; the top bar indicates a physical input, and the bottom bar indicates an existing recorded track. In other words, the top bar indicates a physical input has been routed to a recording track in the Input Mixer, and the bottom bar indicates an existing track has been routed to a recording track in the Track Mixer. Figure 4.2 shows the default routing for a new song. Notice that the physical inputs are automatically routed to their corresponding recording tracks. Figure 4.3 shows that recording track 1 is the destination for physical Input 1 (assigned in the Input Mixer) and recording track 2 is the destination for recording track 1 (assigned in the Track Mixer).

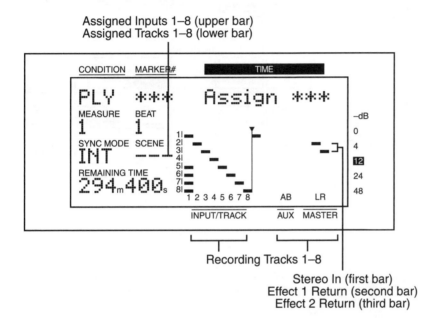

Figure 4.1
The Routing display on the VS-880EX.

Assigned Inputs 1–8 (upper bar)
Assigned Tracks 1–8 (lower bar)

Recording Tracks 1–8

Stereo In (first bar)
Effect 1 Return (second bar)
Effect 2 Return (third bar)

❋ **ROUTING DISPLAY**

Setting the contrast level of the display to a high number can help you better interpret the routing matrix.

Now let's look at the other half of the Routing display in Figure 4.1, which is to the right of the vertical bar. This part of the Routing display shows the routings for the Effects Return Mixer. There are three routings that can be shown in this part of the display: the Stereo Input routing, the Effect 1 Return routing, and the Effect 2 Return routing. Here's where the display needs a bit of inter-pretation. The bottom of this part of the display doesn't have any numbers, but the positions of any bars in this display directly correspond to recording tracks. In other words, a bar directly right of the vertical line represents something being routed to recording track 1. The Stereo In routing, Effect 1 Return routing, and the Effect 2 Return routing will correlate to the numbers 1, 2, and 3 on the far left of the routing screen. Figure 4.4 shows that recording track 3 is the destination for the Effect 1 Return, and recording track 7 is the destination for the Effect 2 Return.

Figure 4.2
After a new song is cre-
ated, each physical input
defaults to being routed
to its corresponding
recording track.

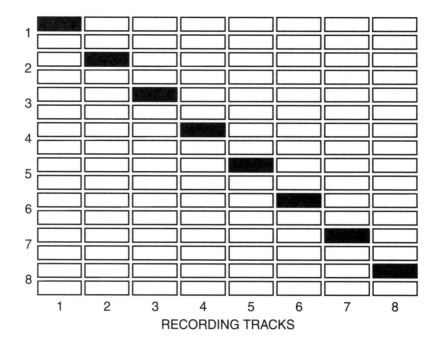

RECORDING TRACKS

Figure 4.3
Input 1 is routed to
recording track 1, and
recording track 1 is routed
to recording track 2.

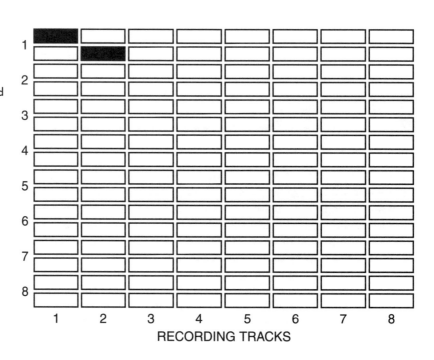

RECORDING TRACKS

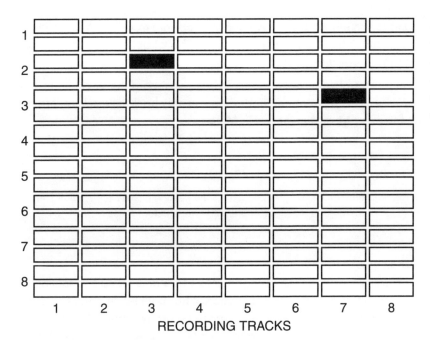

Figure 4.4
The Effect 1 Return is routed to recording track 3, and the Effect 2 Return is routed to recording track 7.

Now let's go back and look at all the routing shown in Figure 4.1. The left side of the display shows that Inputs 1–8 are routed to their corresponding recording tracks 1–8, and recording tracks 5–8 are routed to recording track 1. The right side of the display shows that the Stereo Input is routed to recording track 1, the Effect 1 Return is routed to recording track 6, and the Effect 2 Return is routed to recording track 7.

Creating Your Routings

Now that we've seen the Routing display in all its glory, let's get on to the task of setting up our routing to record. Let's start with a simple example: We want to record a guitar track. We'll need to plug our guitar into one of the analog input jacks on the back of the VS. Which input jack? It doesn't matter, since we'll route that input to a particular recording track. For our example, let's plug the guitar into the Input 1 analog jack, with the intent to record the guitar to recording track 4.

Because we are routing a physical input to a recording track, we have to be in the Input Mixer. Since we want this input to end up on recording track 4, we hold down the STATUS button above track 4, and the display shows the Routing display. While continuing to hold down the STATUS button above track 4, press the SELECT button above track 1. You have told the VS to record on recording track 4 and indicated that the source will be coming from Input 1. When you do this, the SELECT button above track 1 will flash, and the appropriate bar in the Routing display will flash as well. Release both buttons, and pat yourself on the back—you've just performed your first routing within the VS.

You can unassign routings in the same way. Hold down the appropriate track's STATUS button, and press any SELECT buttons that are flashing. This will cause the SELECT buttons to stop flashing, meaning that you've cleared that particular routing.

Figure 4.5 shows a complete picture of what we've done. When you record the track, Input 1 is controlled by the fader for track 1 in the Input Mixer, and when you play back the track, recording track 4 is controlled by the fader for track 4 in the Track Mixer.

> ### ❋ CLEARING ALL ROUTINGS
>
> To quickly clear all routings, hold any track's STATUS button until the Routing display appears and then press CLEAR. Doing this clears all routings in the Input, Track, and Effects Return Mixers.

Routing Stereo Tracks

When we routed our guitar track, we routed a mono signal. Now let's also set up our routing to record a keyboard part along with the guitar part. Our keyboard has both left and right outputs, which send a stereo signal across these outputs, so we'll want to record two tracks for the keyboard. We could record each keyboard output to a separate track, resulting in two mono signals that we'd probably pan hard left and hard right when we mix. This will certainly work, but if we want to apply EQ or effects to the keyboard tracks, we'd have to make sure we applied the same settings to both mono tracks.

The VS provides a way to work with true stereo tracks via the Channel Link parameter. You may link adjacent odd and even numbered inputs and/or tracks, as in 1-2, 3-4, 5-6, and 7-8. When you link tracks, the VS refers to them as tracks a, b, c, and d, respectively. When you link inputs, they become Inputs a, b, c, and d. Figure 4.6 shows how the Channel Link parameter affects whether tracks are mono or stereo. We'll look at more details about Channel Link when we cover mixing, so for now let's get our stereo keyboard tracks recorded.

We routed the guitar to record on recording track 4, so now we'll route the keyboard to record on recording tracks 1 and 2. Since the guitar is plugged into physical Input 1, let's plug the keyboard into physical Inputs 3 and 4. To simplify our routing, let's link Inputs 3 and 4 together in the Input Mixer. To do this, make sure you are in the Input Mixer and in the Play Condition and then press the SELECT button above track 3. Now use the ←← and →→ parameter buttons until you see IN3 Channel Link=OFF. Use the jogwheel to set the value to ON. Notice how the display now shows INb Channel Link=ON. Because we linked Inputs 3 and 4, the VS refers to this pair as Input b. Now that we've linked our inputs, we also need to link our recording tracks. To do this, switch to the Track Mixer, make sure you are in the Play Condition, and then press the SELECT button for track 1. Use the ←← and →→ parameter buttons to get to TR1 Channel Link=OFF, and then use the jogwheel to set the value to ON. The display shows this pairing as track a. Now

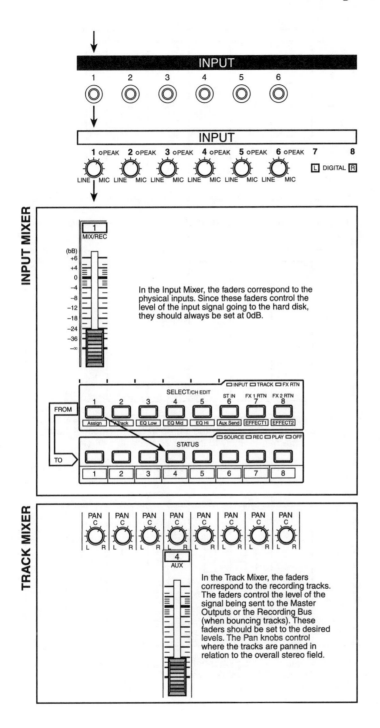

Figure 4.5

Using the Input Mixer and Track Mixer to route Input 1 to recording track 4.

In the Input Mixer, the faders correspond to the physical inputs. Since these faders control the level of the input signal going to the hard disk, they should always be set at 0dB.

In the Track Mixer, the faders correspond to the recording tracks. The faders control the level of the signal being sent to the Master Outputs or the Recording Bus (when bouncing tracks). These faders should be set to the desired levels. The Pan knobs control where the tracks are panned in relation to the overall stereo field.

Figure 4.6

The Channel Link parameter determines whether tracks are mono or stereo.

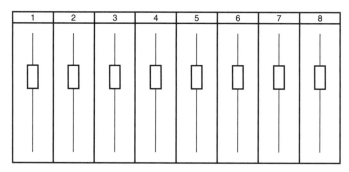

When Channel Link is OFF, each track is independent of any other track.

This example represents setting Channel Link = OFF for each track.

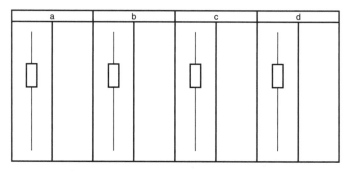

When Channel Link is ON, each odd-even track pairing becomes a stereo track. A single fader controls the level of the stereo track, and most of the track parameters apply to the stereo track as a whole.

This example represents setting Channel Link = ON for each even-odd track pair.

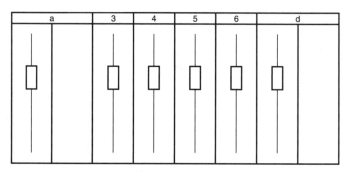

This example represents setting Channel Link = ON for tracks 1–2 and tracks 7–8. The remaining tracks are set to Channel Link = OFF.

that we've told the VS that our inputs are linked and our recording tracks are linked, we need to route them to each other. Switch back to the Input Mixer, make sure you are in the Play Condition, and hold down the STATUS button above track 1. Remember, we start our routings based on the recording track, which in this case is track a. While continuing to hold down the STATUS button above track 1, press the SELECT button above track 3. You have told the VS to record on recording track a and indicated that the source will be coming from Input b. When you do this, the SELECT button above track b will flash, and the appropriate bars in the Routing display will flash as well. Figure 4.7 shows the Routing display after Routing the guitar input and the keyboard inputs.

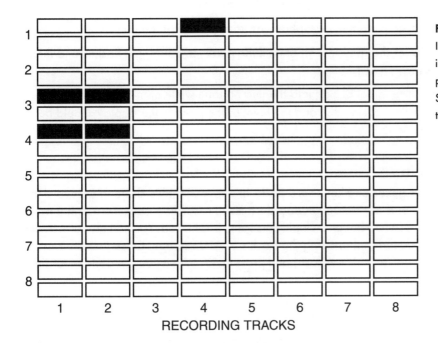

Figure 4.7
Input 1 is routed to recording track 4, and Stereo Inputs 3–4 are routed to Stereo recording tracks 1–2.

RECORDING TRACKS

❋ **TRACK PARAMETERS**

When in the Play Condition, pressing any track's SELECT button brings up the list of track parameters for that track. You can navigate through the track parameters by using the ←← and →→ parameter buttons. You can also jump to a particular parameter by holding the SHIFT key and pressing one of the SELECT buttons. Once you are editing a given track's parameters, pressing SHIFT and SELECT invokes a particular parameter, which is labeled below the SELECT button. For example, if you first press track 5's SELECT button and then press SHIFT and track 3's SELECT button, you will jump to the EQ LOW parameter for track 5.

Setting Input Levels

Now that we have our devices plugged in to the VS inputs and have routed those inputs to recording tracks, we need to set the input levels in the Input Mixer. The level of the signal coming in is controlled via the Input knob. Each analog input has a corresponding Input knob and peak indicator at the top of the recorder section. By default, the peak indicator will light up when the signal is greater than –6dB. You can change the level at which the peak indicator lights up via SYSTEM → SYS System PRM? → SYS Peak Level=.

Here's a simple approach to setting proper input levels in the Input Mixer:

1. Play the instrument or sing into the microphone as you will during the recording.

2. Adjust the Input knob for that physical input until the peak indicator light flashes and then turn the Input knob down a tad.

3. Continue to play the instrument or sing into the microphone while monitoring the peak indicator. It should flash occasionally, and the level of the input in the display should be between –12dB and –4dB.

Recording the Tracks

Now it's time to record our guitar and keyboard parts. In our routing, we decided to record the guitar to recording track 4 and our stereo keyboard tracks to recording track a. To arm a track to record, press the track's STATUS button multiple times until it lights red. You can also arm tracks by holding down the REC button and pressing the track's STATUS button. Once you are ready to record, press the REC button (it will now flash) and press PLAY. When you are done recording, press STOP.

Advanced Recording on the VS-880/890 Series

In the previous section, we saw how to route tracks and do basic recording. Now let's look at some additional recording techniques.

Overdubbing Tracks

Overdubbing is the process of recording new tracks while listening to already recorded tracks. When overdubbing, you'll set your routings and input levels the same as when you recorded the basic tracks. Since you'll want to hear the existing tracks while recording the new track, you'll want to be in the Track Mixer. Now you can adjust the playback levels of the existing recorded tracks, as well as the new track that you'll be recording. Remember, it's always best to use the Track Mixer for adjusting levels, as fader adjustments in the Input Mixer may affect the level of the signal before it gets recorded.

Following our working example, we have our stereo keyboard on recording track a and our guitar on recording track 4. While you were busy reading this, I went ahead and recorded a stereo percussion track to recording track d and a bass guitar on recording track 5. Now it's up to you to record a lead vocal on recording track 3. Once you've configured the proper routing in the Input Mixer, you'll want to adjust the playback levels of all these tracks in the Track Mixer. Once you've set the playback levels, go ahead and record the lead vocal.

Punch-In Recording

Now when we listen back to the guitar, keyboard, and lead vocal tracks, we realize the vocal came in a bit too late on the first line of one of the verses. We can fix this by punching in just before the verse and punching out just after the first line is sung. There are a number of different ways to punch in on the VS, so let's review them.

Manual Punch-In

To do a manual punch, put the vocal track back into record mode, position the song to a location before the part you want to re-record, and press PLAY. When you get to the point where you want to punch in, press the REC button. When you do this, the REC light will be red, and the VS drops into REC mode. When you get to the point where you want to punch out, press the REC button again; the REC light will turn off, and the VS will drop out of REC mode.

Footswitch Punch-In

If you have a momentary-type of footswitch, you can connect it to the VS and use it to punch in. Connect the footswitch to the ¼" footswitch input jack on the back of the VS, then set up the footswitch to enable punch-in recording via SYSTEM → SYS System PRM? → SYS FootSw =. Use the jogwheel to set the value to Record. The footswitch will operate just like the REC button. In our example, you'd press the footswitch at the point you want to punch in, and the VS will drop into REC mode. When you want to punch out, press the footswitch again, and the VS will drop out of REC mode.

Auto Punch-In

The VS can also be set up to automatically punch in and punch out at precise points. There are three ways to set the Auto Punch points:

❋ **Using locators:** Place a locator at the point in the song where you want to punch in and place another locator at the point where you want to punch out. While holding down AUTO PUNCH, press the locator corresponding to the punch-in point and then press the locator corresponding to the punch-out point.

❋ **Using markers:** Set two markers as you did for using locators. Set one for the punch-in point and one for the punch-out point. Move to the marker for the punch-in point, hold AUTO PUNCH and press NEXT. Without releasing AUTO PUNCH, press PREVIOUS.

❋ **Programming points during song playback:** While the song is playing, press and hold AUTO PUNCH. When you reach your desired punch-in location, press TAP. Continue to hold AUTO PUNCH. When the desired punch-out point is reached, press TAP again. Press STOP.

When you are ready to record using Auto Punch-In, press the AUTO PUNCH button so that it lights up. Position the song to a location before the punch-in point, press REC, and then press PLAY. When the VS gets to the Auto Punch-In point, it will automatically drop into REC mode, and when it gets to the Auto Punch-Out point, it will automatically drop out of REC mode.

Once you have set your Auto Punch-In and Punch-Out points, you can fine-tune these points if necessary. To do this, press the LOCATOR button multiple times until you see LOC APin and use the jogwheel to adjust the punch-in point. To change the punch-out point, press the LOCATOR button multiple times until you see LOC APOt and use the jogwheel to adjust value as necessary.

Auto Punch-In with Loop Playback

The VS has the ability to play back in a looping capacity. You set up loop points in the same way you set up Auto Punch points, except that you hold down the LOOP button instead of the AUTO PUNCH button when setting the points. To have the VS play back in a looping mode, press the LOOP button until it lights up, position the song to a point before the start of the loop, and press PLAY. When the VS reaches the end of the loop, it will automatically jump back to the start of the loop and continue playing. The VS will continue to loop until you press STOP.

You can use both LOOP and AUTO PUNCH together to practice the punch-in. To do this, make sure your LOOP points are before and after your punch-in points, as shown in Figure 4.8. Now press LOOP so that it lights up, press AUTO PUNCH so that it lights up, position the song to a point before the start of the loop, and press PLAY. The song will play the material between the loop points, allowing you to practice along with it. When you are ready to record the punch-in, press the REC button, and the VS will drop into REC mode when it reaches the punch-in point.

Figure 4.8
Using loop playback with
Auto Punch-In.

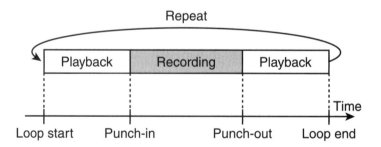

Track Sheets

OK, I'll admit that track sheets aren't really an advanced recording technique, but the more you record, the more you'll appreciate them. Figure 4.9 shows the track sheet for our working example so far. Whenever I begin a recording session, I have a blank track sheet next to my VS workstation. There are two important things to keep in mind when using track sheets: Always keep it up to date, and always write in pencil. As we'll see later, you'll probably want to move some tracks around within the VS, and you'll need to reflect those changes on the track sheet as well.

	Track 1 a	Track 2	Track 3 b	Track 4	Track 5 c	Track 6	Track 7 d	Track 8
Link	CHANNEL	CHANNEL						
V-1	STEREO KEYS	STEREO KEYS	LEAD VOX	GUITAR	BASS			
V-2								
V-3								
V-4								
V-5								
V-6								
V-7								
V-8					OH–L	OH–R	KICK	SNARE
	Track 1	Track 2	Track 3	Track 4	Track 5	Track 6	Track 7	Track 8

Song: VS Power! VS-880EX Example 1 _____ Artist: Chris Skelnik
Date: 2005 Mode: MT1 Drive #: 0 Song #: 1 Length: _____ (mins/secs) AutoMix ☐

LOCATOR / SCENE / NOTES

	LOCATOR	SCENE	NOTES
1			
2			
3			
4			
5			
6			
7			
8			

Figure 4.9

VS-880EX track sheet for our working example.

Exploiting V-Tracks

We've got most of our basic tracks recorded, so now let's record a lead guitar part. The guitar player isn't exactly sure what he wants to play during the guitar solo, so he wants to record a few different takes and then decide which parts are best. Now is the time to understand how V-Tracks work.

From our track sheet, you can see that every track we've recorded so far has been on V-Track 1. The VS defaults to using V-Track 1 for every track, but it's easy to change to record to any V-Track. Let's verify that recording track 6 is set up to record on V-Track 1. You can only change V-Tracks in the Track Mixer, so toggle to it and make sure you are in the Play Condition. Now, press the SELECT button above track 6, and use the ←← and →→ parameter buttons until you see TR6 V.Track = 1. Whenever you bring up the V-Track setting for any track, the display will show the V-Track matrix, as shown in Figure 4.10. This display is similar to the routing display, as the recording tracks are shown across the bottom and the V-Tracks are shown along the left. In the V-Track Routing display, each recording track/V-Track combination can show two bars; the top bar indicates that recorded material exists, and the bottom bar indicates the currently selected V-Track. In our example, we can see that V-Track 1 is currently selected for recording track 6, and no recorded material exists on that recording track/V-Track combination. If you want to change the V-Track, use the jogwheel to select it. When done, press the PLAY/DISPLAY in convention sheet button to return to the Play Condition.

Figure 4.10

The V-Track matrix display.

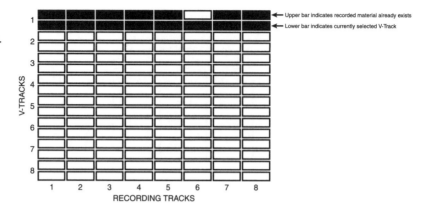

From here on out, I'll abbreviate the combination of a recording track/V-Track as "track r-v," where "r" is the recording track and "v" is the V-Track. In other words, "Track 6-1" represents recording track 6/V-Track 1.

Since recording track 6-1 doesn't have any material on it, and V-Track 1 is the currently selected V-Track for recording track 6, go ahead and record the first take of the lead guitar there. For the next take, let's use recording track 6-2. Press the SELECT button above track 6 and use the ←← and →→ parameter buttons to get to TR6 V.Track = 1. Use the jogwheel to change it to TR6 V.Track = 2. Now record the second take. To record the third take, change to use recording track 6-3 and then record it.

In the chapter on editing and mixing, we'll see how to create composite, or "comp," tracks using multiple takes that are stored on different V-Tracks.

Recording Dry, Listening Wet

Now let's move on to recording a backup vocal track. The singer wants to hear only the lead vocal and the rhythm guitar while recording the backup vocal track. Oh, one more thing: The singer wants to hear some reverb on the lead vocal part while it plays back and also wants to hear some reverb on the backup vocal part as it's being sung but doesn't want to record the reverb.

OK, first things first. Let's figure out where to put this backup vocal track. Since the singer wants to hear the lead vocal (track 3-1) and the rhythm guitar (track 4-1), we want to record the backup vocal on something other than recording track 3 or recording track 4. Remember, during recording or playback, you can only select one V-Track per recording track, so we can't record the new vocal track on those recording tracks. For now, let's set up our routing and track parameters to record this backup vocal track to recording track 5-2.

Now let's get some reverb dialed in for these vocal tracks. We first need to select one of the internal reverb effects. If you are using the VS-880 or VSR-880 and don't have the Effect Expansion Board installed, then you won't be able to use any of the internal effects. To select one of the reverb effects, press the EFFECT button. Each effect board contains two stereo effect processors, called EFFECT1 and EFFECT2. Let's use EFFECT 1 for this example, so continue pressing the EFFECT button until you see FX? EFFECT-1 PRM? and then press the YES button. Use the jogwheel to select one of the 200+ built-in effects. A good choice for vocals in this situation is effect A10=RV:Vocal Plt. Select A10 using the jogwheel and then press the YES button. Now that we've selected our reverb effect, we want to use it on the vocal tracks. While it's technically possible to apply the reverb to the new backup vocal track within Input Mixer, I prefer to do this in the Track Mixer. In the Track Mixer, press the SELECT button for track 3, and use the ←← and →→ parameter buttons until you see TR3 EFFECT1 = Off. Use the jogwheel to set the value to PstFade. This will send the signal to the reverb after it has passed though the track fader. Now do this same procedure for track 5.

So, we're set up to record to 5-2, and we have our reverb dialed in and configured in a send/return fashion for tracks 3-1 and 5-2. The default path for the effect return is the Mix bus, meaning we'll be able to hear the reverb in the headphones and/or monitors, but it won't be recorded. The only thing left to do is adjust how much of the effect return signal is mixed in with the original signal, and this is done in the Effects Return Mixer. Press the FADER[EDIT] button until it lights red, press any track's SELECT button, and use the ←← and →→ parameter buttons until the display reads RTN FX1 TRNLev =. The default value is 100, and you can adjust it by using the jogwheel or by using the fader for track 7. Notice that the label FX1 RTN is printed just above track 7's SELECT button, indicating that when the Effects Return Mixer is active, track 7 controls the return level for EFFECT1. Likewise, track 8 controls the return level for EFFECT2. Let's change the value to 70 by using the fader, then press the PAGE[DISPLAY] button to return to the Play Condition.

Now, since the singer only wants to hear the vocal tracks and the rhythm guitar tracks, we can adjust the levels of these tracks accordingly in the Track Mixer. Finally, mute the remaining tracks by pressing the STATUS button repeatedly for those tracks until it no longer lights up. Now you can record the backup vocal track dry, and the singer will be able to hear the reverb on the lead vocal and backup vocal track while recording.

Recording Wet

We've been working on this recording session for a while, and it looks like we're done. No, wait, what's that? The guitar player wants to add an acoustic guitar track. That's easy enough, right? Well, he also wants to record the guitar wet using a chorus effect, but he doesn't have a chorus pedal. The VS has a number of internal chorus effects, so we'll use one of them and record the acoustic guitar wet.

❄ **WET OR DRY?**

When you record wet, you can't go back and remove the effect if it's not to your liking. Because of this, I'm a fan of recording dry whenever possible. However, there are times when you might want to record wet. If you know you want to use a number of different effects during mixdown, you can save some time by recording wet. You might also record wet if you are using one of the guitar amp simulator effects and know that you want a particular type of guitar sound recorded.

One trick when recording wet is to record the dry signal to one recording track and the wet signal to a different recording track. That way, if you later decide that the wet track isn't what you wanted, you still have the dry track, and you can apply effects to that dry track during mixdown.

Let's set up the necessary routing and track parameters to record this acoustic guitar track to recording track 6-4. Since we used EFFECT1 for our reverb, let's use EFFECT2 for our chorus effect. Press the EFFECT button a few times until you see FX? EFFECT-2 PRM? and then press the YES button. Use the jogwheel to select A71=CH:Lt Chorus and then press the YES button. Chorus effects are normally used as insert effects, so let's set up the effect this way. To do this, we need to insert the effect into the Input Mixer. By inserting the effect in the Input Mixer, the effect gets applied before the signal is recorded. If we mistakenly inserted the effect in the Track Mixer, we'd hear the effect, but it wouldn't be recorded.

In the Input Mixer, bring up the track parameters for track 1 and use the ←← and →→ buttons until you see IN1 FX2 Ins = Off. Use the jogwheel to set the value to Insert and then press the FADER[EDIT] button to return to the Play Condition. Now when you record the acoustic guitar track, it will be recorded wet with the chorus effect. Figure 4.11 shows our track sheet now that we've recorded all these tracks.

Additional Recording Topics for the VS-880/890 Series

Before we move on to editing and mixing on the VS workstations, let's cover a few more topics related to recording.

Song Templates

Each time you create a new song, you might begin to use the same routings, effects, and track parameter settings. If this is the case, you should consider creating a song template. A song template is a song that has all these routings, effects, and track parameters pre-defined, but contains no audio data. Song templates can also contain system settings, such as synchronization parameters and the master clock setting. To create a song template, first create a new song, then

Song: VS Power! VS-880EX Example 1   Artist: Chris Skelnik

Date: 2005   Mode: MT1   Drive #: 0   Song #: 1   Length: _____ (mins/secs)   AutoMix ☐

Link	Track 1 [a]	Track 2	Track 3 [b]	Track 4	Track 5 [c]	Track 6	Track 7 [d]	Track 8
	CHANNEL	CHANNEL						
V-1	STEREO KEYS	STEREO KEYS	LEAD VOX	GUITAR	BASS	LEAD V1		
V-2					BKP VOX	LEAD V2		
V-3						LEAD V3		
V-4						ACOUSTIC		
V-5								
V-6								
V-7								
V-8					OH–L	OH–R	KICK	SNARE
	Track 1	Track 2	Track 3	Track 4	Track 5	Track 6	Track 7	Track 8

	LOCATOR		SCENE		NOTES	
1						
2						
3						
4						
5						
6						
7						
8						

Figure 4.11
VS-880EX track sheet for our working example after recording all the tracks.

customize all the settings that you'd normally do. Name the song "Template" or something similar, then save the song.

Now, each time you want to create a new song, you can use the "Template" as a model. To do this, select the song "Template," and then perform Song Copy. When the copy is done, the true "Template" song is still active, so you'll want to select the new "Template" song, name the song appropriately, and save the song.

One thing to keep in mind when using Song Copy is that you cannot rename the song as part of the copy. Therefore, when you perform Song Select, you'll see two songs with the same name. Another thing to know is that the VS doesn't have a "Save As" function, so once you begin modifying parameters or recording within a song, you can't save a new version of the song without wiping out the old version of the song.

EZ Routing

EZ Routing is a way to create internal templates that contain routing, track parameter, effect, aux, and master block settings. The VS comes with three pre-defined EZ Routing templates and allows you to create 29 user-defined templates. You can apply EZ Routing templates for recording, mixing, and bouncing tracks.

To access the EZ Routing templates, or to create your own, press the EZ ROUTING button. Each time you press the EZ ROUTING button, the display will cycle though the following EZ Routing choices.

* EZR Recording: Apply or create templates for configuring the Input Mixer for recording tracks.

* EZR Bouncing: Apply or create templates for configuring the Track Mixer for bouncing tracks.

* EZR Mix Down: Apply or create templates for configuring the Track Mixer for mixing tracks.

* EZR Mastering: Apply or create templates for configuring the Track Mixer for mastering.

* EZR User Routing: Apply user templates.

* EZR SaveCurRouting: Save all current routing as a user template.

* EZR DelUserRouting: Delete an existing user template.

If you tend to use the same routing, track, and effect settings for your songs, EZ Routing can save you time and effort. While EZ Routing can be helpful, there are some limitations. For example, you cannot have one input routed to multiple recording tracks. Also, system-level settings cannot be saved as EZ Routing templates. I tend to use my own song templates rather than EZ Routing templates, but that's just a matter of personal preference.

STATUS Button Indicators

When you press a track's STATUS button, the button will change color. Green means the track is in playback mode, red means the track is in record mode, orange means the track is in "monitor source" mode, and no light means the track is muted. When you are performing a manual punch-in, you can toggle between hearing the already recorded material and the input signal by pushing the recording track's STATUS button while the song is playing, but before you drop the VS into REC mode. We'll use our punch-in scenario from before, when we punched in a vocal on recording track 3-1. In our manual punch-in mode, the STATUS button is red for track 3, and we press PLAY. We will hear the previously recorded material on track 3 until we push the REC button. However, if we press track 3's STATUS button while the song is playing back, the STATUS button will alternately flash orange and red, and we'll hear whatever noise the vocalist is making. Pressing track 3's STATUS button again toggles back to hearing the previously recorded material.

If you always want to hear the input source instead of the already recorded material in this situation, you can do so via SYSTEM → SYS System PRM? → SYS Record Mon=SOURCE.

Recording from the Digital Inputs

You can connect external digital devices to the VS and record from them. When you do this, you bypass the internal pre-amps and A/D converters built in to the VS. The digital inputs are stereo signals, and they are identified as physical Inputs 7 and 8. When connecting external digital devices to the VS, the sample rate of the external device should match the sample rate of the VS song, and the VS will need to sync to the "clock" of the external digital device. You can change the clock on the VS via SYSTEM → SYS System PRM? → SYS Master Clk =. The default is

INT, meaning the VS is using its own internal clock. To sync the clock to the external device, turn the jogwheel counterclockwise if the device is connected to the VS using a digital coaxial cable, or clockwise if the connection is via a digital optical cable. Routing signals from an external digital device isn't any different than routing from the analog inputs.

Using the Internal Compressor Effect While Recording

A common technique when recording dynamic signals is to use a compressor between the input source and the recording medium. On the VS workstations, this would equate to using the compressor as an insert effect in the Input Mixer. However, keep in mind that the input source will have already gone through the A/D converters on the VS before the compressor can process it. If the signal coming into the VS causes the A/D converters to clip, the compressor will be trying to compress a distorted signal, and the results will be less than optimal. For this reason, many VS owners use an external compressor between the input source and the VS and use the internal compressors on the VS during mixdown.

5 } Editing on the VS-880/890 Series

After recording your tracks, you'll probably want to edit them. The VS-880/890 workstations include a number of powerful track-editing tools, allowing you to edit and manipulate your audio. Before we look at the different track-editing tools, let's first look at some functions that can help us when we begin editing tracks.

Locators

You can set and recall various location points within a song by using locators. These locations are set and recalled using the dedicated LOCATOR buttons on the VS workstation, allowing you to quickly and easily jump to a specific location within a song. The VS-880/890 workstations allow for up to 32 locators per song. There are four locator banks, and each bank can contain eight locators. There are four dedicated LOCATOR buttons under the LOCATOR label in the recorder section. These buttons—labeled LOC 1/5, LOC 2/6, LOC 3/7, and LOC 4/8—set and recall locators one though four. When used with the SHIFT key, they set and recall locators five through eight.

To set a locator within the current locator bank, press the appropriate LOCATOR button. You can set LOCATOR buttons whenever the VS is in the Play Condition. For example, suppose the song is playing, and you want to mark the beginning of each verse. When the first verse begins, press LOC 1/5. When the second verse begins, press LOC 2/6, and so on. If you want to use location five, hold SHIFT and press LOC 1/5.

Recalling a locator is easy; just push the appropriate LOC button, and the VS will automatically jump to that specific point in time. You can recall locators while the song is in the Play Condition. To clear any locator, hold the CLEAR button and then press the appropriate LOC button. Remember, you'll also need to hold the SHIFT button to recall or clear locators five through eight.

Each new song on the VS defaults to using locator bank one. To change to a different locator bank, hold down the LOCATOR Edit Condition button. The current locator bank will be shown in the display, and the corresponding LOC button will flash. Pressing any other LOC button will switch to that locator bank.

I commonly use locators to mark the beginning of verses and choruses within a song. By doing this, I can quickly jump to these parts of the song. In the previous chapter, I mentioned that locators could be used to mark Auto Punch-In and Loop Playback points. Locators can also be used to mark points that can then be used in the various track-editing functions. As you become more familiar with setting and recalling locators, you might consider using each locator bank to hold specific types of locators. For example, locator bank one could be used for the locator points related to verses and choruses, and locator bank two could be used for track-editing points.

Markers

Markers are similar to locators, except that you can't directly jump to a particular marker by pushing a button. You can have up to 1,000 markers per song. The TAP, PREVIOUS, and NEXT buttons are used to set and navigate between markers. These buttons are just below the four dedicated LOCATOR buttons.

When the VS is in the Play Condition, you can set a marker by pressing the TAP button. Markers are kept in sequential order relative to the timeline, starting with zero. If you place a new marker before an existing marker, all subsequent markers automatically get incremented, as shown in Figure 5.1.

Figure 5.1
Markers are assigned
sequentially relative to
the timeline.

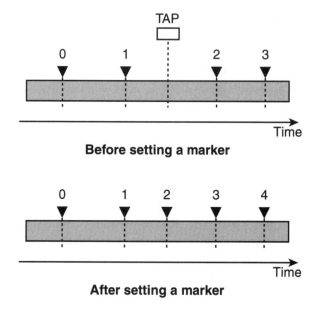

Before setting a marker

After setting a marker

To navigate to the previous or next marker, press the PREVIOUS or NEXT button. If the song is positioned to a specific marker, you can clear that marker by holding the CLEAR button and pressing TAP. Any subsequent markers after that point in time automatically get decremented. If the song is not positioned to a specific marker and you hold CLEAR and press TAP, then the previous marker in the timeline is removed. To clear all markers, hold SHIFT, hold CLEAR, and press TAP. The VS will prompt you with Clear ALLMarker? in the display. Press YES to confirm that you want to clear all markers.

❄ **CLEARING ALL MARKERS**

If you clear all markers, you will also clear any Automix markers you might have set. If you are using regular markers and Automix markers, and you want to clear only the regular markers, you will need to manually clear each regular marker. Clearing any or all markers is not an UNDOable operation.

I typically use markers to set specific points of interest within a song. For example, when listening back to my recorded tracks, I might drop in markers when I hear a bit of sibilance in a vocal track, or when I hear some unwanted background noise before the guitar player starts a solo. I can then scroll through each marker and decide what action I want to take to fix these problems.

Editing Tracks

The VS-880/890 workstations include seven track-editing functions. Repeatedly pressing the TRACK Edit Condition button cycles through the following choices:

- ❄ Track Copy: Copy a section of audio within the same V-Track or to a different V-Track.
- ❄ Track Move: Move a section of audio within the same V-Track or to a different V-Track.
- ❄ Track Exchange: Swap any two V-Tracks.
- ❄ Track Insert: Insert blank space into a V-Track.
- ❄ Track Cut: Remove a section of audio from a V-Track, shifting any subsequent audio forward in time.
- ❄ Track Erase: Replace a section of audio on a V-Track with silence.
- ❄ Time Compression/Expansion: Shrink or lengthen a section of audio on a V-Track.

For each of these track-editing functions, you will need to set one or more edit location points, select the track-editing function you wish to apply, select the appropriate V-Track(s) you want the function applied to, and then execute the function.

Setting Your Edit Location Points

Each of these track-editing functions works in conjunction with one or more edit location points. These edit location points define the beginning and end of audio sections, as well as specific reference points within a section of audio. There are four types of edit location points used in track editing:

* ❋ START: Defines the beginning of a section of audio.
* ❋ END: Defines the end of a section of audio.
* ❋ FROM: Defines a reference point within the source section of audio.
* ❋ TO: Defines a reference point within the destination section of audio.

Each of these location points is a specific point in time. When you invoke a particular track-editing function, you can set these location points by using the jogwheel or by using the NUMRICS button. You could also use previously defined locator points to set these track-editing location points. However, the VS workstations have another set of locators that are used to specifically set the START, END, FROM, and TO edit location points. These edit location points can be set as follows:

* ❋ START: hold the TRACK Edit Condition button and press LOC 1/5
* ❋ END: hold the TRACK Edit Condition button and press LOC 3/7
* ❋ FROM: hold the TRACK Edit Condition button and press LOC 2/6
* ❋ TO: hold the TRACK Edit Condition button and press LOC 4/8

> ❋ **EDIT THE BEAT**
>
> You can enter any of your edit location points in terms of measures and beats. When the VS in is the Play Condition, press the ←← parameter button multiple times until the measure or beat flashes. Turning the jogwheel will now move the timeline according to either measures or beats, depending on which is flashing.

You can set the track-editing location points whenever the VS is in the Play Condition. You can use the Preview and Scrub functions to locate precise points in time, and once you have located these points, you can set them as the track-editing location points.

Preview
Preview will play a small section of audio before and/or after the current point in time. The default for the preview length is one second, but you can change it via SYSTEM → SYSTEM PRM? → SYS PreviewLen =. To preview the section of audio before the current point in the timeline, press the PREVIEW TO button. Pressing the PREVIEW FROM button previews the section of audio after the

current point. Holding down either the PREVIEW FROM or PREVIEW TO button and then pressing the other invokes PREVIEW THRU, as shown in Figure 5.2.

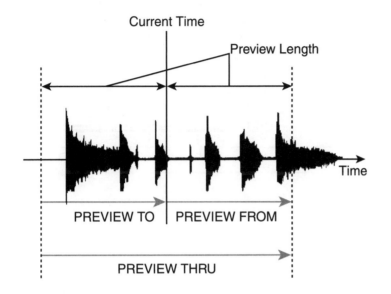

Figure 5.2

The preview functions play back short sections of audio before and/or after the current point in time.

Scrub

Scrub is similar to Preview, but it will repeatedly play a small section of audio within a single track. The default for the Scrub length is 45 ms, but you can change it via SYSTEM → SYSTEM PRM? → SYS Scrub Len =. To invoke the Scrub function, the song must be stopped. Press the SCRUB button, then press the SELECT button for the track you wish to hear. The display will now show a representation of the track's waveform , as shown in Figure 5.3, and you'll hear a small section of audio being played repeatedly. When you are in Scrub mode, you can also use the PREVIEW TO and PREVIEW FROM buttons. To exit Scrub mode, press the SCRUB button or the STOP button.

Selecting the V-Tracks to Edit

Three of the track-editing functions—Track Copy, Track Move, and Track Exchange—work with source V-Tracks and target V-Tracks. Before you invoke one of these three functions, you must have selected the proper source V-Tracks, as you cannot change the source V-Track designation in these three functions. In other words, if you want to copy something from track 1-4 to someplace else, you must first make sure that V-Track 4 is selected on recording track 1 and so on then execute the Track Copy function. When using any of these three functions, the SELECT buttons represent the source recording tracks, and the STATUS buttons represent the target recording

Figure 5.3

Invoking the Scrub function brings up a representation of the waveform in the display.

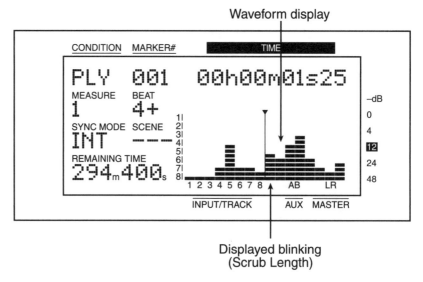

Waveform display

Displayed blinking
(Scrub Length)

tracks. Once you have specified the target recording track, you can use the jogwheel to select the appropriate V-Track within that target recording track.

The rest of the track-editing functions—Track Insert, Track Erase, Track Cut, and Track Comp/Exp—work with source V-Tracks only. When you invoke one of these functions, the STATUS button represents the recording track you wish to apply the function to. You can then use the jogwheel to select the appropriate V-Track within this recording track. You can apply the track function to all V-Tracks within a given recording track by turning the jogwheel until the V-Track is represented with an asterisk (*). For example, if you selected all V-Tracks on recording track 1, the display would show 1-*, and all the V-Tracks on recording track 1 would flash on the display. Additionally, you can apply the track function to all V-Tracks across all recording tracks by turning the jogwheel until both the recording track and V-Track are shown as asterisks (*-*). When you do this, all V-Tracks across all recording tracks will flash on the display.

The Track-Editing Functions

Now that we've seen how to set our edit location points and what those edit location points represent, let's talk about each of the track-editing functions in more detail.

Track Copy

Track Copy will copy a section of audio from a currently selected V-Track to another location. You can copy audio within the existing V-Track, to a different V-Track within the same recording track, or to a V-Track on a different recording track. If audio already exists at the destination, it will be overwritten. You can also have multiple copies of the data placed in the destination V-Track.

There are a number of situations where you might want to use Track Copy. For example, you can copy an entire track so that you end up with two tracks of exactly the same audio. Then, you could process each track differently in terms of EQ, effects, etc., and then blend them together during mixdown.

Another use for Track Copy is when you want to compile, or "comp," multiple takes together. In the recording examples from the previous chapter, we recorded three takes of the lead guitar. We could copy individual sections of the various lead guitar takes to a new V-Track, resulting in a new V-Track that contains the best parts of the individual takes.

You can also use Track Copy when working with loops. Suppose you recorded four measures of a drum track. You could use Track Copy to copy those four measures to a new V-Track and specify the number of copies as 10. The resulting new V-Track would contain 40 measures of the drum track.

Track Copy works well when you've set up a tempo map and have recorded your tracks using the tempo map. You could, for example, sing the chorus one time and then use Track Copy to copy it to the remaining chorus parts.

❊ **UNDERSTANDING THE FROM AND TO POINTS**

Track Copy and Track Move require you to specify START, END, FROM, and TO points. The START and END points define the segment you want to copy or move. The FROM point is a location within the START to END range—a reference point or anchor point somewhere within that range. The TO point is a location outside of the START to END range where you want the audio to be placed.

Track Copy and Track Move always align the FROM point to the TO point. Here are a few ways to effectively use the FROM and TO points.

If you want the target audio to start at the exact same location as the source audio, set the FROM and TO points to be the same as the START point.

If you want the target audio to start at a different location as does the source audio, you'll normally set the FROM point to be the same as the START point.

However, there are instances where you might want to set the FROM point to be different than the START point. Since the FROM point is within the range defined by the START and END points, you could set the FROM point to be a reference point somewhere within the START to END range. For example, say you imported a sound effect of a car skidding and then crashing, and you want the crash to line up with the beginning of the third chorus. In this case, you could define the START and END points to be the beginning and the end of the sound effect audio, the FROM point to be the location of the crash in the source audio, and the TO point to be the location of the third verse.

Remember, the FROM point gets aligned to the TO point, so if you specify a FROM point that is different than your START point, the TO point should not be the point where you want the audio to start. Instead, the TO point should be where you want the FROM point to be aligned in the target track.

Track Move

Track Move is similar to Track Copy, except the section of audio on the source V-Track will be replaced with silence. Like the Copy function, if audio already exists at the destination, it will be overwritten.

Track Move is useful when you simply want to realign audio that has already been recorded. In the tracks we've already recorded, suppose all the instruments play a final note, then the drummer does a small drum fill, and then all the instruments play a final note at the very end of the drum fill. During recording, the bass and guitar parts might not have been played at the exact point where the drummer hits the crash cymbal at the end. You can use Track Move to move the last note of the guitar and bass tracks to line up with the exact spot of the cymbal crash.

Another way I've used Track Move is when audio has been brought into the VS from an external source. For example, during one of the collaborative projects I worked on, I received an audio CD containing keyboard tracks. I played these tracks from a CD player into the VS, and then used Track Move to align them so they were in sync with the existing tracks in the song.

Track Exchange

Track Exchange allows you to swap any two V-Tracks. When you use Track Exchange, all audio on the selected V-Tracks is swapped. You can swap recorded audio with blank audio by selecting a V-Track that doesn't have any audio recorded on it. Track Exchange is the only track-editing function that does not use any location points, as it works with V-Tracks as a whole.

Let's go back to our recording example and see how Track Exchange and Track Copy can be used to create our comp track of the lead guitar. We have three takes of our lead guitar part residing on tracks 6-1, 6-2, and 6-3. Since we can only select one V-Track per recording track, we cannot currently play back all three takes of the lead guitar track, as they all reside on the same recording track. This is where we can use Track Exchange. Let's exchange track 4-1 with 6-2, and track 3-1 with 6-3. Figure 5.4 shows our track sheet after performing this operation.

We can now listen to each version of the lead guitar part at the same time, since they are on different recording tracks, and use Track Copy to build our composite lead guitar tracks. Figure 5.5 shows how we can build this composite lead guitar track on track 5-8 from pieces of the existing lead guitar tracks using Track Copy. Once we've built our new comp track, we can then use Track Exchange to put our lead vocal and rhythm guitar tracks back where they belong. We can then use Track Exchange again to swap track 5-8, which is our new comp track, with 6-5, which is an empty track. This way, all of our individual lead guitar tracks and our new comp lead guitar track reside within recording track 6, as shown in Figure 5.6.

Song: VS Power! VS-880EX Example 1   Artist: Chris Skelnik

Date: 2005   Mode: MT1   Drive #: 0   Song #: 1   Length: _____ (mins/secs)   AutoMix ☐

	Track 1 [a]	Track 2	Track 3 [b]	Track 4	Track 5 [c]	Track 6	Track 7 [d]	Track 8
Link	CHANNEL	CHANNEL						
V-1	STEREO KEYS	STEREO KEYS	LEAD V3	LEAD V2	BASS	LEAD V1		
V-2					BKP VOX	LEAD VOX		
V-3						GUITAR		
V-4						ACOUSTIC		
V-5								
V-6								
V-7								
V-8					OH–L	OH–R	KICK	SNARE
	Track 1	Track 2	Track 3	Track 4	Track 5	Track 6	Track 7	Track 8

	LOCATOR	SCENE	NOTES
1			
2			
3			
4			
5			
6			
7			
8			

Figure 5.4
VS-880EX track sheet for our working example after using Track Exchange.

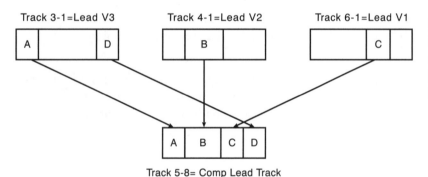

Track 3-1=Lead V3   Track 4-1=Lead V2   Track 6-1=Lead V1

Track 5-8= Comp Lead Track

Figure 5.5
Use Track Copy to build a composite track from the best parts of the existing lead guitar tracks.

❋ AUDIO VS. TRACK PARAMETERS

When you invoke Track Copy, Track Move, or Track Exchange, you are only working with audio. None of the track parameters, such as EQ settings or effect settings, can be copied, moved, or exchanged. Track parameters are defined at the recording track level, whereas these three track-editing functions work at the V-Track level.

Track Insert

Track Insert will insert blank space into a V-Track at a point you specify via the TO point. All data after the TO point is shifted backward in time. If you are using a tempo map, this is an easy way

Figure 5.6

VS-880EX track sheet for our working example after building the lead guitar comp track.

Song: VS Power! VS-880EX Example 1   Artist: Chris Skelnik

Date: 2005   Mode: MT1   Drive #: 0   Song #: 1   Length: _____ (mins/secs)   AutoMix ☐

	Track 1 [a]	Track 2	Track 3 [b]	Track 4	Track 5 [c]	Track 6	Track 7 [d]	Track 8
Link	CHANNEL	CHANNEL						
V-1	STEREO KEYS	STEREO KEYS	LEAD VOX	GUITAR	BASS	LEAD V1		
V-2					BKP VOX	LEAD V2		
V-3						LEAD V3		
V-4						ACOUSTIC		
V-5						COMP LEAD		
V-6								
V-7								
V-8					OH–L	OH–R	KICK	SNARE
	Track 1	Track 2	Track 3	Track 4	Track 5	Track 6	Track 7	Track 8

	LOCATOR	SCENE	NOTES
1			
2			
3			
4			
5			
6			
7			
8			

to insert additional measures into the middle of a song. I've also used Track Insert to insert space at the beginning of a song, so that I could record a lead-in to the song. Remember that you can insert blank space into all V-Tracks in all recording tracks by setting the destination to *-*.

Track Cut

Track Cut is the opposite of Track Insert. The range of data specified within the START and END points is removed, and all data following the END point is shifted forward in time. You can use Track Cut to eliminate sections of songs, creating a radio-friendly version of your opus.

LOCATORS AND MARKERS ARE STATIC

All locators and markers are assigned to specific points within the timeline. Using Track Insert or Track Cut has no effect on any existing locators or markers. For example, if you have a locator set at 00:02:00:00 and then insert 30 seconds of blank space at the beginning of the song, the locator will still be assigned to 00:02:00:00 within the timeline. After using Track Insert or Track Cut, you may want to clear all your existing locators and markers and reassign them as necessary.

Track Erase

Track Erase is similar to Track Cut, but the source audio is replaced with silence. Track Erase is frequently used to clean up beginnings and endings of songs. In our recording example, we might consider using Track Erase to also remove background noise from the vocal track when the vocalist isn't singing. Another example of using Track Erase would be to clean up any noise that exists on the lead guitar track between the time you pressed the REC button and when the lead begins.

Track Expansion/Compression

Track Expansion/Compression allows you to lengthen or shorten a piece of audio. While this sounds great in theory, you want to use it sparingly, as it can produce unwanted artifacts in the resulting audio. The recommendation is that the compression or expansion range is within 93% to 107%. There are a number of parameters specific to this function, including whether or not to keep the pitch of the audio the same, the type of source material, and the resulting amplitude of the new audio.

This function can be used to stretch or expand samples that you have recorded into your VS. If you plan on using Track Copy to create longer patterns from these samples, I'd suggest that you first use Track Expansion/Compression, verify the results, and then use Track Copy.

Undo

As mentioned earlier, the VS workstations use non-destructive editing. This means that every track-editing function, as well as every recording operation, can be quickly and easily undone. This is especially helpful when performing track-editing functions.

Every time you perform a recording operation or a track-editing function, a historical record is kept with the VS. The VS-880/890 workstations can store up to 999 of these historical records per song. To recall a specific historical record, use the UNDO button. When you press the UNDO button, the VS will ask what historical record it should retrieve. Unfortunately, these UNDO records are neither named nor time stamped; they are just listed sequentially. Because of this, I'd highly recommend that you either keep track of each time you record or edit a track, or that you only go back to UNDO level once each time.

Let's look at an example of the Undo function, using the tracks we've already recorded. Suppose we performed a Track Erase to clean up the beginning of track 3-1 and then performed another Track Erase to clean up the end of track 3-1. If we perform UNDO LEVEL=1, we'd undo the cleanup of the end of the track. If we instead perform UNDO LEVEL=2, we'd undo the cleanup of the end of the track and the beginning of the track.

If you perform an undo and realize you've made a mistake, you can redo the last undo. Hold the SHIFT button and press UNDO to invoke the Redo function. The last undo you performed will be redone. You do not have a choice as to which undo point you'd like to have restored; only the last Undo function can be redone.

However, the way that undo and redo work in conjunction with each other can be confusing. Let's go back to our example above, where we used Track Erase twice and then we performed UNDO LEVEL=2. When we play back the track, none of the cleanup editing we did is there, as it was undone by the UNDO LEVEL=2. Now let's do a Track Erase at the beginning of track 4-1. Now, just for fun, let's perform the Redo. Remember, Redo can only restore the last Undo, which involved the edits to the beginning and ending of track 3-1. So what happens to the edit we performed on track 4-1 after we redo the last undo? Nothing. The edit we performed on track 4-1 is still intact. Redo only applies to the edits or recordings that were originally undone.

Confused yet? Mixing Undo and Redo operations can lead to a great deal of confusion, especially if you don't keep track of every edit and/or recording. My advice is to use extreme caution when undoing something other than the most recent edit or recording, as it's easy to undo something you didn't intend to. Instead of undoing a recording, it's best just to re-record the track without undoing whenever possible.

As I mentioned earlier, only track-editing functions and recording processes can be undone. You cannot use the Undo function to remove setting markers, changes to effect settings, changes to system settings, a.

Song Optimize

Each time you record new material, hard disk space gets used, and historical entries are written out that serve as the basis for the Undo function. All of the Undo history is kept with a song until you perform the Song Optimize function.

Song Optimize removes all the historical records used by the Undo function. If you've done a lot of punch-ins or overdubs, the amount of hard drive space reclaimed after Song Optimize can be significant. The down side to Song Optimize is that you will not be able to undo any recording or editing done before the Song Optimize operation. Because of this, the VS will prompt you multiple times when you invoke the Song Optimize function, just to make sure you are really sure that you want to perform this function.

Although the manuals specifically state that you cannot undo the Song Optimize function, the VS will allow you to perform the undo. The problem is, if you do invoke the Undo function immediately after the Song Optimize function, all audio is removed. In this case, immediately performing the Redo function will bring all the audio back.

6 Mixing on the VS-880/890 Series

When it comes to mixing, there are a lot of opinions on the subject. I've read various articles and books on the topic of mixing, and one thing I've learned is there isn't any "right way" to mix. I'm not going to tell you how to mix; there are plenty of resources that explain these topics. Instead, I'm going to explain how to mix on the VS workstation.

Planning Your Mixing Strategy

When it comes time to start working on your mix, you need a game plan. The VS workstations allow you to record a lot of tracks, but there are certain limitations when it comes to mixing all those tracks. Since the goal is to get your song burned to an audio CD, I find it helpful to start at the end of the process and work my way backward.

The first step is to determine where you are going to create the audio CD. You can connect a SCSI CD burner to the VS and use it to create your audio CD. If you choose this option, you must end up with a stereo pair of tracks. When you instruct the VS to create this audio on CD, you cannot apply any effects or signal processing changes during the burn. In other words, the audio that exists on these tracks is what gets burned to CD.

Another option would be to create the audio CD on an external device, such as a stand-alone audio CD burner or a computer. Usually this is accomplished via a digital connection between the VS and the external device, although you could use an analog connection as well. If you choose to create your audio CD on an external device, there is no need to bounce all your tracks down to a stereo pair (see "Bouncing Tracks," later in this chapter, for an explanation of this process). You can mix all your tracks on the fly, applying effects and signal processing changes, and the resulting audio will be passed to the external device.

> ❈ **BURN BABY BURN**
>
> A SCSI CD burner allows you to do three things: back up your song, restore your song from a backup, and create an audio CD. A stand-alone audio CD burner can simplify the process of creating an audio CD, as you do not have to bounce all your tracks to a stereo pair before the burn. However, a stand-alone audio CD burner cannot be used for backup and restore functions.

The next step is to determine if you want to apply internal effects to your tracks. If you are using a VS-880 or VSR-880, you'll need to have the optional Effect Expansion Board per convention installed in order to apply any internal effects. You can only have two effects active at any time, so if you want to use more than two different effects in your song, you'll need to bounce tracks with effects. I'll cover the details of how to bounce with effects, as well as use external effect processors, a bit later. For now, you should consider which tracks you think you'll want to apply effects to and whether the effects will be inserted or applied in a send/return loop, as this can affect how many tracks you'll need to bounce.

Assuming that you do need to bounce tracks, you'll next want to determine which tracks should be bounced together. My approach is to bounce logical groups together. For example, if I had six tracks for drums, I'd bounce these tracks together. If I had three background vocal tracks, I'd consider bouncing them together. Another approach is to bounce foundational tracks together, such as drums, bass guitar, and maybe rhythm guitar. As with mixing, there is no "right way" to bounce tracks, but if you bounce tracks using these approaches, you'll probably find your final mixing steps to be simpler and more intuitive.

Finally, you should make sure that any necessary track editing has already been done and that your track sheet is up to date.

Now let's apply these planning steps to the example we've been working with. For this example, we will use the SCSI CD burner to create the song, so we'll need to eventually bounce everything down to a stereo pair of tracks. In terms of effect processing, let's plan on compressing the snare and kick drum tracks and adding a bit of reverb to some of the drum tracks. We'll also plan on using some reverb on the lead vocal and background vocal tracks. The bass guitar track also needs a bit of compression applied and may need to have some extensive EQ applied as well, so we'll use one of the internal EQ effects instead of the track EQ, as the internal EQ effects provide more flexibility.

Take a look back at Figure 5.6, which shows our track sheet. We have a total of 12 tracks that will eventually need to be bounced down to a stereo pair. Since we recorded this song in MT1 mode, we have a total of eight tracks to work with at any one time. Working backwards, this means our last bounce could bounce six tracks down to two.

Another philosophy I use when mixing is to save the more complicated fader movements for the last bounce. For this song, the keyboards play one solo, and the lead guitar plays another solo.

I already know that I'll want to adjust the levels of these tracks at various times throughout the mix, so I'll leave them for the last bounce, if possible. The same is true of my lead vocal track: I'll want to adjust the level to work within the dynamics of the song, so I'll leave that for last, as well. Since our keyboards are already in stereo, my approach will be to get to the point where the lead vocal is on its own track, the lead guitar is on its own track, and everything else is on a stereo pair of tracks. To get to this point, I'll need to bounce the drum tracks, the bass guitar track, the rhythm guitar track, the acoustic guitar track, and the background vocal track to a stereo pair. If you think about it, except for the background vocal track, these tracks are the foundation of the song, and that's where we'll begin. Again, this is the way I'd mix the song; it's not the only way, it's just my way.

Before we begin bouncing and mixing, let's look at a few features and functions that can aid in these tasks.

Track Parameters

Each track contains a number of parameters, which you can use to manipulate the audio signal of the track in various ways. Let's take a look at some of the parameters that are commonly used during mixing and bouncing.

- ❄ ATT: Allows you to adjust the attenuation of the signal from – 12dB to +12dB. Normally, this parameter is used to boost the level of a signal that was recorded too low.

- ❄ Phase: Allows you to invert the phase of the signal. Using multiple microphones to record a single source can cause phase cancellation, and you can flip the phase of one or more tracks to help correct it.

- ❄ MIX Level: Allows you to increase or decrease the level of the track. Adjusting the track fader changes this value.

- ❄ Pan: Allows you to place the track somewhere within the stereo field. Adjusting the track Pan knob changes this value. Panning tracks in various places within the stereo field can result in a more clear and full sound.

- ❄ EQ Switch: Allows you to turn on EQ settings for the track. Once you enable EQ on the track, you have access to a low-band shelving EQ, a mid-band parametric EQ, and a high-band shelving EQ. The mid-band EQ is only available when you select the 3-band EQ in the Master Block. As a general rule, it's best to use EQ to cut frequencies rather than boost them.

- ❄ Ofs Level and Ofs Bal: These parameters are only available when you have configured two mono tracks as a stereo track via the Channel Link parameter. For stereo tracks, the odd-numbered track fader controls the offset level, and the even-numbered track fader controls the aux send level. Also, the odd-numbered Pan knob controls the offset balance. When you are working with stereo tracks, these offset parameters control the level and balance of the stereo track. If you want to adjust the levels and panning of the left and right channels independently, you'll need to adjust the Pan and MIX Level parameters. In most cases, you'd leave the Pan and MIX Level parameters alone and just adjust the offset parameters as necessary.

Scenes

Scenes provide a way to save a variety of mixer settings, including fader levels, panning, routings, effect settings, and more. The VS-880/890 workstations allow you to have up to eight scenes per song. One important restriction is that scenes cannot be recalled while a song is playing back.

When you create a scene, the VS stores a snapshot of:

* Current track parameter settings, such as fader level, panning, EQ, V-Track, and effect assignments
* Current signal routings
* Current track status, such as whether the track is disabled, set for playback, or armed for recording
* Current effect parameter settings
* Current Master Block settings, such as master balance, master aux level, and master insert effect settings

WHAT'S MISSING FROM SCENES

Scenes store a variety of mixer settings, but not all mixer settings. For example, none of the settings in the Effects Return Mixer are stored as part of a scene. In the Master Block, the Master Level setting is not stored within a scene. Within the track parameters, the MIX SW is not stored within a scene. Finally, many of the global settings in the SYSTEM menus are not stored within a scene.

To access one of the eight available scenes, press the SCENE button so that it is lit. The dedicated LOC buttons are now used as scene buttons. There are four LOC buttons, corresponding to scenes 1-4, and holding the SHIFT button and pressing the corresponding LOC button allows you to access scenes 5-8. To store a scene, press the corresponding LOC button so that it is lit. For example, to store the current settings and routings as SCENE 3, press the LOC 3/7 button. To recall a scene, press the corresponding LOC button, and the settings and routings stored within that scene will be instantly recalled. Remember, you can only recall scenes when the song is not playing.

To delete a scene, verify that the SCENE button is lit, then hold the CLEAR button and press the appropriate LOC button. Once a scene is stored, you cannot save new settings or routings within that scene. Rather, you must first delete the scene, then store the scene with the new settings or routings.

Scenes are useful for a variety of scenarios. In a previous chapter, I described how I've used scenes to quickly switch from recording a track to playing back that track within the mix. In our recording examples, we could have easily used scenes in much the same way. For example, when we were recording the lead guitar takes, we could have created a scene where the rhythm guitar, keyboard, percussion, and bass guitar tracks were in playback mode, and the lead guitar track was armed for recording. After the lead guitar was recorded, we could have created another scene in which all the tracks were in playback mode, and the level of the lead guitar was adjusted to fit within the current mix. When we wanted to record another take of the lead guitar, we could simply recall the first scene, change the V-Track setting, and record another take of the lead guitar part. If we didn't use scenes, we'd need to readjust levels, track status, and so on. Using scenes recalls all these things with the touch of a button.

Scenes are also handy when you are bouncing or mixing tracks. For example, if you wanted to bounce a number of background vocal tracks to a stereo pair of tracks, you could create a scene that includes the necessary settings and routings. After you perform the bounce, you can play back the new tracks, and if you don't like the results, you can undo the bounce, recall the scene, tweak the parameters as necessary, and perform the bounce again.

Scenes are also a great way to try out different mixes. Since scenes can store effect parameter settings, scenes can also be used to try out different effect settings across some or all tracks. For example, you could have one scene that is the dry mix, another scene that adds reverb to the vocal tracks, and another scene that inserts a compressor across the entire mix. We'll use a variety of scenes as we work through some examples in this chapter.

Automix

Automix is a function that allows you to create automated mixes. Automix allows you save various mixer and track parameter settings as Automix markers at location points in the timeline of the song. Every time the VS encounters an Automix marker during playback, these settings are instantly recalled. Automix can be used to dynamically change effects, perform sweeping pans, insert fade-ins and fade-outs, and more.

On the VS-880/890 workstations, you can have one set of Automix data per song. In certain ways, Automix is similar to using scenes. However, since Automix is designed for mixing, it does not store any routing information. In addition, not all track parameter settings are stored as Automix data, as shown in Table 6.1.

Table 6.1 Automix Compatibility for VS-880/890 Track Parameters

Track Parameter	Stored as Automix Data?
Assign	No
Attenuation	No
Phase	No
Mix Switch	No
Offset Level	Yes
Mix Level	Yes
Offset Balance	Yes
Mix Pan/Balance	Yes
V-Track	No
All EQ Settings	No
Aux Switch	No
Aux Level	Yes
Aux Pan/Balance	Yes
Channel Link	No
Fader Link	No
Effect 1/2 Insert Switch	No
Effect 1/2 Insert Send Level	No
Effect 1/2 Insert Return Level	No
Effect 1/2 Send Switch	No
Effect 1/2 Send Level	Yes
Effect 1/2 Pan/Balance	Yes

There are a few things to note about Table 6.1. None of the track EQ parameters are stored with Automix. That means you cannot dynamically change EQ settings via the track parameters with Automix. However, if you needed to change EQ settings during playback, you could create your own custom EQ effect patches and use Automix to enable these effect patches during playback.

Speaking of effects, notice that Automix does not store the switching on or off of the effects within a given track. For example, we want to apply reverb as a send/return effect to the vocal track only during the choruses. Ideally, we'd like to set that track's Effect 1 Send Switch = OFF for the verses and then set it to PstFade for the choruses. Unfortunately, Automix can't perform this switch. But we could set the Effect 1 Send Switch to PstFade at the beginning of the song and set the Effect 1 Send Level to zero. We could then use Automix to set the Effect 1 Send Level of the track to an appropriate level for the choruses and then set it back to zero outside of the choruses. This scenario works for send/return effects as the send levels can be stored in Automix, but it will not work for insert effects, as none of the effect insert parameters for a track can be stored in Automix.

Another thing to understand about Automix is that although it can dynamically switch effects during playback, it cannot change any parameters within the effects. For example, the reverb we want to apply to the lead vocal track is effect A10 RV:VocalPlt. However, we want to change the reverb time from the default of 2.2 seconds to 2.8 seconds. If we program Automix to use the A10 effect patch, we cannot tell it to change the reverb time. Instead, we have to save a version of the A10 effect patch with our new reverb time as a user effect. Then we can use that user effect with Automix, and the reverb time will be 2.8 seconds.

Enabling Automix

To enable Automix for recording or playback, press the AUTOMIX button so that it is lit. The SELECT button above each track shows the Automix status of that track:

- ❄ Lit solid: Track is enabled for Automix playback.
- ❄ Lit flashing: Track is enabled for Automix recording and playback.
- ❄ Not lit: Track is not enabled for Automix.

To toggle a track's Automix status, hold the AUTOMIX button and press the track's SELECT button. By default, the first time you enable Automix in a song, the tracks will be in Automix playback status. Before recording Automix data, be sure to set the tracks to Automix recording and playback status. Automix can be enabled for each available track in the Input Mixer and Track Mixer, and Automix can be enabled in the Effect Return Mixer to store various settings within that mixer mode. In addition, various settings within the Master Block can be stored in Automix. On the VS-880EX, the EZ ROUTING button represents the Master Block, and holding down the AUTOMIX button and pressing the EZ ROUTING button will toggle through the Automix statuses for the Master Block.

You can enable any or all tracks for Automix. I typically enable everything for Automix, as the total number of events and markers is the same regardless of how many tracks are enabled for Automix.

After you enable Automix, you have the choice of performing Realtime Automix or Snapshot Automix. Both have their advantages, so let's look at both in more detail.

Realtime Automix

Realtime Automix records changes you make to the track faders and the track settings while the song plays. Realtime Automix is great for songs that only need minor fader adjustments during playback. As the song plays, each fader or parameter change you make causes an Automix marker to be created.

To perform a Realtime Automix, be sure you have Automix enabled, then do the following:

* Press the ZERO transport button to position yourself at the beginning of the song.
* Adjust the track faders, track parameter settings, master fader, and so on as necessary for the beginning of the song.
* Hold AUTOMIX and press the TAP button. This places a Snapshot Automix marker at the beginning of the song. Doing this records the current fader and parameter settings into Automix.
* Hold AUTOMIX and press REC. The upper-left corner of the display will alternate between PLAY and MIX, indicating that you are in Realtime Automix mode.
* Press PLAY and make the required fader and parameter adjustments as the song plays.
* When done, press STOP. The display will revert back to the Play Condition.

When you play the song, the adjustments you made will be played back. If you're not happy with the adjustments, you can re-record the Automix data, but you must first delete all the existing Automix data. To do this, go to SYSTEM → SYS Scene/AutoMix ? → SYS A.Mix Erase ? → SYS Erase, and now use the cursor buttons and jogwheel to specify the range of Automix markers to erase. Next, press the →→ parameter button, and when prompted with SYS EraseMode, choose MARKER. This will remove all Automix events and markers you've recorded within the range specified.

> ### USING SCENES WITH AUTOMIX
>
> If you have created a scene with particular settings, you can easily recall those settings and use them within your Automix.
>
> When using Realtime Automix, you could have a scene with all your initial settings for the song and recall this scene before placing the required Snapshot Automix marker at the beginning of the song. If you wanted to use other scenes with Realtime Automix, you would need to stop the song at the location where you wanted to recall the scene. Then, after recalling the scene, create another Snapshot Automix marker, re-enable Realtime Automix, and continue.
>
> When using Snapshot Automix, you can use scenes, as well. Since snapshots are normally created when the VS is not playing the song, simply position the song at the proper location, recall the scene, then perform the snapshot.
>
> Keep in mind that Automix does not record all the parameters that can be stored as a scene.

If you're happy with most of the Automix but would like to modify a part of it, you can edit your Automix by using Snapshot Automix.

Snapshot Automix

Another way to create Automix data is via snapshots. With Snapshot Automix, you can capture all your fader and parameter settings for a point in time. To do this, move to the point where you want to change your settings, make those changes, and then record those settings into Automix. Then move to the next point in time, make the appropriate changes, and record those settings into Automix. When you finish recording your Automix data, you can play back the song, and the VS will recall the appropriate settings at the appropriate point in time. One advantage of Snapshot Automix is that you can create your snapshots in any sequence within the song. Since Automix markers are a type of marker, they follow the same rules as regular markers, meaning they are tied to a specific location within the song and are automatically kept in sequence according to the timeline of the song.

To perform a Snapshot Automix, be sure you have Automix enabled, then do the following:

- ❄ Press the ZERO transport button to position yourself at the beginning of the song.

- ❄ Adjust the track faders, track parameter settings, master fader, and so on as necessary for the beginning of the song.

- ❄ Hold AUTOMIX and press TAP. This places a Snapshot Automix marker at the beginning of the song. Doing this records the current fader and parameter settings into Automix.

- ❄ Position the song to the location where you want to make a change to a fader or track parameter, make the necessary change, then set an Automix marker by holding AUTOMIX and pressing TAP.

- ❄ Repeat the above for all desired locations and changes.

When you play the song, the adjustments you made will be played back. If you're not happy with the adjustments, you have a couple of different options. Just like with Realtime Automix, you could erase all the existing Automix data and re-record it all. However, every time you take a snapshot, an Automix marker gets created. If you want to change the Automix data at a given Automix marker, use the PREVIOUS and NEXT marker buttons to position yourself to the appropriate Automix marker, make the changes, then hold AUTOMIX and press TAP. By doing this, you are overwriting the existing Automix data at that particular Automix marker.

 FINE TUNING AUTOMIX

When using Snapshot Automix, I'll frequently play the song until I get to the part I want to change, then press STOP. From here, I'll use the PREVIEW TO and PREVIEW FROM buttons, along with the jogwheel, to move to the exact point in time where I want to set a snapshot.

As we get further into the details of mixing and bouncing, we'll use Snapshot Automix with our example song.

One final note on Automix: When placing Automix markers, the markers must be 0.1 seconds away from each other. When using Realtime Automix, the VS will not create subsequent markers within 0.1 second of each other. When using Snapshot Automix, if you attempt to place a new Automix marker within 0.1 seconds of an existing Automix marker, the Automix data at the existing Automix marker will be replaced.

Gradation

Gradation allows you to create a smooth transition between two consecutive Automix markers. I normally use this for level and pan changes, but you can use it for a variety of transitions.

To create a Gradation, be sure you have Automix enabled, then do the following:

❋ Position the song at one of the existing Automix markers.

❋ Hold AUTOMIX and press the NEXT marker button to create a transition between the current Automix marker and the next Automix marker. Conversely, you could hold AUTOMIX and press the PREVIOUS marker button to create a transition between the current Automix marker and the previous Automix maker.

❋ The VS will prompt you with "Gradation OK?" To perform the Gradation, press YES.

After creating the Gradation, the VS will automatically place a number of additional Automix markers between the original two. These additional Automix markers will increment or decrement the values of the parameters as necessary to create the transition.

❋ **GETTING REAL WITH GRADATION**

People tend to think that you can only use Gradation with Snapshot Automix. While that's the most common way to use Gradation, you could certainly use it with two consecutive Automix markers created with Realtime Automix. Remember, both Snapshot Automix and Realtime Automix are creating Automix markers, and Gradation can be used between any two consecutive markers.

Here's a quick example of using Gradation to create a fade out at the end of a song. Position the song to the point where you want the fade out to begin and take a snapshot. Now, move to the point where you want the song to go silent. At this point, pull the Master Fader all the way down, and take another snapshot. While positioned at this last Automix marker, hold AUTOMIX and press the PREVIOUS marker button, and answer YES to the Gradation prompt. When you play back the song, the level of the Master Fader will continue to be reduced between the two original Automix markers, creating a smooth fade out.

Automix Considerations

Automix is one of the greatest features of these VS workstations, but it can be overwhelming at times. Here are some pointers for using Automix successfully.

❋ **TOP OF THE POPS**

So you're listening to your Automix, and you notice that there is a spot where the bass guitar pops a note that is too loud. This can be easily fixed using Automix. Add an Automix marker just before the note to reduce the level, and then add another Automix marker just after the note to bring the level back. (It's easiest if you place the "after" marker first.) Find the spot just after the bass pop and take a snapshot. That marker will have all the same settings as whatever Automix marker precedes it in the timeline of the song. By placing this marker first, the settings for this marker will automatically bring the track back to the same settings it was at up until this point. Now, go back in time to just before the bass pop, reduce the level of the bass track, and take a snapshot.

First, be sure to keep detailed notes about your tracks before you invoke Automix. For example, I normally have a timeline or layout of the song with changes noted. The times don't need to be exact; you just want them as a point of reference when you get started. I typically use Snapshot Automix and start out taking snapshots of the big changes first, then going back and doing the minor changes. Here's an example of some notes from a recent session:

- ❋ Intro: Keep acoustic out.
- ❋ End of first verse: Bring acoustic in—set level to approximately 85.
- ❋ Start of second verse: Bring lead vocal down a bit.
- ❋ Last chorus: Bring up keyboards—set level to approximately 75.

Consider clearing all existing markers before you begin recording your Automix. While you can certainly have regular markers along with Automix markers, going back and editing existing Automix markers can get confusing as to whether the marker location is a regular marker or an Automix marker. Remember, once you clear all your markers, you can't get them back. For me, by the time I'm ready to mix, I've got my detailed notes—I don't need to reference any regular markers to move to specific points in time.

Another suggestion is to create a scene for things that Automix doesn't record. For example, Automix doesn't record any individual track EQ settings or the ATT setting. Once I've played around with the song and have the proper EQ and ATT settings for my tracks, I'll create a scene to save those settings. When I begin my Automix, I can recall that scene and take a snapshot so that I'll always have the same starting point.

Finally, plan out your use of effects with Automix. Remember, Automix cannot record changes within an effect patch. For example, if you are using a reverb effect and want to change the reverb time from 1.0 second to 3.0 seconds at a certain spot, Automix can't record that. Instead, you could create two different user effects—one with reverb time set at 1.0 second and the other with reverb time set at 3.0 seconds—and use Automix to switch between the effects. For that matter, any effect patches that you modify need to be saved before starting Automix; otherwise, when you select that effect in Automix, it will pull up the version of the effect patch as it was last saved.

Bouncing Tracks

The process of mixing one or more tracks together and recording that new mix on one or more new tracks is called "bouncing." You can bounce tracks to reduce your overall track count or when you want to submix a group of tracks for easier mixing. Bouncing can also be used to free up the effect processors in cases where you want to apply more than two effects to the song. Bouncing can also be used to create a copy of a track that has different signal processing or effects applied to it. For example, you could bounce a snare drum track with some extreme EQ and compression settings to a new track and then blend the original and processed versions together during mixdown.

Mono and Stereo Bouncing

Before we get into the mechanics of bouncing, let's review mono tracks versus stereo tracks. When you bounce tracks, you need to decide whether the destination tracks should be mono or stereo. By default, each of the eight tracks on the VS-880/890 series is a mono track.

You can configure tracks as stereo tracks via the Channel Link parameter. You may link adjacent odd- and even-numbered tracks, as in 1-2, 3-4, 5-6, and 7-8. When you link tracks, the VS refers to them as track a, b, c, and d, respectively. We covered linking inputs for stereo sources in Chapter 4, "Basic Recording on the VS-880/890 Series," and the same concept applies for bouncing. Now that you know how to configure tracks as stereo tracks, the question becomes one of when to bounce to mono tracks and when to bounce to stereo tracks. Here are some guidelines to help you answer that question.

- When bouncing multiple single-track sources that will be positioned in the same place within the stereo field, bounce them to a mono track.
- When bouncing multiple single-track sources that you want to be spread across the stereo field, bounce them to a stereo track.
- When bouncing tracks that are already linked, set up the destination tracks as linked in order to preserve the stereo image found in the source tracks.
- When bouncing a single track with a mono effect, bounce it to another mono track.
- When bouncing a single track with a stereo effect, bounce it to a stereo track.

The determining factor in deciding whether to bounce to a mono track or a stereo track is positioning within the stereo field. Any time you bounce multiple tracks to a mono track, you've lost the ability to pan the original source tracks differently. In our recording example, we have four tracks for drums. If we bounce these four tracks to a single track, we lose the stereo separation of our two drum overhead mics. If we instead bounce these four drum tracks to a stereo track, we can keep the stereo field intact.

Creating Your Routings

To bounce tracks, you'll need to set up the appropriate routings in the Track Mixer. As with all routing configurations in the VS, we start with our destination tracks and then route source tracks to them.

> ✷ **CLEAR 'EM OUT**
>
> Get in the habit of clearing any existing routings before you do a bounce. If you don't do this, it's easy to accidentally bounce the wrong tracks, especially if you have to perform a number of bounces. By clearing out any existing routings before you begin creating the routings needed for the new bounce, it makes the routing display much easier to read.
>
> To quickly clear all existing routings, hold down any track's STATUS button and then press CLEAR.

In the chapter on recording, we took a detailed look at routing, so you should already be familiar with the various components of the routing display. To route tracks for a bounce, press and hold the STATUS button for the destination track and then press the SELECT button for each source track. Remember, if you want to bounce in stereo, you must set Channel Link to ON for the destination tracks. For example, suppose we have recorded four background vocal tracks, and we want to pan each to specific points within the stereo field. If these background vocals are on tracks 1-4, we could link a pair of tracks and bounce these four tracks to a stereo track. Figure 6.1 shows an example of the routing display after routing tracks 1-4 to stereo recording track c.

You can also perform multiple bounces in a single step. For example, suppose we wanted to bounce the snare drum track with an EQ effect and a compressor effect inserted. In this case, we'd be bouncing a mono track to another mono track. We could perform this bounce at the same time as the bounce of the four background vocal tracks to stereo recording track c. In order to do this, we would need to use tracks 7 and 8 for the snare drum bounce. If the snare drum is on a V-Track within recording tracks 1-6, simply use Track Exchange to swap it with a V-Track on recording track 7 or 8. Figure 6.2 shows the routing display after routing tracks 1-4 to stereo recording track c and routing track 7 to track 8.

Figure 6.1
Bouncing tracks 1–4 to stereo track c in the Track Mixer.

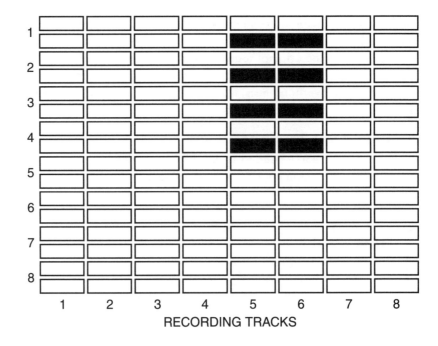

RECORDING TRACKS

Figure 6.2
Bouncing tracks 1–4 to stereo recording track c and bouncing track 7 to track 8 in the Track Mixer.

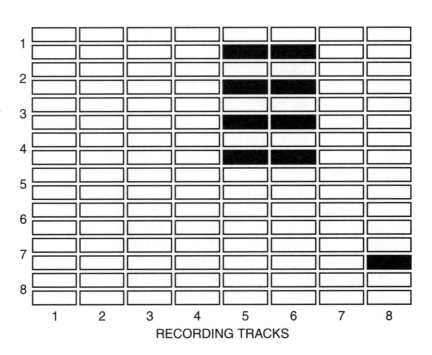

RECORDING TRACKS

Previewing the Bounce

Now that you've set up your routing, make sure you have the proper V-Tracks selected on each recording track before continuing. Next, play the song and adjust the faders and parameters on the source tracks as necessary. You can experiment all you want at this point, as nothing is being recorded. Once you've got the mix of your source tracks where you want it, you're ready to do the bounce.

Let me point out a few things about how the destination tracks get recorded. When you are bouncing tracks, the fader position of the destination tracks does not affect the recording level. The recording level is determined by the sum of the levels of the source tracks. During the bounce, any adjustments you make to the source tracks will be recorded on the destination tracks. However, if you make any adjustments on the destination tracks, you are only adjusting the playback of what is being recorded, and you are not affecting the signal that is being recorded. Let's review the example of bouncing four background vocal tracks to a stereo track. Figure 6.3 shows the signal flow between the four source tracks, the stereo destination tracks, and the monitors for this bounce.

When previewing the bounce, you can monitor the actual signal being recorded on the destination tracks. To do this, switch the display to PreFader mode. Next, repeatedly press the STATUS button on the destination tracks until it lights orange. The destination tracks are now in the monitor source mode, and you'll be able to monitor the recording levels. You can now view the recording level of the destination track. If it's too strong, reduce the levels of the source tracks; if it's too weak, increase the levels of the source tracks.

However, when you preview the song with the destination tracks in monitor source mode, or when you actually perform the bounce, what you hear may not be what is actually recorded. Remember, you will hear the signal after it has been recorded and passed through any track parameters for the destination track. In our example, suppose you had applied some EQ to track c. When you perform the bounce of tracks 1–4 to stereo track c, you will hear the effect of the EQ being applied to the destination track, even though the recorded signal does not contain this EQ. In this case, you'd want to turn off the EQ on stereo track c when monitoring or performing the bounce. These are times when you should consider using scenes; create one scene for the normal track conditions and another scene for monitoring the bounce.

When I set up a bounce, I set the STATUS button for the destination tracks so that it is not lit and adjust my source tracks based on what I hear out of the monitors. To verify the levels are correct, I'll switch the destination tracks to monitor source mode, check the levels in the PreFader display, and then perform the bounce.

Performing the Bounce

When you're ready to do the bounce, simply position the song to where you want to start, arm the destination tracks in record ready mode, press REC, and then press PLAY. When you

Figure 6.3

When bouncing tracks, the settings on the source tracks determine what is recorded on the destination tracks.

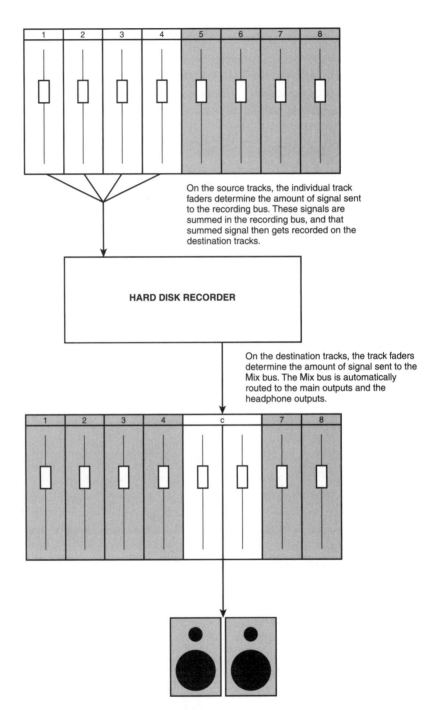

On the source tracks, the individual track faders determine the amount of signal sent to the recording bus. These signals are summed in the recording bus, and that summed signal then gets recorded on the destination tracks.

HARD DISK RECORDER

On the destination tracks, the track faders determine the amount of signal sent to the Mix bus. The Mix bus is automatically routed to the main outputs and the headphone outputs.

are done, press STOP. You can now play back the bounced version of the tracks and decide whether you want to keep it or redo the bounce. At this point, you'd want to mute the source tracks and just listen back to the destination tracks. Here's another place to use scenes; create a bounce scene that contains all the settings and routings for the bounce, and then create a playback scene. If you decide to redo the entire bounce, you can recall the bounce scene and redo the bounce.

❋ **SEEING RED (AND GREEN)**

If you attempt to arm a destination track in record ready mode and the STATUS button alternates between flashing red and green, it means you have routed a track to itself. While the VS will allow you to bounce a track to itself, I'd recommend you don't do this, as you'll overwrite the original track with the bounced version. The only way to get the original track back is to use the Undo function.

If you find that you accidentally routed a track to itself, you can unassign it in the routing display.

Bouncing Using the Internal Effects

When you want to bounce tracks with effects, you'll need to perform the same routing as a regular bounce and make the necessary adjustments to the source tracks. Next, you'll need to determine which effects you want to use and then decide if you want to use the effects as insert effects or send/return effects.

❋ **BOUNCING USING EZ ROUTING**

Don't forget that you can use EZ Routing when bouncing tracks. Although there are some limitations when using EZ Routing, you can perform many of your bounces, including those with effects, via the preset EZ Routing templates or by creating your own.

Selecting and Editing Effects

To select one of the internal effects, press the EFFECT button. Each effect board contains two stereo effect processors, called EFFECT1 and EFFECT2. Repeatedly pressing the EFFECT button toggles between selecting EFFECT1 and EFFECT2. After selecting which effect processor you want, use the jogwheel to select one of the 200+ built-in effect patches. When you find an effect patch you want to use, press the YES button to load it into the effects processor.

All effect patches contain one or more effect blocks. For example, effect A23 DL:MediumDly is a delay effect patch, and it contains the Delay effect block followed by the EQ effect block. With all the internal effect patches, the order of the effect blocks is fixed. In other words, you cannot customize effect A23 such that the EQ effect block comes before the Delay effect block. However, you can modify the parameters within the effect blocks and even disable the individual effect blocks within an effect patch. To modify the effect, press the →→ parameter button after selecting the effect. You can now use the ←← and →→ parameter buttons to scroll though all the individual parameters within each effect block, and you can modify them using the jogwheel.

After changing the parameters within an effect block, you can save the modified version of the effect patch as a user effect. On the VS-880EX, you can have up to 100 user effects, and these are labeled U00 though U99. To save a modified effect as a user effect, continue pressing the →→ parameter button until you see Save User Patch? and then the press YES. Now, select one of the U00 through U99 effect slots and press YES to save your modified effect patch in that user effect slot. By default, the 100 user effect patches already have copies of the first 100 preset effects stored. In order to differentiate between the copies of the preset effects and my own modified versions of the effects, I change the name of the effect when I save it. You can change the name of the effect by editing it, pressing the →→ button until you see NAM=, and using the cursor buttons and the jogwheel to change the name. Be sure to save the effect when you are done renaming it.

> ❄ **EFFECTS AND SCENES**
>
> Scenes have the ability to store effect block parameter changes. If you want to modify an effect patch but do not want to save it as a user effect, consider saving it within a scene. Whenever you recall that scene, the effect will be loaded into the effects processor, and the changes you made to the effect parameters will be reapplied.
>
> If you want to use these effect settings in other songs, it's best to store the effect as a user effect, as you cannot copy scenes from one song to another. Also keep in mind that if you want to use Automix, you'll need to store the modified version of the effect as a user effect, as Automix does not record individual effect parameter changes.

Bouncing with Insert Effects

To apply an insert effect during a bounce, bring up the track parameters for the source track and use the →→ parameter button until you see FX1 Ins = OFF. Setting this value to Insert will insert the effect patch loaded into the EFFECT1 effects processor into this track. If you'd rather use the effect loaded into the EFFECT2 effects processor, change the FX2 Ins = Insert parameter instead. Once you insert an effect into a source track, it will automatically be applied during the bounce.

Remember that the effect processors are stereo effect processors. This is important when using insert effects, as it is possible to use a single insert effect on two different tracks. When you use an insert effect on a mono track, you can configure the effect so that it can be used by two mono tracks at the same time. However, when you use an insert effect on a stereo track, the settings within the effect get applied to both channels of the stereo track, and the insert effect cannot be used on any other track. When you choose to use an insert effect on a mono track, the insert parameters can be set as follows:

✳ Insert: The track signal gets routed to one side of the effect, and the other side is not usable on any other track. This is the only option available if you are inserting the effect on a stereo track.

✳ InsertL: The track signal gets routed to the left side of the stereo effect, leaving the right side free to be used by another track.

✳ InsertR: The track signal gets routed to the right side of the stereo effect, leaving the left side free to be used by another track.

✳ InsertS: The track signal gets routed to the left side of the stereo effect, and the output of the left side then gets routed to the right side of the stereo effect.

✳ **SERIAL KILLERS**

When you select the InsertS option for an insert effect, both sides of the stereo effect get processed serially. That means you can serially insert one of the 2-band parametric EQ patches on a mono track and use it as a 4-band parametric EQ. The same concept applies to the 5-band graphic EQ patches; inserting them serially gives you a 10-band graphic EQ for a mono track. Another popular way to use a serial insert is with a compressor effect. You could set the left side of the compressor to just tame the extreme peaks and then use the right side of the compressor to manipulate the sound of the track.

Here's an example of using the same insert effect across two different mono tracks. Let's set up EFFECT1 as a compressor, and on our snare drum track, set FX1 Insert value to InsertL. Now call up the kick drum track and set the FX1 Insert value to InsertR. Now you can edit the compressor effect and modify the settings for the left side of the effect and for the right side of the effect. Each group of settings is independent of the other, allowing you to have one set of compression settings for the snare track and another set for the kick drum track.

Bouncing with Send/Return Effects

Bouncing tracks with send/return effects is a bit more complicated than using insert effects, as you'll need to create some routings in the Effects Return Mixer. To start, bring up the track parameters for the source track and use the →→ parameter button until you see EFFECT1 Send = OFF. If you want to use EFFECT2 for send/return effects, then navigate to EFFECT2 Send = OFF. Use the jogwheel to select either PreFader or PostFader. Most send/return effects are configured as PostFader, meaning the track fader determines the amount of signal sent to the effect.

FALLING OFF A CLIFF

Configuring a send/return effect as PreFader can produce some interesting results. My favorite is the "falling off a cliff" effect for vocal tracks. As you reduce the level of the vocal track, the amount of reverb remains consistent, resulting in a sound that seems to fall away from the listener.

Send/return effects can be shared across multiple tracks at the same time. The amount of signal sent to the effect can be controlled within each track's parameter settings. The EFFECT Send value allows you to determine how much of the track's signal gets sent to the effect. In addition, the overall return level from the effect can be set in the Effects Return Mixer. Let's return to the example of bouncing four vocal tracks to a stereo track. Let's say we wanted to apply a reverb effect to all four background vocal tracks as part of the bounce. Once we set up the reverb effect, we can control how much reverb gets applied to each of the four vocal tracks by adjusting each track's Effects send level. We can also adjust how much of the overall reverb gets returned from the effects processor by adjusting the effect return level in the Effects Return Mixer.

When applying send/return tracks during a bounce, consider bouncing to a stereo track. A number of the internal send/return effects, such as reverb, generate a return signal that is in stereo. If you apply a reverb effect while bouncing to a mono track, the reverb gets collapsed and will not sound as natural and full.

A WORD ABOUT REVERB EFFECT PATCHES

Effects that are based on the Reverb, Gated Reverb, Vocoder, and Voice Transformer algorithms are only available for use in the EFFECT1 effects processor. These include effect patches A00-A21, A80, A97, B79-B85, and B97-B98. This usually isn't a problem with most effect patches, but there are times when you might wish to use two different reverb patches at the same time. In these cases, consider using the patches based on the Reverb2 algorithm, such as B00-B19 and B90, in the EFFECT2 effects processor. Both the Reverb and Reverb2 algorithms contain an EQ effect block and a reverb effect block. In the Reverb algorithm, the EQ effect block comes before the reverb effect block; they are in the opposite order in the Reverb2 algorithm.

Once you've set up the send/return effect and have configured one or more tracks to use it, you will need to route the output of the effect to the same tracks that you are bouncing to. The output signals from send/return effects get routed to the Mix bus by default. To have these output signals included in the bounce, you'll need to route them appropriately in the Effects Return Mixer. To do this, press the FADER[EDIT] button until it lights red. Now we need to perform our effects routing, and just like all routings, we start with the destination tracks. Press and hold the STATUS button for the tracks you are bouncing to, and then press the SELECT button on track 7. When you are in the Effects Return Mixer, track 7 controls settings for EFFECT1, and track 8 controls settings for EFFECT2. By routing the output of EFFECT1 to the same destination tracks that you are bouncing to, the destination tracks will be recorded with the effects applied to them.

This can often confuse new VS users, as they will hear the effect through the monitors while doing the bounce, but the effect will not have been recorded on the destination tracks. Remember, if you are bouncing tracks, and you want to apply effects during the bounce, you must route the output of the effect to the destination tracks in order for the effect to be recorded on the destination tracks.

After Bouncing with Effects

After you have performed the bounce with effects, you need to remember to un-route the outputs of the effects from the destination tracks. If you follow my guideline of clearing all your routings before and after every bounce, you won't have any problems. If you forget to un-route the outputs of the effects, it will seem as though the effects aren't working. They are working; the outputs of the effects are just being routed to a particular track instead of being routed to the Mix bus.

Also, remember to configure any source tracks so that they are not using the effects after the bounce. If you used insert effects on any tracks, be sure to set the FX1/FX2 Ins = parameter to OFF after the bounce. Likewise, for tracks using send/return effects, set the EFFECT1/EFFECT2 Send = to OFF after the bounce. Unfortunately, there is no way to automatically reset just these settings for a track; you must do it manually.

Bouncing Using External Effects

You can easily incorporate external effect processors with your VS workstation. To send signals from the VS to the external device, you'll want to connect the Aux Send outputs from the VS to the inputs of the external device. The outputs of the external device are then brought into the VS via the analog input jacks, and they are recorded as new tracks.

To route a track to the Aux Send, bring up the track parameters and use the ←← and →→ parameter buttons until you see AUX Sw = OFF, and use the jogwheel to select either PreFade or PostFade. You can then edit additional track parameters that control the amount of signal sent to the Aux Send as well as the panning of the signal across the stereo Aux Send outputs. The Aux Send knob, which is located above the Master fader, controls the overall level of the Aux Send signal.

> ❄ **USING DIGITAL EFFECT DEVICES**
>
> If your external effect device has digital inputs and outputs, you can route signals between the external device and the VS digitally. The external effect device must be able to be configured as the Master Clock in order for this to work properly. On the VS, you'll need to bring up the Master Block settings and change the appropriate Digital Output setting from MIX to AUX.

I've used external compressors and reverb units this way with great success. However, there are two important things to note. First, doing this can introduce a bit of latency in the resulting signal. If you are going to blend the effect output signal with the original source signal, play them back without any other tracks and see if you can hear any latency. If you do, you can use the track-editing tools to eliminate any latency. Second, if you are using the external device as an insert effect, you'll want to set the MIX Sw = OFF on all tracks you are routing to the external effect device. If you don't do this, you'll hear both the source tracks and the affected tracks while you are recording the outputs of the effect. When you are done, remember to go back and set the Mix SW = ON for all your source tracks.

Putting It All Together

We've gone through a lot of concepts in this chapter, so let's put them to use in our recording example. Let's review our mixing and bouncing strategy for our existing 12 tracks:

* Apply compression to the snare drum, kick drum, and bass guitar tracks
* Apply reverb to the lead vocal and background vocal tracks
* Apply corrective EQ to the bass guitar track
* Final bounce must be to a stereo pair so that we can burn the song using the SCSI CD burner
* We want the source tracks for the final bounce to be the stereo keyboard, lead vocal, lead guitar, and all remaining tracks

As we work through bouncing and mixing all these tracks, I'm just going to cover the high-level steps. For example, I'm not going to list the specific compression settings being used or the amount of reverb applied to certain tracks. Even if I did give you those details, they probably wouldn't apply to your situation (and that's not the point of this exercise). However, once you understand how to perform the mixing and bouncing tasks, you'll be able to apply your specific settings with ease.

Again, let me reiterate that the method I'm showing for bouncing and mixing these tracks is how I'd do it; you may do it differently, and that's OK.

Since we're going to perform a number of bounces and will use Track Exchange quite frequently, I'm not going to show the track sheet after every bounce. Instead, where appropriate, I'll list the relevant tracks that we need to worry about. Also, although not specifically listed, you can assume that I'll clear all routings and effect assignments between each bounce, as well as arm the source tracks for playback and the destination tracks for recording.

Feel free to flip back to Figure 5.6 to see our track sheet as it exists before we begin our bouncing and mixing steps.

Step 1–Bounce the Drum Tracks with Effects

In this step, we'll bounce the existing four drum tracks to stereo recording track a. We'll also apply compression to the snare and kick drum tracks, and we'll apply varying amounts of reverb to all the tracks as part of the bounce. We'll perform this bounce as follows:

❋ Assign patch A96 DualComp/Lim to EFFECT1, configuring the left side for compressing the snare track and the right side for compressing the kick drum track.

❋ Assign patch B06 R2:MediumRm to EFFECT2, adjusting the parameters as necessary.

❋ On track 8 (snare track), select V-Track 8, set FX1 Ins=InsertL, and set EFFECT2 Send=PstFade.

❋ On track 7 (kick drum track), select V-Track 8, set FX1 Ins=InsertR, and set EFFECT2 Send=PstFade.

❋ On tracks 5 and 6 (drum overhead tracks), select V-Track 8, and set EFFECT2 Send=PstFade. These tracks were not recorded as linked tracks, therefore you'll need to do these adjustments on each track.

❋ On track a, verify that Channel Link is ON, and select V-Track 8. We'll bounce the drum tracks to a set of V-Tracks on this stereo track.

❋ In the Input Mixer, route mono tracks 5-8 to stereo track a.

❋ In the Effects Return Mixer, route the output of EFFECT2 to stereo track a.

❋ Adjust faders, track EQ, and panning as necessary on recording tracks 5-8.

❋ Save this configuration as Scene 1.

❋ Perform the bounce.

❋ When done, Track Exchange 1-8 with 7-1 and 2-8 with 8-1.

After this bounce and Track Exchange, we have the stereo drum tracks on 7-1 and 8-1, and tracks 1-8 and 2-8 are empty. Go ahead and Channel Link tracks 7-8 so they become track d.

Step 2–Bounce the Rhythm Tracks with Effects

In this step, we'll bounce the new stereo drum tracks, along with the bass guitar, acoustic guitar, rhythm guitar, and background vocal tracks, to stereo recording track a. We'll also apply EQ changes to the bass guitar track and apply reverb to the background vocal track. These effects will be included in the bounce.

Before we begin, we need to use Track Exchange to swap our lead vocal track on 3-1 with our background vocal track on 5-2. Since we want to include the bass guitar track and the background vocal track, and both of those tracks exist as V-Tracks on the same recording track, we need to move one of them to a different recording track in order to do the bounce.

Now we have background vocals on 3-1, rhythm guitar on 4-1, bass guitar on 5-1, acoustic guitar on 6-4, and our stereo drum mix on track d-1. Here's how we'll set up this bounce:

* Assign patch B50 PEQ:Bass1 to EFFECT1, adjusting the parameters as necessary.
* Assign patch A11 RV:Soft Amb to EFFECT2, adjusting the parameters as necessary.
* On track 3 (background vocal track), select V-Track 1, and set EFFECT2 Send=PstFade.
* On track 4 (rhythm guitar track), select V-Track 1.
* On track 5 (bass guitar track), select V-Track 1, and set FX1 Ins=Insert.
* On track 6 (acoustic guitar), select V-Track 4.
* On stereo track d (stereo drum mix), select V-Track 1.
* In the Input Mixer, route mono tracks 3-6 to stereo track a and route stereo track d to stereo track a.
* In the Effects Return Mixer, route the output of EFFECT2 to stereo track a.
* Adjust faders, track EQ, and panning as necessary on tracks 3-6 and track d.
* Save this configuration as Scene 2.
* Perform the bounce.
* When done, Track Exchange 1-8 with 3-2 and 2-8 with 4-2.

After this bounce and Track Exchange, we have the stereo rhythm tracks on 3-2 and 4-2. Go ahead and Channel Link tracks 3-4 so they become track b.

Step 3–Perform Final Bounce with Automix

After the bounce in step 2, we are left with the following relevant tracks:

* Stereo Track a-1 = Keyboard Tracks
* Stereo Track b-2 = Rhythm Tracks
* Mono Track 5-2 = Lead Vocal Track
* Mono Track 6-5 = Lead Guitar Track

We'll bounce all these tracks to a new stereo pair on recording track d. Before we do the bounce, let's set up Automix to create a custom, automated mix using Snapshot Automix. In this mix, we want the keyboards boosted during the keyboard solo, and we want all the instruments to fade out during the outro of the end of the song, leaving just the vocal track in the mix. Here are the high-level steps for creating this Automix.

* Adjust all track faders and parameters as needed for the beginning of the song.
* Assign patch A10 RV:Vocal Plt EFFECT1, adjusting the parameters as necessary, then save this effect as U10 SampPlate.

- ❄ On stereo track a (keyboard tracks), select V-Track 1.

- ❄ On stereo track b (rhythm tracks), select V-Track 2.

- ❄ On track 5 (lead vocal track), select V-Track 1, and set EFFECT1 Send=PstFade.

- ❄ On track 6 (lead guitar track), select V-Track 4.

- ❄ Save this configuration as Scene 3.

- ❄ Enable Automix as necessary, and take a snapshot at the beginning of the song.

- ❄ Position the song to the beginning of the keyboard solo, adjust the fader of the stereo keyboard track to increase the level, and then take a snapshot.

- ❄ Position the song to the end of the keyboard solo, adjust the fader of the stereo keyboard track to decrease the level, and then take a snapshot.

- ❄ Position the song to the beginning of the outro and take a snapshot.

- ❄ Position the song to the third measure of the outro, pull the faders all the way down on all tracks except the lead vocal track, and take a snapshot.

- ❄ While positioned at this last Snapshot Automix marker, perform a Gradation between the previous Automix marker and this Automix marker. This will create the fade of all the instruments.

Now we can play back the song and verify that the mix is the way we want it. Once we are satisfied with the Automix, set up the destination stereo recording track d appropriately and route all the source tracks to it. Also, remember that before you perform the bounce, you'll need to route the outputs of EFFECT1 to stereo recording track d so that the reverb is included in the bounce. By now, you should be able to perform those steps on your own, so we'll consider this song mixed—nice job!

In the next chapter, we'll see how to create this final stereo mix on an audio CD.

7 } Finishing Your Project on the VS-880/890 Series

Now that we've completed mixing our song, there are a few more things to consider. First, we'll look at applying effects across the entire mix to help put the finishing touches on the song. We'll then look at backing up our song, as well as recovering a song. Finally, we'll look at a variety of utility processes, such as upgrading the operating system and techniques to send tracks to a computer.

Mastering Your Song

The term "mastering" gets thrown around a lot these days. In this section, I'm going explain how to apply certain effects, such as EQ and compression, to your entire mix. Some people call this mastering; I call it applying effects across the entire mix. To me, mastering is a very specialized skill, and few people have the appropriate gear, environment, and most of all, ears to be a mastering engineer.

Not everyone can afford to have his songs mastered in the true sense. But you can use tools such as EQ, compression, and limiting to put a bit of sparkle and pizzazz into your final mix.

Using Internal Effects

Once you've bounced all your tracks down to a stereo pair, you can now apply effects across the mix. This procedure isn't any different than applying effects during a bounce, as that is essentially what you are doing. Most of the time, you'll want to consider using EQ and compression across the mix, as this can give you a tighter, more balanced sound. However, don't be afraid to experiment with other effects as well.

❁ ❁ ❁

Using the Mastering Tool Kit

The VS8F-2 Effect Expansion Boards include an internal effect algorithm called the Mastering Tool Kit, or MTK, as a way for VS users to master their projects. Sorry, VS-880 users—the MTK is not available on the VS-880 workstations.

To help you get started with mastering, Roland provides 19 MTK presets. These presets on the VS-880EX are listed as effects C10 through C28. As with any preset, you can change the settings within the MTK to customize a MTK preset to your liking. To get the most out of the MTK effect, you first need to understand everything that is included in the MTK.

The MTK contains nine different effect blocks, and just like all internal effects, the order of the effect blocks cannot be changed. Here is a description of each of the nine effect blocks within the MTK:

* EQ (Equalizer): This effect block offers a 4-band EQ. The high and low bands can be configured as either shelving or parametric EQs, and the two middle bands are parametric EQs. You can also adjust the level of the signal before and after the 4-band EQ.

* BC (Bass-Cut Filter): This effect block contains a bass-cut filter, which you can use to reduce low-end frequencies that can muddy up your mix.

* ENH (Enhancer): This effect block allows you to add a phase-shifted signal to the original signal. With this type of effect, a little goes a long way, so use it sparingly (unless you are purposely trying to get a unique sound).

* IN (Input): This effect block provides a way to split the input signal into three separate frequency ranges, each of which can them be processed independently by the compressor and expander effect blocks. You can also set the look-ahead time used by the compressor and expander effect blocks. The level of the signal can be adjusted before the frequency splitting step.

* EXP (Expander): This effect block gives you the ability to apply an expander to each of the three frequency ranges defined in the Input block. Each instance of the expander has its own settings.

* CMP (Compressor): This effect block is the heart of the MTK, providing a way to apply a compressor to each of the three frequency ranges defined in the Input block. Each instance of the compressor has its own settings.

* MIX (Mixer): This effect block controls the level of each of the three frequency ranges after passing through the expander and compressor effect blocks. This effect block then merges all three frequency ranges back together.

* LMT (Limiter): This effect block contains a limiter, which you can place in the signal path to restrict any excessive signal peaks.

❄ OUT (Output): This is the last effect block in the MTK, and it allows you to choose if you want to dither the signal. You can also adjust the level of the signal returned from the MTK.

Now that you know the effects that the MTK contains, here are a few ways to use the MTK. The most common way to apply the MTK is as an insert effect. In our recording example, if we wanted to apply the MTK, we'd need to assign one of the MTK presets to the EFFECT1 effects processor and make adjustments to the effect parameters as necessary. Then we'd need to bounce our final stereo pair of tracks once again so that the MTK effect gets applied to the destination tracks. Remember, the process that burns the audio CD won't include any effect processing that is active at the time, so we need to have our MTK effect applied during a bounce.

This is certainly a great way to use the Mastering Tool Kit. However, this shouldn't limit the ways in which you consider using the MTK. Individual tracks, stereo tracks, or even submixes can be processed using the MTK. Likewise, interesting results can be obtained when using the MTK in a send/return configuration. In addition, you could use the MTK and only activate certain effects blocks within the MTK, like the Enhancer or the Limiter. Experimenting with the MTK can lead to interesting and innovative results.

❄ **LOOK OUT FOR LOOK-AHEAD**

The Input block of the MTK contains a look-ahead setting, D-Time, which can be adjusted between 0ms and 10ms. The input signal is delayed by the amount specified in D-Time before being processed by the Expander and Compressor effect blocks. Setting this value to 10ms allows the expanders and compressors to react more quickly, which can improve their effectiveness.

If you are using the MTK when bouncing tracks, remember that the destination tracks will be delayed in time by the value specified in D-Time. For example, setting D-Time to 10ms will result in the destination tracks being roughly 30 subframes behind the source tracks in the timeline.

Be aware that the MTK uses both stereo effect processors. This means that you must assign the MTK to EFFECT1. Once you've assigned the MTK to EFFECT1, if you try to assign an effect to the EFFECT2 effects processor, you'll see the message Can't Use FX2.

Mixing to an External Source

One of the advantages of mixing down to an external source such as a stand-alone audio CD burner is that you don't have to bounce all of your tracks down to a stereo pair. If you are mixing to an external source, you can apply effects to the entire mix without having to bounce all of your tracks to a stereo pair first. You do this by inserting effects into the Master Block. When effects are inserted into the Master Block, they get applied to the entire mix, and the main outputs and the digital outputs contain the effected signals.

If you want to insert two different effects using this method, bring up the Master Block settings, use the ←← and →→ parameter buttons until you see MST FX1 Ins Sw = OFF, and then use the jogwheel to change it to ON. Do the same for the FX2 parameter as well. Now when you play the song, the entire mix gets processed by both effects.

If you are bouncing tracks and have effects inserted into the Master Block, the effects will not be applied during the bounce. Also note that the Master Block only allows for effects to be inserted. You cannot use effects in a send/return manner within the Master Block.

Burning Your Song to a CD via the SCSI Burner

The end goal of your recording is to get the song created on a CD. In the beginning of the previous chapter, I discussed the two most common ways to do this: via the SCSI CD burner and via a stand-alone audio CD burner. If you have a stand-alone audio CD burner connected to your VS workstation, simply play the tracks on the VS while recording on the stand-alone audio CD burner. If you want to burn via the SCSI CD burner, you must have first bounced all your tracks, effects, and signal processing down to a stereo pair. Let's walk through the process of getting that final stereo pair burned to a CD.

> ❋ **CD TALK**
>
> Throughout this section, I'll refer to burning and backing up to CD via the SCSI CD burner. The VS workstations can write to regular CD-R discs and CD-RW discs, provided your CD burner supports writing to CD-RW discs. If you use CD-RW discs when creating audio CDs, understand that most regular CD players cannot play CD-RW discs. If you use a CD-RW disc for backups, and the disc already contains data, the VS cannot append data to it. Rather, it will delete all existing data on the CD-RW disc before writing the backup to the disc.

SCSI CD Burner Limitations

The ability to connect a CD burner to your VS workstation provides a way to both create audio CDs and back up your work. However, there are some important things to understand regarding the CD burner.

First, the CD burner must have a SCSI port, and only certain brands of SCSI CD burners will work. All of the Roland-branded burners will work, but they are expensive. You can save some money by purchasing a SCSI CD burner manufactured by Plextor. All Plextor SCSI CD burners, up to the 12×10×32 model, will work with the VS-880/890 workstations. If you were considering purchasing a SCSI CD burner made by any other manufacturer, I'd recommend against it, unless you know that it is already being used by a VS workstation. The VS operating system only supports a particular list of SCSI CD burners. You can think of the operating system of your VS like the operating system found on some older computers. When you connect peripheral devices to these computers, you need to install a driver in order for the device to be recognized by the operating system. The VS is similar, except that you cannot install your own drivers; the only drivers available are those included within the operating system.

TRIPLE DIP

If you are using an external Plextor burner, the PARITY and TERM dip-switches on the back of the unit should be set to ON. All other dip-switches should be set to OFF.

One exception is the Plextor model PX-412Ce. On this particular model, you will need to set the BLOCK dip-switch to ON in order to for the burner to work properly.

Regardless of the write speed available on the actual SCSI CD burner, the VS limits the actual write speed to a maximum of 4×. This is another reason why the older Plextor models are attractive, as most people don't want to spend hundreds of dollars for a new SCSI CD burner only to find that it can't burn faster than 4× speed.

Preparing to Burn

Before you actually burn your song to CD, there are a number of things to consider. First, your song must have been recorded using a sample rate of 44.1kHz in order for it to be burned to the SCSI CD burner. If you used a different sample rate for your song, you'll have to record the song to an external device. Also, remember that if you apply any effects or signal processing changes —or change any track parameters such as level, pan, EQ, and so on—these changes will not be applied during the burn.

Also know that when the song gets burned to CD, the VS assumes the song starts at 00:00:00:00. If you have blank space before your song actually starts, consider using Track Cut so that the true beginning of your song starts in the 0.2–0.5-second range. The same principle applies to the end of your song. Figure 7.1 shows an example of using Track Cut to eliminate blank space at the beginning and end of a song.

The process of burning the song to CD requires additional space on the internal hard drive. When you perform the burn, the VS first creates a CD-R image file on the internal hard drive and then writes this image file to CD. To put this in perspective, attempting to burn a four-minute song to CD can take 10 minutes or more. The VSR-880 and VS-890 workstations provide a feature called the mastering room, which provides a simpler method for getting your song burned on CD. When you enable the mastering room function, you can bounce six tracks down to two, insert effects to the entire mix via the Master Block, and have the resulting two tracks be created in CD-R image format. Data existing on the Mastering Tracks can then be more quickly burned to CD.

When you burn your song to CD, you'll have the option of choosing Disc-At-Once (DAO) or Track-At-Once (TAO). If you are burning a single song at a time, choose TAO. TAO will place two

Figure 7.1

Use Track Cut to eliminate blank space before burning to CD.

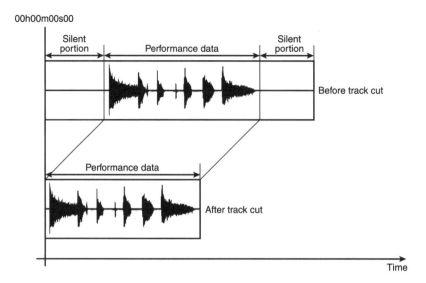

seconds of silence after each song. If you eventually want more than one song on this CD, and you do not want a two-second gap between songs, you'll need to use DAO. If you use DAO, you'll need to have the final stereo pair of tracks for each song on the same V-Tracks within a song. This works well if you've recorded a live concert of multiple songs as a single song within the VS. However, if you had recorded multiple individual songs that you wanted to burn using DAO, you'd need to have all of these songs created as one long song in the VS. Unfortunately, the VS-880/890 workstations don't provide a function to combine multiple songs into one song. The only way to accomplish this would be to record each song to an external recording device, such as a DAT or stand-alone audio CD burner, and then record each song back-to-back into the VS within a single song. If you are using DAO, you need to place song markers at the beginning of each song. To place a song marker, hold the SONG Edit Condition button and press TAP. The VS automatically assumes a song marker at 00:00:00:00, so you only need to do this for subsequent songs.

❋ **BURNING DAO**

If you want to burn a CD using DAO, consider doing it on your computer. Although you can burn using DAO on the VS, it is a very time-consuming and laborious process. Instead, burn your songs on the VS using TAO, then convert them to individual .WAV files on your computer. Then you can use CD burning software on your computer to burn these to a CD using DAO.

Performing the Burn to CD

To burn your song to CD, press the SONG Edit Condition button multiple times until you see SNG CD-R Write ?, and then press YES. The VS will search for the SCSI CD burner, and it will briefly show some information about the CD burner in the display.

Next, you'll be prompted with SNG Disc at Once ? If you want to burn using DAO, press YES; otherwise press the →→ parameter button to see the SNG Track at Once? message and press YES to burn using TAO. We'll use TAO in this example; using DAO is similar. Next, you'll see the message SNG Write + Finalize? If you want to finalize the CD after this song is burned, press YES. If you want to be able to burn additional songs to this CD, press the →→ button until you see the SNG Write w/o Fin.? message and press YES.

At this point, the display will show useful information about the size of the song you want to burn, the amount of space remaining on the hard drive, and the amount of space remaining on the CD, as shown in Figure 7.2. After reviewing the display and verifying there is enough room on the CD and hard drive to perform this operation, you're ready to select the pair of tracks to burn to CD. Press the SELECT button for the track that represents the left side of the stereo pair, press the YES button, and press the SELECT button for the track that represents the right side of the stereo pair. During this step, you cannot change which V-Track is selected for a given track. For example, if you want to burn from tracks 7-2 and 8-2, but V-Track 1 is the currently selected V-Track for tracks 7 and 8, pressing track 7s SELECT button will show 7-1 in the display, and you will not be able to select 7-2. Instead, cancel out of this procedure, select the appropriate V-Tracks, and invoke this procedure again.

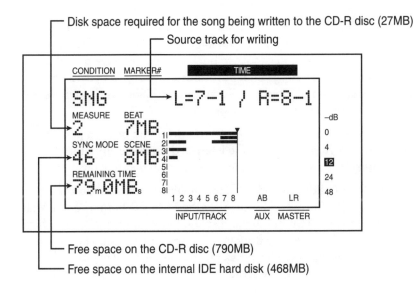

— Disk space required for the song being written to the CD-R disc (27MB)

— Source track for writing

— Free space on the CD-R disc (790MB)

— Free space on the internal IDE hard disk (468MB)

Figure 7.2

The display shows current song size and free space information when creating your song on CD.

After selecting the appropriate tracks, press the →→ parameter button. You can now select the write speed for the burn. Remember, the VS can only burn at a maximum of 4× speed. After selecting the speed, press the →→ parameter button, and when prompted with SNG CD-R Write Sure?, press YES. You'll then see a couple of additional prompts, so press YES a few times. At this point, the VS will begin converting the song to the required CD-R image file, and once that is complete, the burn to CD will begin. When the burn is completed, you will be prompted to burn another copy of the song. If you press YES, the VS will not need to convert the song, as the CD-R image file will still be available. However, once you answer NO to the Write Another? prompt, the CD-R image file gets deleted from the hard drive.

Backing Up Songs to CD

You've put a long of hard work into your recording, editing, mixing, and mastering, so be sure to make regular backups. When you back up your song to CD, you are backing up all of your audio and the VS internal data surrounding that song. This internal data includes things such as locators, scenes, markers, Automix data, track parameter and effect settings, and Undo history.

> ❄ **SELECT YOUR PART**
>
> When you choose to back up a song to CD, you can only back up songs that are in the currently selected partition. When you choose to recover a song from CD, you can only recover the currently selected partition. Before you perform a backup or recover, make sure you have first selected the proper partition. Use the Drive Select function within the System menu to change partitions.

Backups can only be made of songs that reside on the internal hard drive. If you are using external SCSI hard drives, you'll first need to copy songs back to the internal hard drive before you can back them up. During the backup process, you can choose to back up either one song or all songs within a partition. This means if you had three songs on a particular partition, you could not back up Song 1 and Song 3 in a single step. Also, the backup works on a partition level, so there isn't any way to back up all songs in all partitions in a single step.

When you create a backup, the CD is automatically finalized as part of the backup procedure. Additionally, since the backup contains your audio and the internal data in a proprietary format, this CD is not playable on a CD player, and the data cannot be read on a computer.

To perform the backup, press the SONG Edit Condition button multiple times until you see SNG CD-R Backup? and then press YES. The VS will search for the SCSI CD burner, and it will briefly show some information about the CD burner in the display. Now you can choose which song to back up by using the jogwheel. If you want to back up all songs, turn the jogwheel counter-clockwise until you see CDR Bak = All Song xxx, where xxx represents the total number of songs in the current partition. Figure 7.3 shows the display screen when selecting one song versus selecting all songs.

Song Number   Song Name

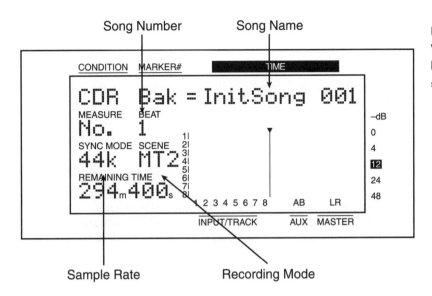

Figure 7.3
When performing a backup, you can select one song or all songs.

Sample Rate   Recording Mode

Total number of songs in the current drive (3 songs)

At this point, if you press the YES button, the backup will begin. However, there are two additional settings that you can control, and these are only available if you press the →→ parameter button after selecting the song to back up. The first setting is the Verify option, and the default is ON. If you set Verify = ON, the VS will back up the song data to CD and then compare the backup version to the original version. If Verify finds any differences, you will receive a warning message, and you should perform the backup again. Using Verify will increase the amount of time it takes to perform the backup function. The next setting is the write speed, and the default is 1×. Changing this to 4× is a good idea, as the backup process will be faster. However, if your song data is fragmented across the hard drive, the VS may not be able to send data to the burner fast enough. This can result in a Function Failed message. If your backups fail when writing at 4× speed, try reducing the write speed to 2×.

If the amount of song data to back up is more than what will fit on a single CD, the VS will span the backup across multiple CDs.

❄ **THE BACKUP SHUFFLE**

When you execute a backup, the VS first compares the free space on the CD to the amount of song data to back up. If the song data is greater than the amount of space on the CD, the VS will prompt you to Insert Disc 2. Here's a tip: If you are using CDs with the same amount of available space, such as 700MB, just reinsert the exact same CD. During this process, nothing is being written to the CDs; the VS is just determining how many CDs will be required to back up the song data. Once that is done, it will prompt you to Insert Disc 1, and now it will begin writing the backup data to the CD.

Recovering Songs from CD

The steps in recovering a song from CD are similar to the steps for performing a backup. Press the SONG Edit Condition button multiple times until you see SNG CD-R Recover, and then press YES. The VS will now display all the songs contained on the backup. Now you can choose which song to recover by using the jogwheel. If you want to recover all songs, turn the jogwheel counter-clockwise until you see CDR Rcv=All Song xxx, where xxx represents the total number of songs in the current partition.

At this point, if you press the YES button, the recover process will begin. However, if you press the →→ parameter button after selecting the song to recover, you can select the read speed. The maximum read speed is determined by the burner, and the VS will allow you to select all available read speeds that are supported by your burner. Set this value to the maximum speed allowed by your burner. After you have selected the read speed, press YES.

If you chose to recover a single song, the VS will now begin the recover process. However, if you chose to recover all songs, you will be prompted with INIT IDE.n OK ?, where n is the currently selected partition. If you press YES, all songs on that particular partition are erased, and then all songs from the CD are recovered to the partition. The manual incorrectly states that all songs on the entire hard drive will be erased. The truth is that only the songs on the currently selected partition will be erased.

> **❊ BETTER SAFE THAN SORRY**
>
> If you have a copy of your owners manual, you'll understand when I say that there are some problems with it. One of the biggest issues involves the Drive Initialization process. Let me try to set the record straight.
>
> If you go to SYSTEM → SYS DriveInitialize, the VS will ask which partition to initialize. Regardless of which partition you choose, the entire hard drive will be re-initialized. All data on all partitions of the hard drive will be lost.
>
> If you are recovering songs from a backup CD, and you choose to recover all songs on the CD, the VS will ask if you want to re-initialize the current partition. In this case, only the currently selected partition will be re-initialized, not the entire drive. Saying YES to this particular function only erases the songs on the currently selected drive and does not do anything to songs on any other partitions.
>
> In the manual, the section on recovery states that all songs on all partitions will be erased. In my testing, I found this to be incorrect. I have tested recovering songs to the internal hard drive as well as to external SCSI hard drives. My tests were done with a VS-880EX running version 2.014 of the operating system. Whether you are running the DriveInitialize function or you are recovering songs from a CD, make sure you have a backup of all your data. The only thing worse than accidentally wiping out your hard drive is not having a backup when you do.

Updating Your Operating System

The last operating system upgrade to any of the VS-880/890 workstations came in 2002. The most current version of the operating system for these workstations is shown in Table 7.1.

Table 7.1 Most Current Operating System for VS-880/890 Workstations

VS Workstation	OS Version
VS-880	3.205
VS-880EX	2.014
VSR-880	1.032
VS-890	1.1014

During the startup sequence, the display on the VS workstation shows the version of the operating system. Unfortunately, it only shows the first two digits after the decimal point. For example, I'm running v2.014 on my VS-880EX, and the startup display shows v2.01. To see the actual version of the operating system, you need to boot up the VS in a special way.

With the workstation powered off, hold down the STATUS and SELECT buttons above track 1 and then power up the VS. The display will show the full version number, along with some other information, and will then proceed to boot as normal.

If you want to upgrade your operating system, you will first need to download the files from the Roland Web site. You can upgrade your operating system via MIDI or via a SCSI ZIP drive. There are specific download files for each of these, and there are specific files for PC and MAC. Be sure to read the instructions in the text file included with these download files.

If you are upgrading your operating system via MIDI, you can use a hardware sequencer or your computer. If you use your computer, be sure to also download the SMF player from the Roland Web site, as this will allow you to play the MIDI files to the VS. You'll also need the appropriate MIDI cable connected between your computer and your VS workstation. When you are ready to do the upgrade, you'll need to start up the VS in a special manner. With the workstation powered off, hold down the STATUS and SELECT buttons above track 7 and then power up the VS. The display will read System Update ? Press YES, and the VS will display Waiting MIDI EX. You'll now need to play the MIDI files through your sequencer or through the SMF player on your computer. There are 16 MIDI files, and they must be played in order. Again, see the instructions in the text file included with the download. When all the data has been transmitted and applied, the VS will prompt you to reboot.

If you are upgrading your operating system via a SCSI ZIP drive, be sure it is in fact a SCSI ZIP drive. Connecting a parallel-port ZIP drive to your VS workstation can cause damage to the ZIP drive and to the VS. You will also need to be able to connect the SCSI ZIP drive to your computer in order to copy the download files to the ZIP disk. If you are having problems performing this task, you can obtain a ZIP disk containing the necessary files from Roland. When you are ready to do the upgrade, verify that the SCSI ZIP drive is connected to the VS and powered up, then power up the VS. The display will read Update SysPrg Press YES, and the VS will begin reading the upgrade data from the SCSI ZIP drive. When all the data has been transmitted and applied, the VS will prompt you to reboot.

When you are ready to do the upgrade, you'll need to start up the VS in a special manner. With the workstation powered off, hold down the STATUS and SELECT buttons above track 7 and then power up the VS. The display will read System Update ? Press YES, and the VS will begin receiving the upgrade data from the MIDI port or from the SCSI ZIP drive.

Interfacing the VS Workstation with a Computer

There are a number of ways to transfer your tracks between the VS and a computer. The exact setup and configuration details depend on the specific hardware and software you are using on the computer. I'll provide an overview of the process from the VS side, and you'll need to fill in the details related to the computer side.

Analog and Digital Transfers

If you want to transfer the signal on the Mix bus to the computer, simply make the appropriate analog or digital connection between the VS and computer, press record on your audio software recorder, and press PLAY on the VS. This is a common technique for mixing down tracks and sending the resulting stereo pair to a software audio editor on the computer. On the other hand, if you want to transfer tracks from the VS so that you can mix the tracks on the computer, you'll have to transfer all of the individual tracks. To do this, you can sync the VS and the computer and then play a subset of tracks on the VS while recording them on the computer. If you set up your sync parameters correctly, each track you transfer from the VS to the computer should line up in the timeline.

If you can't sync the VS and computer, you can record a short reference point at the beginning of all your tracks on the VS. For example, you could put a handclap or single snare hit at the beginning of all your tracks. After you transfer all your tracks to the computer, use your software audio editor to visually align all the tracks via the reference point in the beginning of each track.

If you want to transfer audio from the computer to the VS via the digital connections, make sure your soundcard or external transfer device can output using a 44.1kHz sample rate. Many of the consumer models of these devices can only output from the computer at a 48kHz sample rate.

SCSI Transfers

If your computer has a SCSI port, you may think that you could simply connect the VS to the computer via SCSI. This is not recommended, and doing so can possibly damage your computer or your VS. The VS never transfers audio via the SCSI port, only data.

However, there is one interesting way to use SCSI devices with both the VS and a computer. You can connect external SCSI hard drives and external SCSI ZIP drives to the VS and then copy data to and from the internal hard drive on the VS to the external drives. Once you've got data on the external drive, disconnect the SCSI device from the VS and connect it to the computer. Each VS partition on the external SCSI device will be listed as a separate drive on the computer, and you can copy files from the SCSI drive to the computer hard drive. Doing this is an alternative to performing the backup function on the VS. Once the data is on your computer, you can burn it to a CD, but you will not be able to recover the data on that CD directly to the VS via the recover function.

If you originally recorded the song on the VS using MAS mode, it can be read as audio data by a number of software audio editors once you get the data onto the computer. While this seems like good way to get audio data to the computer, there is a catch. Every time you record a new piece of audio on the VS, that audio gets stored in its own file on the hard drive. So every time you record, punch in, overdub, and so on that audio gets stored in a different file. The internal names for these data files are random. Therefore, when you look at these files on the computer, you'll have no way to know which file represents which track or which file represents which punch-in or overdub. The workaround for all of this would be to bounce each of your tracks to a new track so that all the individual audio parts are present as a single audio part in the new track. Then, erase all the original tracks, leaving just the new bounced-down versions. Finally, use

Song Optimize to really delete all the old tracks. The only tracks remaining will be the newly bounced-down tracks, and these will all be complete audio tracks.

Syncing Multiple VS Workstations

Synchronizing multiple VS workstations is an easy and affordable way to add more tracks to your current VS. In fact, I use three VS-880EX synced together, giving me a 24-track recorder. To sync up two machines, you will need a MIDI cable and a digital audio cable. In this setup, one VS must be the master and the other the slave. Connect the MIDI-Out from the master to the MIDI-In on the slave, and connect the digital out from the master to the digital in on the slave. There are a few system-level settings that need to be changed on each machine as well. Finally, on the slave machine, set the Stereo In setting to Digital and the Master Clock to DIGIN1 or DIGIN2, depending on which digital port you are using. To change the Stereo In setting, switch the mixer to the Effects Return Mixer, then press the SELECT button above track 6 two times. Use the jogwheel to select RTN StereoIn = Digital. You can change the Master Clock via SYSTEM → SYSTEM SYS PRM ? → SYS MasterClk = and use the jogwheel to select the proper value.

Now, when you press PLAY on the master, both machines will play. The output of the master will be brought into the slave machine via the Stereo In setting, meaning you can control each track on each machine via its fader.

If you sync multiple VS workstations, remember that you'll need to back up each machine separately. You'll also want to plan out your recording session in terms of which tracks should end up on which machine. This comes into play during mixdown, as effect processors cannot be shared between the machines.

Miscellaneous Utilities, Functions, and Parameters

Before we close out the chapters on the VS-880/890 series, I wanted to mention a few miscellaneous utilities, functions, and parameters. Although you probably won't use these utilities and functions on a regular basis, you should know that they are available. Likewise, many of the parameters can be left at their default values, but there may be times when you want to change them.

Drive Check

This utility will scan your hard drive to see if there are any damaged or unusable clusters. It will also check for clusters that are cross linked, meaning a cluster is detected as belonging to more than one song. It will also check some of the internal file structures that are used to store information on locators, markers, effects, Automix, and so on. To execute the Drive Check utility, press the SYSTEM Edit Condition button repeatedly until you see SYS Drive Check ?, and then press YES and follow the prompts.

System-Level Parameters

There are a number of system-level parameters that control the operation of various functions. These are found via SYSTEM → SYSTEM SYS PRM? We've already covered some of these in previous chapters, but here are a few more:

❊ Marker Stop: When set to ON, the VS will play back or record until it reaches the next marker, and then it will stop.

❊ Fade Length: When punching in or punching out within a track that already contains audio, the VS will attempt to do a very quick fade-in/fade-out between the audio passages. If you hear noise between these audio passages, you can adjust the fade length. The default is 10ms. Using multiple microphones to record a single source can cause phase cancellation, and you can flip the phase of one or more tracks to help correct it.

❊ Shift Lock: When set to ON, pressing the SHIFT key once lights up the SHIFT key and keeps the SHIFT key activated. To deactivate it, press the SHIFT key again so that it is not lit.

❊ Fader Match: This setting has two values: NULL and JUMP. When you switch between mixer modes, the fader may not match the actual level you had previously set for that fader. The default is Jump, meaning as soon as you adjust any fader, the level you previously set automatically jumps to the new level. Null means that the fader must first be moved to the previously set level before you can adjust the level to something different.

Mute and Solo

By holding the SHIFT key and pressing the EZ ROUTING/SOLO button, the VS will enter Solo mode. During this time, pressing any track's SELECT button puts that track in Solo. To exit Solo mode, hold SHIFT and press EZ ROUTING/SOLO again. To enter Mute mode, hold the EZ ROUTING/SOLO button and press the SELECT button for the tracks you wish to mute. When you release the EZ ROUTING/SOLO button, these tracks remain muted, even if their track STATUS button is lit for playback.

These functions should be used with caution. Once you invoke Solo mode for a track in the Input Mixer while recording, you effectively mute the other input signals, and they will not be recorded. I personally don't see much value in the Mute function. I can just as easily mute tracks by pressing their STATUS button. Also, there is no indicator visible if you mute a track via the Mute mode.

Vari Pitch

This function changes the playback speed of the tracks, allowing you to record new tracks at a higher or lower speed. This is useful when you change the pitch of previously recorded tracks to match the pitch of tracks you want to record. To change the playback speed, hold SHIFT and press the VARI PITCH button, then use the jogwheel to adjust the value. The value is shown in terms of sample rate, so you'll need to cross reference the key you want to the appropriate sample rate.

8 Introduction to the VS-1680/1880 Series

In early 1996, Roland introduced the VS-880 eight-track digital recorder. It was perceived by many as one of the biggest breakthroughs in the digital recording world at that time. Using Roland's own patented compression scheme (RDAC), the VS-880 was able to squeeze more recording time than previously possible from an eight-track hard disk recorder. Although some looked at this as a drawback because they thought it compromised the sound quality, the overwhelming popularity of the VS880 made it one of the most popular eight-track hard disk recorders of all time.

Roland continued to provide support for their beloved VS-880, which included new effects algorithms, the ability to play back six (as opposed to the original four) tracks of uncompressed tracks, Automix, and even a CD writer system. Finally, the VS-880 user was able to create musical works from beginning to end and walk away with a tangible, finished product that was ready to play in his favorite audio listening system.

Even though Roland's programmers were able to squeeze so much power from the little VS-880, it seemed that it would only be a matter of time before a new unit was needed. That is how the VS-1680 was born.

Larger LCD for Easier Viewing

The VS-1680 addressed many of the shortcomings of its little brother. One major concern was the VS-880's tiny LCD. The VS-1680's LCD boasts a resolution of 320×240 dots, which is a huge improvement in comparison. This new and improved screen can host graphics, icons, and even a mini waveform display for detailed editing. If the LCD's lighting is not to your particular liking, there is a small contrast knob directly to the right side of it, allowing for a very wide range of adjustments.

At the very top of the screen, you will find a large time indicator complete with a bar/measure display. The display resembles a sequencer arranger window with scrolling parts moving across

Figure 8.1
The Roland VS-1680.

the screen. Tiny blocks represent recorded data. These blocks show which tracks, including virtual tracks, are active or have something recorded on them.

You can also switch to a song information display that lists all manner of detailed information about your song such as song name, recorded sample rate, recording mode, song size, and remaining time on the selected hard drive's partition.

If you press an Input or Track Select button, you activate a graphical display of associated parameters for that track. These screens show things like volume levels, EQ, effects, and pan, to name a few. Each channel has a STATUS button, which switches light colors between track monitor (green), input monitor (yellow), record (red), and mute (off). Hold the button down for a moment and a graphical screen will materialize, illustrating the signal routing with lines drawn between the active connections. From here you can redirect an input to a track by holding down the appropriate buttons. A line appears on the screen verifying that the connection is made. It's this sort of attention to detail that helps make such a powerful and complex machine manageable. The graphics are clear but never over-fussy, and they are the key to an easy grasp of signal flow.

 CONNECTING TO AN EXTERNAL VGA MONITOR

The VS-1680 cannot be connected to an external VGA monitor. At the time of this writing, the only models that support external VGA use are the VS-2000, VS-2400, and VS-2480.

Recording Modes

The VS-1680 features two additional recording modes that are not present on the VS-880: Multi-Track Pro (MTP) and Live 2. These two modes still use Roland's RDAC compression scheme.

The only recording mode on the VS-1680 that does not use RDAC is MAS mode. When Mastering mode is used, the VS-1680's track count is reduced to only eight tracks on playback. To get the best overall performance from your VS-1680, it is recommended that you use the new 24-bit MTP mode. I owned a VS-880 for five years before I upgraded to a VS-1880, and I must say that MTP mode does sound richer and fuller than the VS-880 to my ears, though admittedly, this sort of thing is subjective to each user. The following is a table that shows the approximate recording times in minutes for the available sample rates and recording modes. This information is based on one track using a hard drive partition of 2GB.

Table 1.1   Recording Modes Versus Available Time Guide

Recording Mode	48.0kHz	44.1kHz	32.0kHz
MTP	742	808	1114
Mastering	370	404	556
MT1	742	808	1114
MT2	990	1078	1484
Live 1	1188	1292	1782
Live 2	1484	1616	2228

❋ **MTP AND MT1 TIMES ARE THE SAME**

You may notice the calculated times for MTP and MT1 are the same on the table. Roland insists that even though the times are the same, their engineers have been able to extract greater performance at exactly the same cost.

It's important to note that Roland's recorders do not place any restrictions on the way you divide up the available recording time. In other words, there is no fixed length. The VS-1680 does not care if you want to record for three or four hours on just two tracks or divide the time amongst 16 tracks using all 256 virtual tracks.

Two Fully Independent Mixers

The VS-1680 is unique in that it has a built-in 26 channel digital mixer that is divided into three main sections.

❋ Input Mixer

❋ Track Mixer

❋ Master Block

This is especially helpful during mixing because the two independent mixers can work side by side for a total of 26 channels of automated digital mixing. This is great when you need to bring in additional parts to the master mix, like tracks from a MIDI sound module or even tracks from another multitrack recorder. Just connect the additional sound sources to the Input Mixer and you're ready to go.

The Input Mixer and the Track Mixer work independently. Each mixer has separate control over a wide variety of things, including status, EQ, effects (loop and insert), channel link, virtual tracks, attenuation, phase, meter, pan (referred to as MIX), fader level, solo, mute, and aux. Let's take a closer look at the three main components of the VS-1680's digital mixer and their functions.

Input Mixer

In the recording chain, the Input Mixer appears first, before the recorder section. Every new track recorded on the VS-1680 travels through the Input Mixer, then to the recorder, then to the Track Mixer. The buttons on the top row of the VS-1680 are the INPUT SELECT buttons. There are 10 INPUT SELECT buttons that correspond to the VS-1680's eight analog inputs and two digital inputs. Use these buttons if you want to print your effects during the recording process.

For example, let's say you want to print a reverb effect while recording through Input 1. You would select the first Input button and apply your effect and route the effect return to that input channel. When you are done recording, your track will be printed with the selected reverb effect. This cannot be changed. The effect now becomes part of the recorded track.

Track Mixer

The Track Mixer appears after the recorder section. This mixer handles signals that have already been recorded or are being recorded to one or more of the VS-1680's 16 digital tracks.

> ❄ **REMEMBERING TIP FOR THE INPUT AND TRACK MIXER**
>
> An easy way to remember the difference between the Input and Track Mixer is this: Think of the Input Mixer as the one that handles the audio signal *before* it is recorded. Think of the Track Mixer as the one that handles the audio signal *after* it is recorded.

Any effects you apply to this mixer are not part of the recorded signal and can be changed at any time before final mixdown.

Routing signals from the Track Mixer is really easy. The track output can be re-routed to facilitate many different applications. For example, you can route the track output back to the recording bus for track bouncing or re-recording. You can also route the tracks to individual outputs for transferring to other multitrack recorders using the Direct Out function.

At all times, it is important that you always know which mixer you are working in. There are several ways to keep track of which mixer is selected. One way is to use the FADER/MUTE button, shown in Figure 8.2.

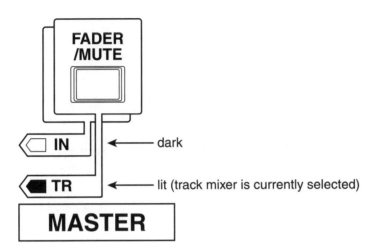

Figure 8.2
FADER/MUTE button.

The FADER/MUTE button allows you to easily switch back and forth between the Input and Track Mixers. When TR is lit, the faders are used to control Track Mixer channels 1-16. This is the setting you will use most often during mixdown.

When IN is lit, the faders now control the 10 Input Mixer channels (8 analog and 2 digital), the Stereo Input, plus the ⅓ effects return and the 2/4 effects return.

Whenever a new song is created, this feature defaults to the track setting. Another way to switch between the Input and Track Mixer is by using the INPUT SELECT and TRACK SELECT buttons. For example, if you have the FADER/MUTE button set to TR and you need to access the Input Mixer for channel 1, just press the INPUT SELECT button above channel 1. From there, you can easily get back to the Track Mixer for channel 1 by pressing the TRACK SELECT button above channel 1. This does not change the function of the fader. In the above example, when switching to various channel views, the white faders are still active as Track Mixer faders.

Master Block

The Master Block, as seen in Figure 8.3, works like a patch bay. It allows you to determine which signals appear at each of the physical output connections. The Master Block has inputs and outputs just like on a physical patch bay. Each of the inputs can be routed to any of the physical outputs.

To enter the Master Block, press the EDIT/SOLO button. Use the cursor buttons to move around in the Master Block and use the TIME/VALUE wheel to change the settings.

Figure 8.3

The Master Block can route any of the inputs on the left to any of physical outputs on the right.

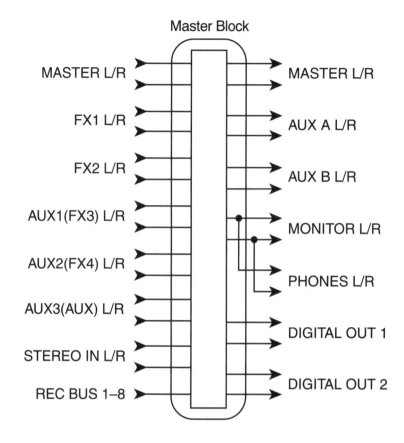

Master Block

MASTER L/R → → MASTER L/R

FX1 L/R → → AUX A L/R

FX2 L/R → → AUX B L/R

AUX1(FX3) L/R → → MONITOR L/R

AUX2(FX4) L/R → → PHONES L/R

AUX3(AUX) L/R → → DIGITAL OUT 1

STEREO IN L/R → → DIGITAL OUT 2

REC BUS 1–8 →

In the diagram above, the MONITOR LR and PHONES LR are connected. The reason is because the signals in the VS-1680 are first routed to the Monitor bus. The Monitor bus is then routed to the Phones output. So in essence, the two knobs (MONITOR and PHONES) are physically connected, with the MONITOR knob taking precedence. That means when you turn the MONITOR knob up or down, you will hear a volume change in your headphones as well. This is the way the VS-1680 is hardwired and cannot be changed. This can be quite frustrating to deal with at times. What I have done to overcome this problem is connect my Stereo Outs to an external mixer, which is connected to my monitors. This bypasses the need to use the MONITOR knob. I control the monitor levels from my external mixer, and that leaves the PHONES and MONITOR knobs on the VS to control the headphone level only. This method gives you more independent control over the Phones and Monitor outputs.

This also works nicely when you are recording vocal tracks and you need to turn off your monitors, but still need to hear audio through your headphones. Instead of dealing with the PHONES and MONITOR knobs, you can just turn your monitors off by lowering the volume on the external mixer.

Also, if you just need to turn off your monitors while maintaining level in the headphones, you can place an A/B switch between your monitors and your VS-1680's monitor out jacks. Connect one side of the A/B switch to your monitors (A) and leave the other side empty (B). When you need to hear your monitors, select the A setting on the A/B switch. When you need to turn the monitors off, select the B setting. This will also keep you from having to physically power down your monitors to record vocal tracks.

Ten Inputs

The VS-1680 gives you 10 inputs that can be routed to any track you want for recording. This includes two XLR inputs, six ¼" inputs, and two digital inputs.

That gives you a total of eight analog inputs and two digital inputs. You can combine signals from the 10 inputs with the 16 tracks of recorded audio to have a total of 26 automated channels being mixed at once.

Notice there are two sets of digital input connections in the previous figure. The VS-1680 gives you the option of using two types of digital inputs—coaxial and optical—but you may only use one type of digital input at once. For each type of digital connector, there is an IN and an OUT. Whether you use the coaxial or optical digital inputs is up to you. I have not been able to hear any noticeable difference between the two.

Also notice that there are seven ¼" analog inputs. The input to the far left is the HI-Z guitar input. It shares the same fader with analog input 8, so that means you may only use the HI-Z guitar input or analog input 8. You cannot use them both at the same time.

THE HI-Z GUITAR INPUT TAKES PRECEDENCE

If you have both inputs connected at the same time, the HI-Z guitar input takes precedence over analog input 8. In other words, you will not hear any sound from analog input 8 until you disconnect the HI-Z guitar input.

Two Effects Cards at Once

Of concern to the VS-880 user was that machine's inability to use more than one VS-8F-1 effects card. That meant you could only use two stereo effects at once. Unlike its little brother, the VS-1680 can hold two effects cards at once. It uses an upgraded effects card called the VS8F-2, which was specifically designed for the VS-1680/1880/2480 series.

On the new card, you will find all the same effects that you loved on the VS-880 effects card. With two VS8F-2 cards installed, a total of four high-quality stereo effects (or eight mono effects) are available for use during recording, bouncing, and mixing.

In January 2004, Roland introduced a brand-new effects card (appropriately named the VS8F-3) at the Winter NAMM show. The new card is available for the VS-1680 and higher models. With the release of the VS8F-3 effects card, a VS owner could add powerful third-party plug-in effects to his VS recorder. Roland includes five free plug-ins with the purchase of the new card. These are:

* Enhanced Mastering Tool Kit
* Stereo Reverb
* Tempo Mapping Effect (Delay)
* Vocal Channel Strip
* Mic Preamp Modeling

The list of third-party effects include powerful plug-ins such as Antares Auto-Tune, Massenburg DesignWorks Hi-Resolution Parametric EQ, Universal Audio VS-1176LN, McDSP Chrome Tone Amp, Universal Audio VS-LA2A, and IK Multimedia T-RackS VS. Each third-party plug-in is specifically designed for use with the VS recorder and sold separately.

Phantom Power

The VS-1680 can power two condenser microphones using its own phantom power at +48 V. The two XLR inputs are the only ones that can be used with the internal phantom power. There is a switch on the VS-1680 that turns the phantom power on and off. It is located on the back of the unit, on the left side of the two XLR inputs.

> **❊ USE THESE PHANTOM POWER PRECAUTIONS**
>
> Only turn on the phantom power when the VS-1680 is turned off. Also, you should not use phantom power with dynamic microphones, as this can result in damage to your equipment.

Markers and Locators

One of the best ways to move around in your song is by using markers and locators. The VS-1680 has 64 locators and 1,000 markers. Markers are used differently from locators on the VS-1680. You will basically use the LOCATOR buttons to jump from one part of your song to another. The markers will be used for a variety of different reasons, such as defining sections of a song for loop recording, storing Automix data and CD indexes, and marking points used for punch-in recording.

You can use a total of 64 locators per song. The VS-1680's 64 locators are organized into eight banks. Each bank has eight locators. This feature is very handy when you want to quickly move from one destination to another within your song during recording or mixing. Each LOCATOR button can be assigned a single time location within your song. Pressing that particular LOCATOR button will move you instantly to the stored time. A nice way to use this feature is to assign each part of your song to a LOCATOR button. For example, you can assign the intro to one locator, the first verse to another locator, the chorus to a third locator, and so on until you have each section of your song assigned to a different LOCATOR button.

To switch from one bank of LOCATOR buttons to another, do the following:

1. Press the BANK button. The LOCATOR buttons now serve as bank changing buttons. The flashing LOCATOR button indicates which bank is the active one. So if LOCATOR button 1 is flashing, that means bank 1 is active. If LOCATOR button 2 is flashing, then bank 2 is active, and so on.

2. Press the LOCATOR button for the bank you want activated. If you want to make bank 1 active, press LOCATOR button 1. If you want bank 2 to be active, press LOCATOR button 2. You can select all the way up to bank 8. After a bank locator is selected, the bank's indicator light goes out.

3. To return to the previously indicated bank, press the BANK button again and then the LOCATOR button to the corresponding bank you wish to activate. For example, if bank 1 is active and you want to get to bank 1, press BANK and then press LOCATOR button 2.

Undo and Redo

One of the greatest advantages of recording in the digital world is that we can use Undo and Redo. With these features, you never have to worry about experimenting with a track. Just about everything you do on the VS-16880 can literally be undone with the press of a button. When you need to undo something that you just did on the VS-1680, just press the UNDO button and the YES button.

The VS-1680 has 999 levels of Undo and one level of Redo. Let's say you recorded a vocal part, and you didn't like it. You then recorded that part four more times using the punch-in feature. That would be a total of five times the part was recorded, as shown in Figure 8.4. To get back to the second time the part was recorded, you would need to select Undo level three.

If you decide that you really don't like the second recording after using the Undo function, just use the Redo function to go back to the fifth or last recording, as shown in Figure 8.5.

If you use Undo to go back to the second of the five recordings and then make a brand new recording, you will not be able to get back to the old recordings 3–5. If you use Undo after making the new recording, you will be able to go back to the original second recording.

Redo works the same way as does Undo. If you use Undo and find that you really did like the change you previously made, you can use Redo to go back to the change. To use Redo, press the UNDO button while holding down SHIFT, and then press the YES button.

Figure 8.4
Recording 5 is the current level. To get back to the second recording, you would need to go back three levels as shown in this figure. Another way to think of it would be 5 minus 3 equals 2.

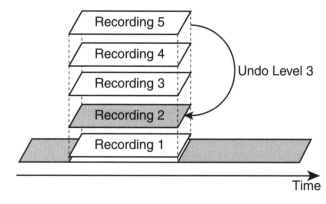

Figure 8.5
Using the Redo function immediately after using the Undo function allows you to go back to the last take you were listening to.

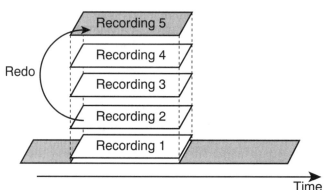

Dedicated Mastering Room

The original VS-880 did not have a way of putting the final touches on your recordings. Coincidentally, neither did the first VS-1680. This process is referred to as mastering your song. This was subsequently addressed in the form of an operating system update for the VS-1680. This was further expanded upon with the creation of the VS-1880.

With the VS-1680 operating system update, you could essentially choose from a list of pre-configured mastering templates to add to your final mix. These templates were created for different styles of music and were labeled that way. They have names such as acoustic, dance, jingle, and mixdown. After you apply a mastering effect to your mix, you can then tweak the effect to custom fit your song. Many times you can use a mastering effect preset as is. Each mastering room effect's label begins with the letters MTK. That stands for Mastering Tool Kit. So each MTK is a chain of powerful signal processors that can be tweaked until your heart's content.

The mastering room was a great add-on feature to the VS-1680. It allows your final mix to be run through a chain of signal processors just like in a real mastering house. It gives you the power to combine processors such as enhancers, EQ, limiters, compressors, and expanders into one stereo effects patch. If you spend some time getting to know how each processor works, you can accomplish some astonishing results using the MTK.

Differences Between the VS-1680, VS-1880, and VS-1824

As with the release of any piece of gear, the users always want more. Roland made some improvements to the VS-1680 and publicly debuted these improvements with the release of a new and improved model: the VS-1880. The VS-1880 is almost identical to the VS-1680, with a few major upgrades. The VS-1824 came out later and was released as an upgrade to the VS-1880. Each upgraded model has its advantages.

VS-1880 Upgrades

The VS-1880 was the first upgraded model of the VS-1680. Even though the two recorders share most of the same architecture, there are a few significant differences.

More Tracks

The biggest and most obvious upgrade the VS-1880 has over the VS-1680 is the higher track count. The VS-1880 boasts 18 individual tracks of digital recording. You may notice that the two recorders share the same number of faders. What Roland did to accomplish two more tracks and keep the same number of faders was convert the single faders 7 and 8 into two stereo linked faders. So on the VS-1880, instead of having eight single faders and four stereo linked faders, it has six single faders and six stereo linked faders, giving you a total of 18 tracks. Just like on the VS-1680, you can unlink the stereo tracks at any time.

❊ **USING THE STEREO LINKED FADERS**

When unlinked, the stereo linked faders control the odd-numbered tracks by default. To control the even-numbered tracks, press the SHIFT key and then move the fader. For example, If you want to control track 7, just move the seventh fader normally. To control track 8, press and hold the SHIFT button while moving the eighth fader.

❊ **USING SHIFT LOCK**

You can set the SHIFT button for one-handed operation by using the Shift Lock feature. This setting can be found under SHIFT → SYSTEM → GLOBAL → SHIFT LOCK → ON. When set to ON, you can press the SHIFT button one time to lock it in place while you move your fader. This feature is also included in the VS-1680 and VS-1824.

24 Bit Internal AD Converters

The internal AD (analog to digital) converters in the VS-1680 are 20-bit. That means when you plug an instrument into the analog inputs of the VS-1680, the analog signal is converted to digital information in a 20-bit format. Generally speaking, the higher the bit rate, the clearer the signal is. The internal processing of the VS-1680 is 24-bit. In other words, if you connect an external 24-bit AD converter to your VS-1680 through the digital inputs, the VS-1680 will recognize and process the 24-bit AD. It's only the internal AD converters that process at 20 bits.

The VS-1880's internal AD converters are 24-bit. So if you plug into the VS-1880's analog inputs, the signal will be automatically converted into 24-bit digital information. For many, this has eliminated the need for buying an external 24-bit AD converter.

❄ WHAT IS A BIT?

You can think of a bit as a piece of information. The more bits (or pieces) you have, the more information you have. The more information you have, the more detailed the sound will be.

Twenty-four pieces of the sound will re-create your song better than only 20 pieces. This is why the VS-1880's internal converters were upgraded to 24-bit.

Dedicated CD/RW—Mastering Button

The VS-1880 has a dedicated button (CD/RW MASTERING button) that takes you directly to the CD writing and mastering functions of the machine. The screen that appears immediately after pressing this button is called the CD/RW Mastering menu, shown in Figure 8.6. SHIFT+CD-RW button bypasses this menu and takes you directly to the mastering room.

Figure 8.6
The CD/RW Mastering menu provides quick access to the mastering room and all the CD/RW functions.

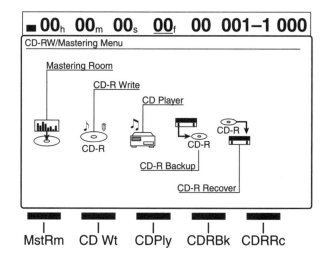

CDR Mode

In order to burn a CD using the Roland CD/RW writer, you must first burn an image file. Once the image file is created, you can then use that to burn your CD. Burning a CD image file is a very time-consuming process. The VS-1880 has a special feature called CDR mode that allows you to bypass the step of creating an image file, shown in Figure 8.7. The CDR mode option is located in the mastering room.

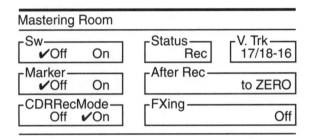

Figure 8.7

Set the CDRRecMode to On when you are ready to burn a CD.

When the CDRRecMode option is set to On, your two-track stereo master will be created in a 16-bit audio format that makes it ready to burn to a CD.

VS-1824 Upgrades

The VS-1824 is almost the twin brother to the VS-1880, with a few improvements.

Built-In CD/RW Drive

When musicians talk about an all-in-one box being able to produce a finished product from beginning to end, the VS-1680 and VS-1880 both lack the ability to burn a CD without the use of external equipment. Roland addressed this concern with the release of the VS-1824. The VS-1824 was the first VS recorder to boast its own onboard CD/RW writer. With the VS-1824, no longer did a VS user have to buy an external CD/RW writer just to burn a CD or back up his song data. As an added plus, the VS-1824 also comes with a SCSI port on the back. This means you still have the option of using an external CD/RW writer with it if you want to.

Improved Fader Layout

As time went by, many users grew tired of having to unlink the defaulted stereo linked faders. Roland quickly addressed this concern with a new and improved fader layout on the VS-1824. Unlike its two predecessors, the VS-1824 comes with zero linked faders. The 12 faders can be used individually in one of two fader banks. The first fader bank allows faders 1-12 to control tracks 1-12. The second fader bank allows faders 7-12 to control tracks 13-18. You also still have the option of linking side-by-side stereo tracks if you want to. In other words, tracks 1-2, 3-4, 5-6, and so on can be linked together in stereo pairs and controlled by one fader.

CD Capture

Since the VS-1824 (also known as the VS-1824CD) has its own onboard CD/RW writer, it only made sense that it would also include the ability to rip songs from a CD using the internal CD/RW writer. This is accomplished by using the CD Capture function. You can now rip songs from your favorite CDs and import them into your VS creations for editing or whatever you like.

9 Advances in Recording with the VS-1680/1880

The VS-1680's user interface has been so logically planned out that, once you know where everything is located, recording on it is a breeze. In this chapter, we will create a new song and record a guitar part. If you play the guitar and have one handy, feel free to grab it now and follow along.

Creating a New Song

Before we can actually begin recording, we have to first designate a space on the VS-1680's hard drive where our new song will be recorded. This is called creating a new song. To create a new song, press SHIFT → F1 (Song) → F2 (New). This brings you to the Song New screen. Here you will set the following parameters:

❋ Sample Rate: If your final product will end up on a CD, the best sampling rate to choose is 44.1k. You can use 48k if you want, but you will still have to convert it to 44.1k before you can burn it to a CD, so I recommend using 44.1k for your recordings.

❋ Record Mode: We covered the different recording modes in Chapter 8, "Introduction to the VS-1680/1880 Series." Use MTP for your recordings to get the best results.

❋ Copy System Parameters: When this is set to On, you can create a new song that will have the same system parameters as the current selected song. Leave this off for now.

❋ Copy Mixer/Scene Parameters: When this is set to On, you can create a new song that will have the same mixer settings and scenes as the current song. Leave this off for now.

❋ Icon: You can select from a group of seven graphic icons to represent your song.

Once you are done making the appropriate selections, press F4 (EXEC). You will be asked, Create New Song, Sure? Press ENTER/YES.

Setting Up a Track for Recording

Now that you have allocated space for your new song, you can begin recording. Let's say you want to record a guitar on track 1. The VS-1680 has a HI-Z guitar input right next to input 8. This input is configured so that you don't have to use any kind of pre-amp if you don't want to when recording a guitar or bass. After the guitar is plugged in, we have to route the input signal to the track on which we want to record. Since we want to record on track 1, we have to route the signal from the guitar HI-Z input to track 1.

1. Press and hold the STATUS button for track 1. You will probably see track 1's INPUT SELECT button start to flash because that is the default setting for a new song.

2. While holding down the STATUS button for track 1, press the INPUT SELECT button for track 1 until it stops flashing.

3. While still holding down the STATUS button for track 1, press the INPUT SELECT button for channel 8. The INPUT SELECT button for channel 8 should now be flashing.

That's it! You're done. At this point, the HI-Z guitar input is routed to track 1.

Setting the Recording Level

Now that we have the input channel properly routed to the desired recording track, we need to set the proper recording level. Plug your guitar into the HI-Z input channel. Press the STATUS button for track 1 until it turns red to arm it for recording.

SHORTCUT FOR ARMING TRACKS TO BE RECORDED

A faster way to arm a track for recording is to press the STATUS button for the desired track while holding down the REC button on your Transport Controls.

You can view the input signal at the PRE or POST fader level, but I suggest looking at the input PRE levels. Press the PAGE button until you see LM In above F2. Press F2 (LM In). Now we can see the recording levels for all the input channels. This next part can be confusing, so pay close attention. If you see POST above F4, then you are on the PRE screen. If you see PRE above F4, you are on the POST screen. F4 tells you what screen you will be on *if you press it*. You can also look toward the top of the screen under the measure/bar counter to see exactly which screen you are on, as shown in Figure 9.1. You can press F3 (LM TR) to view signal levels being recorded to the tracks Pre Fader view if you wish.

Press the INPUT SELECT button for channel 8. This brings us to the Input Mixer screen. If you don't see MIX above A1, press PAGE until you do. In the upper right-hand corner of the screen is the

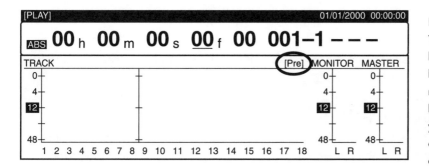

Figure 9.1
You can always tell which levels you are viewing by looking at the indicator right below the measure/bar counter. In this figure, you can see that PRE is circled, showing that we are currently on the PRE levels screen. We need to be on the PRE levels screen for recording. Press F4 to view the POST levels screen, if necessary.

MIX display. Channel 8 defaults to R63. We want to set that to 0. Press the MIX button and then turn the jogwheel until the setting is at 0.

❋ **JOGWHEEL TIP**

If you press and hold the SHIFT button while turning the jogwheel, it advances in increments of 10 instead of one. Use this method as often as you can to cut down on the wear and tear on your jogwheel. When using SHIFT LOCK, as described in Chapter 8, "Introduction to the VS-1680/1880 Series," you only need to press the SHIFT button once. You don't have to hold it down.

Make sure the FADER/MUTE button is set to TR (track). Turn up your guitar and play something. Now slowly turn up the Input Gain knob for input 8 until you see a level on the screen. The ideal level you want is between –12db and –4db.

❋ **TRACK FADER CONTROL**

The fader for track 1 now controls the monitor level only. It does not control the input level. It does not matter what position the fader is set to during recording, so feel free to adjust it to the best possible listening position you can.

We are now ready to record something. Press the REC button, and it will start to flash. That means everything is set and is ready to go. When you are ready to record, press PLAY and play your guitar. When you are finished, press the ZERO button. This takes you back to the beginning of your song. Now press PLAY, and you should hear what you just recorded. Use fader 1 to adjust the playback volume.

You can repeat these steps to record a bass part on any of the remaining tracks using the HI-Z guitar input.

Recording a Vocal Track

The VS-1680 gives you two XLR inputs. These are mainly used for recording vocals. They are also the only two inputs that are phantom powered. You should only turn on the phantom power when using a condenser microphone, as shown in Figure 9.2. Using the phantom power with dynamic microphones can result in damage to your equipment.

Using an External Preamp

The VS-1680's preamps can provide sufficient power to record decent vocal tracks, but adding an external preamp can give your vocal tracks more power at the input gain stage. This will keep you from having to turn the VS-1680's Gain knob almost all the way up to get a decent signal. There are two ways to add an external preamp:

✱ **Go in through the analog inputs:** This way does not bypass the internal VS preamps. Instead, it gives you a mix of the VS preamp and the external preamp. I recommend setting the VS Input Gain knob around the nine o'clock position or less when using this method. Raise the external preamp until the desired recording level on the VS monitor screen is reached.

✱ **Go in through the digital inputs:** This way allows you to bypass the VS preamps. When this method is used, all gain staging comes from the external preamp. You may only use this method with external preamps that have digital in and out connections.

Using an External A/D (Analog to Digital) Converter

It is possible to connect an external A/D converter, such as the one shown in Figure 9.3, to your VS-1680. Some external preamps already have A/D converters built right into the unit. You can use those, or if you find you are unhappy with the quality of the VS-1680's onboard preamps or A/D converters, you can use a preamp with a separate A/D converter. An A/D converter can be connected to either the coaxial or optical digital input on the VS-1680. Even though the VS-1680's internal A/D converters are 20-bit, it can process an external A/D signal at 24-bit. This is another reason why some people choose to add an external A/D converter to their system.

Figure 9.2
Studio Projects C1 Microphone. This is a large diaphragm condenser microphone that can only be used with phantom power. It is an excellent microphone for vocals.

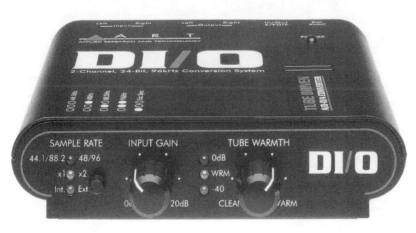

Figure 9.3
Art DIO 2-Channel Analog to Digital and Digital to Analog Converter with Tube Processing. (To learn more about the D/IO and other ART audio products, please visit www.artproaudio.com.)

Compressing a Track While Recording

You can always add external gear to your VS-1680 if you want to, but you don't have to. The VS-1680 is a self-contained, all-in-one unit. It has preamps, A/D converters, and compressors (with the optional VS8F-2 and VS8F-3 effects boards) built right in. If you are having problems controlling a wild vocalist, you can use the VS compressors to smooth out the track.

A good place to start is to use effects patch P221: MTK:VocalCmp. This patch is specifically designed to help bring out the best in a wild vocal track. The following steps detail how I use it on vocals while recording.

> ❋ **INTERNAL COMPRESSORS COME AFTER INTERNAL PREAMP**
>
> You have to be very careful when using the internal compressors to tame vocals. This is because the internal compressors come after the internal preamps in the signal chain. Since the compressor is after the preamp, it cannot control the incoming vocal signal from distorting the preamp if a loud peak is present in the input signal. Only an external compressor can do that. You will have to adjust your input recording level to a point where the vocalist is not distorting the signal, even when he sings at full volume. You can then use the internal compressor to smooth out the signal.

1. Set the Input Peak Level to –6db. Use the following steps: SHIFT → F5 SYSTEM → F2 GLOBAL. Use cursor keys to tab to Input Peak Level. This makes the red clip light above the Gain knob to indicate clipping (lights red) at –6db instead of 0. This setting gives you an advance warning before your signal actually hits 0 and distorts.

2. Allow the vocalist to sing as loudly as he will during his performance, and adjust the Gain knob so that the recording level does not distort or that the red clip signal barely lights up at the loudest volume.

3. Insert P221: MTK:VocalCmp to the vocal input channel using steps 4–12.

4. Hold SHIFT → F3 (FXA) → F1 (FX1) → F2 (Select).

5. Use the jogwheel to scroll to P221: MTK:VocalCmp.

6. Press F4 (Exec).

7. Press the INPUT SELECT button for the input channel to which the microphone is connected.

8. Press PAGE until you see FX1In above F1. Press F1.

9. Press ENTER/YES.

10. Turn the jogwheel to insert the effect. InsL (mono) uses the left side of the effects card, and InsR (mono) uses the right side of the card. Ins (stereo) uses both sides of the card. Since this is a mono track, I suggest using either InsL or InsR.

11. Press PLAY/DISPLAY to exit.

12. Hold SHIFT F3 (FXA) to get back to the effects screen.

The MTK Vocal Compressor is now inserted on the input track. While the vocalist is singing, you can press F5 (Bypass) to hear the vocal without compression. Press it again to hear the vocal with compression. You can edit any parameter of the MTK Vocal Compressor patch by selecting the component with your left and right cursor keys and then pressing F3 (Edit).

❋ **BE CAREFUL WHEN TWEAKING MTK COMPONENTS**

Each component of the MTK patch is powerful. If not used properly, drastic tweaking of these components can ruin a track rather quickly. I suggest you experiment with these settings until you are comfortable with them before making any drastic changes.

You can also record the track without any compression and then add compression to the track at a later time. This is covered later in Chapter 11, "Advances in Mixing with the VS-1680."

Adding Effects to a Track During Playback

Some vocalists like to hear effects while they are recording, but they don't want that effect recorded to the track. Recording an effect to a track is called printing. The VS-1680 makes it easy to record a track without printing an effect, while allowing the vocalist to hear the effect in his headphones at the same time. Use the following steps to add an effect to track 1 that the vocalist will hear, but that will not be printed to the track:

1. Hold SHIFT → F3 (FXA) → F1 (FX1) → F2 (Select).

2. Use the jogwheel to scroll to P060: Reverb.

3. Press F4 (Exec).

4. Route the selected effect's return to the destination track.

5. Press the TRACK SELECT button for the channel onto which the vocal is being recorded.

6. Press PAGE until you see FX1 above F1. Press F1.

7. Use the jogwheel to change the setting from OFF to PST.

8. Use the down cursor to select the reverb send amount.

9. Use the jogwheel to change the reverb send amount from 100 to the desired level.

When the vocalist sings, he will hear reverb on his voice, but the reverb will not be recorded to the track.

Using Virtual Tracks

You can record up to 16 different tracks on each track channel. This gives you a total of 256 tracks. These are called virtual tracks, also referred to as V-Tracks. The VS-1880 and VS-1824 have a total of 288 V-Tracks, since they have two more regular channels. You can think of the V-Tracks as placeholders for different musical takes. Only one V-Track per track channel may be played at a time. You cannot switch V-Tracks during playback.

There are many benefits to using V-Tracks. If your vocalist is struggling to get a good take, you can record multiple takes on different V-Tracks. Later, you can copy and paste the best parts from the different takes to one V-Track. Many refer to this procedure as "comping" a track.

You can also use V-Tracks to keep original tracks safe when you are experimenting with different techniques. For example, if you want to experiment with printing reverb to a track, you can copy the dry track to a different V-Track. Experiment with printing reverb to the active V-Track as much as you want. If you are not happy with your results, you can always go back to the original dry track that you saved on the other V-Track.

This technique can also be used when you are bouncing tracks. Bouncing means to combine several tracks into one track or a two-track stereo pair. Let's say you want to bounce tracks 1, 2, 3, 4, and 5 with effects to stereo pair 9/10. You can copy your original tracks to other V-Tracks so they are safe from your experimenting. When you finish your bounce and then record over tracks 1, 2, 3, 4, and 5 with new material, you may discover that you are not happy with the bounced tracks. No need to worry. You can retrieve the original tracks from the V-Tracks you first copied them to and start over. V-Tracks are a wonderful way to help you get that perfect take!

To select a different V-Track for recording, do the following:

1. Press the TRACK SELECT button for the V-Track you want to change. The Track Mixer screen appears in the display.
2. If V.Trk does not appear above F5, press PAGE until it does. Press F5 (V.Trk).
3. Use the jogwheel to select he V-Track you want to use.
4. Press PLAY/DISPLAY to exit.

Using the Digital Inputs to Record a Track

The VS-1680 allows you to record a true digital source through its digital inputs. This source can be a CD player, DAT machine, another VS recorder, or any other digital source. You have the choice of using the coaxial or optical inputs. There are basically three steps to using the digital inputs:

1. Make your connections. Connect the digital outputs of your digital source to the appropriate digital inputs on the VS-1680.

2. Match the sample rates. The sample rate of the song and the sample rate of the digital source must be the same before the VS-1680 can record the signal. The sample rate for your song is set when you perform the New Song function described earlier in this chapter. If that sample rate does not match your digital source, you can create a new song with the correct sample rate to match the digital source.

3. Set the Master Clock. The VS-1680's internal clock must be synchronized with the digital signal from the digital source before the VS-1680 can record the data.

To set the Master Clock, do the following:

1. Hold SHIFT → F5 (SYSTEM) → F1 (SYSPM).

2. Use the cursor keys to move the cursor to MasterClk.

3. Use the jogwheel to select either DIGIN1 or DIGIN2, depending on whether you are using the coaxial or optical inputs. Digital In Lock should appear in the VS screen.

4. Press PLAY/DISPLAY to exit.

The last thing you'll need to do before recording the digital signal is route the digital input to the desired recording track. If you are trying to record the digital signal to track 1, do the following:

1. Press and hold the STATUS button for track 1. You will probably see track 1's INPUT SELECT button start to flash, because that is the default setting on a new song.

2. While holding down the STATUS button for track 1, press the INPUT SELECT button for track 1 until it stops flashing.

3. While still holding down the STATUS button for track 1, press the DIGITAL SELECT button on the right side of the channel 8 INPUT button. The DIGITAL SELECT button should be flashing now.

You may now record the digital source to track 1 by pressing REC and PLAY. Many SP/DIF digital sources are two channels of digital audio, a left and right or stereo signal. Linked tracks will record both of the incoming digital signals in stereo.

Punch In/Out

There may be times when you are listening back to a recorded track and hear parts that are not recorded well. Instead of redoing the entire track, the VS-1680 allows you to record over the badly recorded part. This is accomplished using the Punch-In/Out technique. Switching from playback to recording while a song is playing is called "punching in." Switching from recording back to playback while a song is playing is called "punching out." There are two ways you can punch in and out on the VS-1680: the manual punch method and the Auto Punch method.

Manual Punch

There are two ways you can use the manual punch method: You can punch in and out with your hand or you can use a footswitch.

Manual Punch by Hand

Use the Transport Control buttons to manually punch in and out, as shown in Figure 9.4.

Figure 9.4

This timeline gives a visual demonstration of how to use the manual transport buttons when punching in and out.

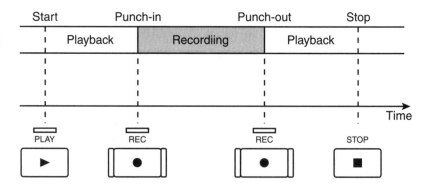

Use the following steps to manually punch in and out:

1. Press PLAY to begin playback of the song.

2. When you reach the exact point in the song that you want to re-record, press REC. The VS-1680 goes into record mode and begins recording the new performance.

3. When you are finished recording, press REC again to punch out.

※ **THE RECORD BUTTON**

Each time the REC button is pressed, the recorder alternately punches in and out.

Manual Punch with Footswitch

There may be times when it is too difficult to perform a manual punch while playing an instrument or engineering. In these cases, it would be convenient to use a footswitch (such as the DP-2 or the Boss FS-5U) to do your punch-ins and -outs, as shown in Figure 9.5.

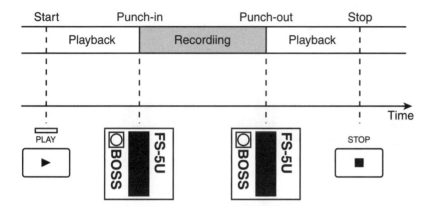

Figure 9.5
This timeline gives a visual demonstration of how to use a footswitch when punching in and out.

Connect the optional footswitch to the VS-1680's Foot Switch (per fig) jack, as shown in Figure 9.6.

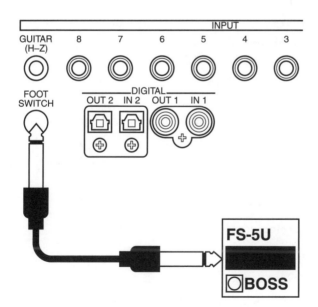

Figure 9.6
The Foot Switch jack is located on the rear of the VS-1680, on the left side of the digital connections.

Set up the VS-1680 to tell the footswitch what functions to perform by doing the following:

1. Hold SHIFT and press F5 (SYSTEM).

2. Press F1 (SYSPM).

3. Press F2 (Prm 2).

4. Use the cursor buttons to select Foot Sw.

5. Use the jogwheel to select Record.

Auto Punch

There may be times when you need to punch in and out at precise, pre-programmed locations. This is called Auto Punch. With Auto Punch, you preset the desired punch-in and -out points and then let the VS-1680 automatically do the punching in and out for you. This is very convenient when you are trying to punch in and out while playing an instrument or singing.

There are three ways to set the Auto Punch:

※ Using locators: Place a locator at the point in the song where you want to punch in and place another locator at the point where you want to punch out. While holding down AUTO PUNCH, press the locator corresponding to the punch-in point, then press the locator corresponding to the punch-out point.

※ Using markers: Set two markers like you did for using locators. Set one for the punch-in point and one for the punch-out point. Move to the marker for the punch-in point, hold AUTO PUNCH, and press NEXT. Without releasing AUTO PUNCH, press PREVIOUS.

※ Programming points during song playback: While the song is playing, press and hold AUTO PUNCH. When you reach your desired punch-in location, press TAP. Continue to hold AUTO PUNCH. When the desired punch-out point is reached, press TAP again. Press STOP.

Choose the method that works best for you in your particular situation. You are ready to re-record your performance after the Auto Punch-In and -Out points have been set. The following demonstrates how to use Auto Punch after the punch-in and -out points have been set:

1. Press the AUTO PUNCH button. The AUTO PUNCH indicator will light.

2. Locate a point a few seconds or measures before the Auto Punch-In point.

3. Press REC. The REC button will start to flash.

4. Press PLAY to begin playback of the song.

5. When the song reaches the Auto Punch-In point, the VS-1680 will automatically start recording. The REC button will turn solid red during recording.

6. When the song reaches the Auto Punch-Out point, the VS-1680 will automatically stop recording. The REC button will go back to flashing.

7. Press the AUTO PUNCH button to disable Auto Punch when you are finished. The AUTO PUNCH indicator will be unlit.

Bouncing

You can take the performance data of several tracks and combine them into one track or a two-track stereo pair. This is called bouncing. You can bounce tracks dry (without effects) or wet (with effects) while controlling the amount of effect(s) for each track. A stereo bounce will also retain all individual pan settings.

Bouncing can be a real asset if you run out of free playback tracks and need some space for additional recording.

In the following example, we will bounce tracks 5, 6, 7, and 8 to stereo pair 9/10 as shown in Figure 9.7.

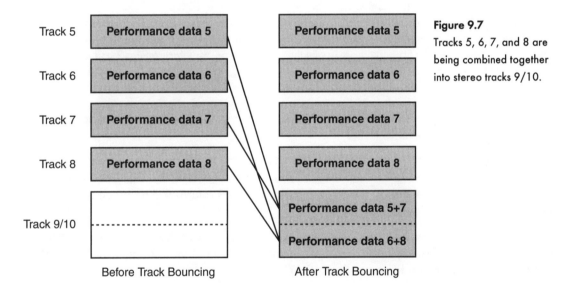

Track 5 — Performance data 5
Track 6 — Performance data 6
Track 7 — Performance data 7
Track 8 — Performance data 8
Track 9/10

Performance data 5
Performance data 6
Performance data 7
Performance data 8
Performance data 5+7
Performance data 6+8

Before Track Bouncing   After Track Bouncing

Figure 9.7
Tracks 5, 6, 7, and 8 are being combined together into stereo tracks 9/10.

In this example, tracks 5, 6, 7, and 8 are called the source tracks. Tracks 9/10 are called the destination tracks.

All panning, EQ, levels, and effects should only be applied to the source tracks. Do not add any effects or EQ to the destination tracks or the bounce will sound different than the source tracks.

To set up the bounce, route the source tracks to the destination tracks as follows:

1. Press the STATUS button for tracks 9/10 (the destination tracks) until it lights orange.

2. While holding the STATUS button for tracks 9/10, press the CLEAR button to clear all previous routings. Once you are comfortable with bouncing, you may bypass this step.

3. Hold the STATUS button for tracks 9/10 and press the SELECT buttons for tracks 5–8 (the source tracks) so that they start blinking.

4. If you have any effects assigned to any of the source tracks, hold the STATUS button for the destination tracks and press the SELECT button(s) for the appropriate effects returns you want to add to the bounce.

You may now monitor the source tracks 5–8 through the destination tracks 9/10.

> ❄ **LOCATING THE SELECT BUTTONS FOR THE EFFECTS RETURNS**
>
> On the VS-1680, the SELECT buttons for effects returns 1 and 3 are above stereo tracks 13/14. The SELECT buttons for effects returns 2 and 4 are above stereo tracks 15/16.
> On the VS-1880 and VS-1824, the SELECT buttons for effects returns 1 and 3 are above stereo tracks 15/16. The SELECT buttons for effects returns 2 and 4 are above stereo tracks 17/18.
> You will have to use the SHIFT button to access the SELECT buttons for effects returns 3 and 4 on all three machines.

Monitor the recording levels on the Pre Level screen as described earlier in this chapter under "Setting the Recording Level."

Record your bounce by changing the STATUS button for the destination tracks from orange to red. Press ZERO to rewind to the beginning of your song. Press PLAY to begin recording. Any changes you make in real time to the source tracks or effects returns will be reflected in your destination tracks. Press STOP when finished.

To hear your bounce, rewind to the beginning of the song. Change the source tracks status to MUTE (STATUS to CLEAR) to retain the levels in case needed again. Change the STATUS of the destination tracks from red to green. Press PLAY.

Recording with MIDI

MIDI stands for Musical Instrument Digital Interface and was created in the early 1980s. It was developed so that the music industry would have a standard protocol that all musical instruments, regardless of the manufacturer, could use to effectively communicate with one another.

The digital recording revolution of the 1990s created an increase in the number of high-quality, one-man project studios. Many of these home studios are located in bedrooms. That usually doesn't leave much room for a full band or to set up a drumkit. MIDI and the use of sequencers provide a way for a single person to program and record many different instrument parts without a band. A sequencer is a device that records MIDI data and plays it back through a MIDI keyboard or other type of MIDI sound module.

All of the VS recorders have fairly extensive MIDI capabilities and can be synced to drum machines, stand-alone sequencers, and computer sequencers.

There are two types of MIDI sync you can use to link your VS to MIDI gear. VS units can slave to MTC only, not MIDI Clock. VS units can generate (act as Master) MTC, and MIDI Clock.

❋ **MTC=MIDI Time Code:** MIDI Time Code is a time-based system that allows MIDI devices to sync together using the actual time frame information (minutes and seconds) of recorded material. This is the most accurate way to sync MIDI gear. It is most commonly used for syncing audio to video productions where absolute accuracy is a must. It is also used when syncing devices to certain software applications that do not work well with MIDI Clock.

❋ **MIDI Clock:** MIDI Clock sends bar/measure/beat information with which devices can communicate. In most cases, this is sufficient to sync basic MIDI gear with your VS recorder.

Recording a MIDI Drum Track

You can sync your VS-1680 to any drum machine that supports MIDI.

To sync a drum machine to your VS-1680, you will need at least one MIDI cable. You can usually get these from any musical instrument store. Use the MIDI cable to connect the MIDI OUT jack of the VS-1680 to the MIDI IN jack of the drum machine. That's it!

No matter which VS recorder you are using, you will always have to set the same three parameters to sync to a drum machine. Those parameters are MIDI Thru set to OUT, Syn Generator set to MIDI Clock, and the Tempo Map set to the desired tempo of the song.

To set those three parameters on the VS-1680, do the following:

1. Hold SHIFT and press F5 (SYSTEM).
2. Press F4 (MIDI). Use the cursor keys and the jogwheel to set MIDI Thru to OUT.
3. Press F6 (EXIT).
4. Press F6 (SYNC).
5. Use the cursor keys and jogwheel to set the Syn Gen to MIDIclk.
6. Press F3 (T.Map). Use the jogwheel to set the correct tempo for your song.

7. Press F6 (EXIT) two times.

8. Press PLAY/DISPLAY to exit the system screen.

Set your drum machine to receive a MIDI Clock signal. The terminology for this setting varies from drum machine to drum machine. It is usually referred to as external sync, slave, or MIDI. Consult your drum machine's owner's manual for the proper setting.

If you have set everything properly, your drum machine will start playing in perfect sync when you press PLAY on your VS-1680.

To make a recording of your drum patterns, connect the drum machine's audio outputs to the VS-1680's analog inputs and route the input signals to whatever tracks you wish to record on. If you want a two-track stereo mix of your drum machine parts, make sure the VS two-track stereo pair is linked together so that the tracks are panned hard left and hard right. You can find the link setting under the TRACK SELECT button and then look for the MIX setting.

When everything is connected and routed properly, check your recording levels on the Pre Level input screen and then make your recording.

❄ **USING PATTERN MODE VERSUS SONG MODE**

If your drum machine is in Pattern mode, it will not stay in sync when you press STOP on the VS-1680 and then press PLAY again. You will need to rewind the VS-1680 to the beginning of the song to get the units back in perfect sync.

The only way to keep the two machines in perfect sync after pressing STOP and PLAY on the VS-1680 is by putting your drum machine in Song mode. This is the mode that allows your drum machine to arrange a series of drum patterns together and play them back as a song. The terminology used for this mode varies from one drum machine to another.

Consult your drum machine's owner's manual to set it to Song mode operation. This is true of any MIDI Clock master device, not just the VS-1680.

Recording with a Sequencer

There are three types of sequencers you can use:

❄ **Software computer sequencer:** This is a computer software application that is specifically designed to record MIDI tracks to your computer. Some examples are Cakewalk, Sonar, Cubase, Logic Pro, and Reason.

❄ **Stand-alone hardware sequencer:** This is a dedicated hardware box that usually only allows for the recording of MIDI tracks. There are some hardware sequencers that have more than one purpose, such as the Akai MPC series and now the Roland MV-8000, as shown in

Figure 9.8. Some examples of hardware sequencers are the Yamaha QX-21, QX-5, and QX-1; the Roland MC-50 and MC-500; and the Alesis MMT-8.

❋ **Keyboard sequencer:** Many keyboards have built-in sequencers. They are usually self-contained units that have all the sounds necessary to make a complete recording. These sequencers can usually trigger sounds from other sound sources. Some examples of keyboards with onboard sequencers are the Korg Triton series, the Yamaha Motif series, the Roland Fantom series, and the Ensoniq EPS16 Plus and ASR-10.

Figure 9.8
Roland MV-8000. This is a complete MIDI production center that provides powerful MIDI sequencing and editing capabilities. It also has extensive sampling features and can be used as a drum machine.

Regardless of which sequencer you decide to use, they all function similarly. They will record MIDI information on up to 16 different MIDI channels, and some will record up to 32 MIDI channels. Each channel is assigned to a different part or "voice." Remember that MIDI is not sound—it is merely information that is transmitted to a device (keyboard or sound module) that can read that information and translate it to a sound you can hear.

To sync your sequencer to your VS-1680, you will need to set the same parameters you did for syncing with a drum machine.

Some software sequencers require that you use MTC. If that is the case, instead of setting the Syn Gen to MIDIclk, you will set it to MTC. Consult your sequencer's owner's manual for setting your sequencer to receive MTC.

Song Templates

A song template is an empty song that has all the routings and parameter settings you want to use already preconfigured.

Now that you know how to create a new song, route inputs, and sync to external MIDI gear, you may discover that it is a hassle to set up these parameters every time you begin a new song. The VS-1680 has preconfigured song templates for recording, mixing down, mastering, and bouncing already laid out for you under the EZ ROUTING button. You can customize these templates to your liking if you wish.

I have found another way—in addition to EZ Routing—to make song templates, and I find this method much easier to work with.

1. Create a new song and set up all the routings, effects, and parameters that you normally use.

2. Name that song something like Song Template using the Song Name function under SHIFT → SONG → NAME.

3. Save that song to a CD-R.

Whenever you need to start working on a new song, just load the Song Template song from your external CD- R/W drive. When you are finished working on the song, change the name and save it to your hard drive.

If you don't have a CD-R/W drive, use the following steps:

1. Create a new song and set up all the routings, effects, and parameters that you normally use.

2. Name that song something like Song Template using the Song Name function under SHIFT → SONG → NAME.

3. Save that song to the VS-1680's hard drive.

4. Load the song from the hard drive.

5. Hold SHIFT → F1 (Song) → F2 (New). This will create a new song.

6. Set Copy System PRM and Copy Mixer/Scene PRM to On.

7. Change the name of the newly created song and save it to the VS-1680's hard drive.

❅ **SOMETHING TO REMEMBER ABOUT USING SONG TEMPLATES ON YOUR HARD DRIVE**

The VS-1680 does not have a Save As function. Changing the name of the template and then saving it does not protect the template on the hard drive from being written over. That is why you have to create a new song, change the name, and then save that to your hard drive.

❅ **COPYING EFFECTS SETTINGS**

Setting the Copy System PRM and Copy Mixer/Scene PRM On does not copy all effects settings. To get all your effects settings to copy to the new song, save them as a scene. When you create your new song with these parameters, the scene containing all your effects information will also be copied over. In the newly created song, select the scene that has the effects settings you want to use. You will learn about setting up scenes in Chapter 11.

10 Advances in Editing with the VS-1680/1880

The VS-1680 has been very logically laid out, making editing very simple. The editing features are divided into two main categories: track editing and song editing. There are many powerful editing features on the VS-1680 that allow you to move and manipulate your recorded audio in many different ways. Don't be afraid to be bold and experiment with the editing features. Remember that you always have the Undo function, so if you mess up something while experimenting, just press the UNDO button and start over.

Track Editing Versus Phrase Editing

On the track level, there are two methods to tackle editing: track editing and phrase editing. Every time you press REC and then STOP on your VS-1680, a section of audio data is recorded. These sections of audio are called phrases. If you start at the beginning of a song and press REC and don't press STOP until the end of the song, you will be left with one long phrase. In contrast, if you punch in and out several times throughout the duration of the song, you will be left with many different phrases. You will have a different phrase for each punch-in and punch-out.

In a track edit, you must tell the VS-1680 where to begin the edit and where to end the edit. That is what the START and END points are for. Most of the track editing functions require you to set four points—START, END, FROM, and TO—however, for functions such as CUT and ERASE, you only have to set the START and END points. In phrase editing, the START and END points are already defined as the start and end of the phrase, respectively.

Phrase editing can work well when doing a lot of punching in and out. The VS-1680 uses the edges of the phrase to define the START and END points on each punch-in and punch-out. In many cases, phrase editing can be a valuable time saver.

To get to your track editing functions, hold SHIFT and press F2 (Track). Use the F1 key to toggle between the track editing and phrase editing functions. For track editing, you will see the following options:

❋ **Track Copy:** Copies selected sections of audio to another location and/or another track if desired. The original audio remains in tact.

❋ **Track Move:** Moves selected sections of audio to another location and/or another track if desired.

❋ **Track Exchange:** Swaps all audio data on two tracks.

❋ **Track Insert:** Inserts blank space at the specified location.

❋ **Track Cut:** Removes audio from a specified location. When the audio is cut, the data between the start and end points is completely removed and the remaining sections of audio are spliced together. This is much different from Track Erase.

❋ **Track Erase:** Erases audio from a specified location. This is similar to recording blank space on an analog recorder, as shown in Figure 10.1.

Figure 10.1
The Track Erase function erases a selected piece of audio and leaves a space. Track Cut, on the other hand, erases the audio and deletes the remaining space, thus joining the remaining pieces (A and C) together.

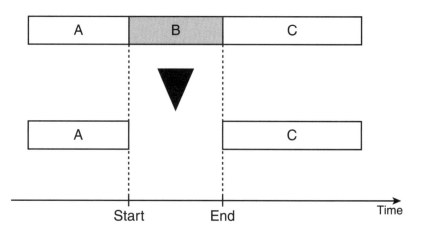

❋ **Track Compression/Expansion:** Allows you to expand or compress the playback time of a track or group of tracks by a specified time. This is usually referred to as time stretching on software editing applications.

❋ **Track Name:** Allows you to give your track a unique name.

❋ **Track Import:** Allows you to copy tracks from other songs into the current song.

Basic Steps for Track Editing

There are two basic steps for Track Editing:

1. Setting the edit points.

2. Performing the steps for the desired track edit function.

After deciding which Track Editing feature you want to use, you must set the edit points. Some features, such as Track Erase and Track Cut, only require you to set the START and END points. Other features require you to set all four editing points: START, END, FROM, and TO.

❋ **Understanding the Difference Between FROM and START**

Setting edit points confuses many people. In most cases, these points will be the same, but these points will be different in some cases.

The best way to help illustrate the difference between the FROM and START points is by envisioning a time bomb that ticks and then explodes. Let's say you want to move the audio so that the beginning of the explosion lands at a certain point in time. In this scenario, the START point will be the beginning of the ticking. The FROM point will be the beginning of the explosion. The TO point will be the position in the timeline where the explosion should occur. We refer to this type of edit as a back-time edit, as shown in Figure 10.2. You don't have to figure out where the ticking should begin in order for the FROM and TO points to line up.

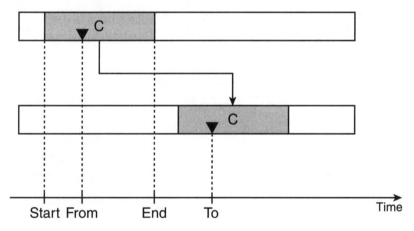

Figure 10.2
This is what a "back-time" edit looks like.

Setting the Edit Points

Before you can make the edit, you have to set the edit points. The first step in setting the edit points is finding the START and END points. These points define the section of material you want to edit. The VS-1680 gives you many different options for setting these points, including the use of locators, Preview, and Scrub.

Setting Ballpark Edit Points

One of the fastest ways to set edit points is by using locators while the song is playing. Start playback of your song, and when it gets to a point where you want to begin your edit, press the START locator button. When it gets to the part where you want to end the edit, press the END locator button. You now have two locator points that define the section you want to edit. This puts you in the editing ballpark. This is a quick way of setting edit points and is very useful in some applications where precise edit points are not needed.

Setting Precise Edit Points

Once you have your ballpark edit points selected, you can then use the Preview section, the Scrub function, and the Waveform display to zoom in to precise edit points.

* **Preview:** You can use this section to audition a short portion of a track.
* **Scrub:** This is another part of the Preview section that allows you to quickly find precise editing points while listening to the audio as it is slowed down. It is similar to rocking a tape head back and forth on an analog tape deck to find the precise point.
* **Waveform Display:** This is a pop-up waveform that gives you a visual representation of the track's audio. You can hear the audio using the Scrub function and you can see it on the Waveform display.

Perform the Steps for the Desired Track Edit Function

Once you set your edit points using the tools just mentioned, it's time to perform the steps necessary to complete the desired track edit function.

All of the track edit screens basically work the same way. When you enter a track edit screen, you must place your chosen time locations for the edit points (START, END, FROM, TO) in the appropriate fields on the screen. In the following example, we will use Track Erase, as shown in Figure 10.3.

※ TRACK CUT AND TRACK ERASE

Remember that Track Cut and Track Erase only use START and END edit points.

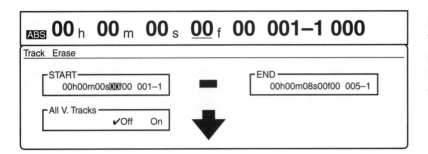

Figure 10.3
Track Erase screen: This is where you enter the START and END points for your edit.

Do the following to perform a Track Erase command.

1. Set the START locator to the beginning of your edit. Set the END locator to the end of your edit.
2. Hold SHIFT and press F2 (Track).
3. Press F2 (Erase) for Track Erase.
4. Use the cursor keys to move the cursor to the START field.
5. Press the START locator to move to the start location.
6. Press F2 (NOW) to lock it in place.
7. Press the down cursor to move to the END field.
8. Press the END locator to move to the end location.
9. Press F2 (NOW) to lock it in place.
10. Press F1 (SelTr) to select the track(s) you want to perform the edit on, or touch the appropriate TRACK SELECT buttons (blinking until selected) to quickly select the tracks to edit.
11. Use the cursor keys to select the track(s) you want to edit. Press F3 (Mark) to mark them for editing.
12. Press F4 (Exec).

Creating a Seamless Loop Using Track Copy

You can use the Track Copy function to create a seamless loop of audio. This is useful when you want the same audio, like a drum machine pattern, to repeat over and over. A great benefit of creating a drum loop this way is that Track Copy does not re-write audio to the hard drive. Therefore, your drum loop will not use up any additional hard drive space.

The key to getting a seamless loop is correctly setting your START and END points. You'll want the START point to be on a downbeat or on a beat that has a clear audible edge. A good, solid bass drum hit is always a good place to set the START point. Once the START point is set, carefully determine where the end of the loop will be. The end of the loop should also be on a good, solid downbeat or on a beat with a clear audible edge. If you make the START point on the second beat of measure two, the END point should also be on the second beat of a measure to ensure a smooth sounding loop of the correct length.

✳ MATCHING EDIT POINTS

When making a loop, the START and FROM points must be the same; likewise, the END and TO points must be the same. I usually increment the TO point 1 subframe beyond the END point, otherwise the start of the next repeated loop is one subframe early and, if there are many repeated copies, eventually the groove will rush ever so slightly due to the 1/3000th of a second loss at the end of the repeated loop.

The smoothness of the loop will greatly depend on the accuracy with which you set the START and END points. If you used a Tempo Map to record your drum beat, finding the precise loop points may be as simple as scrolling the jogwheel to the correct measure numbers you want to use. If you did not use a Tempo Map, you may have to use more precise methods to find the correct loop points. This is when you would use Scrub, Preview, and the Waveform display to help you find the exact loop points.

Here are the steps for creating a seamless loop:

1. Determine the best START and END points using one of the methods previously described.

2. Set locator 1 (START) to the start point. Set locator 3 (FROM) to the same position. These two points should be the same.

3. Set locator 2 (END) to the end point. Set locator 4 (TO) to 1 subframe past the END point. (See note above.)

4. Hold SHIFT and press F2 (Track).

5. Make sure the Track Edit menu appears and not the Phrase Edit menu. If you see the Phrase Edit menu here, use the F1 button to toggle to the Track Edit menu.

6. Press F2 (Copy).

7. Enter the START, END, FROM, and TO points in the appropriate places on the screen. Don't forget to use the F2 (NOW) button to lock each one in.

8. Use the cursor keys to select Copy Time. Enter the amount of times you want the loop to repeat.

9. Press F4 (Exec).

Phrase Editing Features

Phrase editing works similarly to track editing, except you don't have to set all four START, END, FROM, and TO points. You only have to set the FROM and TO points.

The phrase editing features are:

❋ **Phrase Copy:** Copies a phrase from one section to another. Leaves the original phrase intact.

❋ **Phrase Move:** Moves a phrase from one section to another.

❋ **Phrase Trim In:** Trims audio from the beginning of a phrase.

❋ **Phrase Trim Out:** Trims audio from the end of a phrase.

❋ **Phrase Delete:** Erases a phrase and leaves a blank space in its place without moving other phrases on the track. This is similar to Track Erase.

❋ **Phrase Split:** Divides a phrase into two parts.

❋ **Phrase New:** Creates a new phrase from any recorded take in a song.

❋ **Phrase Name:** Names your phrases to help you remember which one is which.

Selecting the Phrase for Editing

Before you can edit the phrase, you have to select it. You can select a phrase from the Play/Display screen and then quickly jump to any phrase-editing window using the following shortcut:

1. Press PLAY/DISPLAY.

2. Use the jogwheel to move to the current time so that it falls somewhere within the phrase you wish to edit.

3. Use the cursor keys to highlight the phrase you wish to edit, as shown in Figure 10.4.

4. Press the PAGE button, as shown in Figure 10.5, until you see the phrase editing functions displayed at the bottom of the window.

5. Choose the desired phrase edit function by pressing the corresponding "F" key.

Figure 10.4

Use the cursor keys to select the desired phrase for editing. In this example, we have selected a phrase that is on track 3. You can tell the phrase is selected by the reverse indication. It is now a light-colored phrase, whereas all the other phrases are dark-colored.

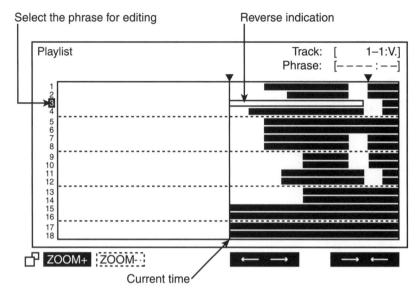

Figure 10.5

Keep pressing the PAGE button until you see the Phrase Edit menu line up across the bottom of the screen. Each function will be above an F key.

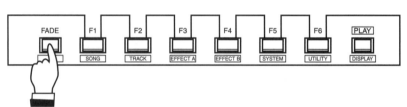

DEALING WITH AUDIO PHRASES LESS THAN 0.5 SECONDS LONG

The VS-1680 cannot play back sections of audio that are 0.5 seconds in length or shorter. If you take a phrase that is three seconds long and erase 2.5 seconds of it, you will be left with a 0.5 second phrase. That phrase cannot be played by your VS-1680.

While making any type of edits, track or phrase, try not to leave any isolated pieces of audio that are 0.5 seconds in length or shorter.

Do not confuse this with setting editing points. You can still choose editing points with a resolution of up to 1/3000th of a second. It is also possible to erase or cut a portion of audio shorter than 0.5 seconds from a larger piece of audio.

Song Editing

Not only can you edit in the VS-1680 on the track level, but you can also edit across entire songs. Song editing in the VS-1680 consists of 3 major areas: Song Arrange, Song Split, and Song Combine.

Song Arrange

Song Arrange is a powerful tool that allows you to experiment with the arrangement of your song. You can use this feature to arrange parts of your song in different ways. For example, let's say you want to try the following arrangement: Intro, verse, chorus, verse, chorus, chorus, bridge, and chorus. Song Arrange allows you to do this very easily. With Song Arrange, you can place a marker at the beginning of each part, then tell it which parts to play in what order. You can arrange and re-arrange your song as many times as you like until you find the right arrangement for you. Song Arrange can be reversed using Undo.

Let's say you recorded an intro, a verse, and a chorus. We will call the intro A, the verse B, and the chorus C. If you wanted to change the playback order of the song to verse B, chorus C, and intro A, it would look like the illustration in Figure 10.6.

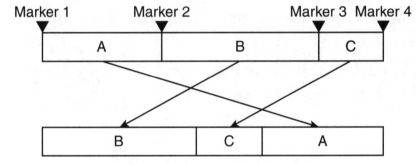

Figure 10.6

By using markers, you can tell song arrange to play back parts A, B, and C as B, C, and A.

To change the arrangement of your parts in Song Arrange, do the following:

1. Mark the beginning and end of each major section of your song with a marker. To place a marker, locate the correct position and press TAP.

2. Hold SHIFT and press F1 (Song).

3. Press F6 (Arrange).

4. Use the cursor keys to move the cursor to START. Use the jogwheel to enter the marker number that defines the start of the first section of your song, as shown in Figure 10.7.

Figure 10.7

Enter the appropriate marker numbers on this screen. You will need to enter appropriate marker numbers for the start position and the end position of each part.

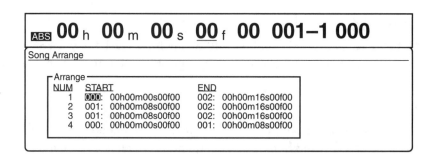

```
ABS  00 h  00 m  00 s  00 f  00  001-1 000

Song Arrange

┌ Arrange ─────────────────────────────────────────
  NUM   START                    END
   1    000:  00h00m00s00f00      002:  00h00m16s00f00
   2    001:  00h00m08s00f00      002:  00h00m16s00f00
   3    001:  00h00m08s00f00      002:  00h00m16s00f00
   4    000:  00h00m00s00f00      001:  00h00m08s00f00
```

5. Use the cursor keys to move the cursor to END. Use the jogwheel to enter the marker number that defines the end of the first section of your song.

6. Press ENTER. This will move the cursor to the second section. Repeat steps 4 and 5 to define the second section of your song, as defined by the audio that plays between the two markers you specify.

You can arrange up to a maximum of 99 separate segments by repeating steps 4 and 5.

❄ **F KEY FUNCTIONS WHILE IN SONG ARRANGE MODE**

F1 (New): Specifies the next segment.
F2 (Clr): Clears all segments.
F3 (Del): Clears the segment where the cursor is positioned.
F4 (Ins): Inserts a segment in front of the current position.
F5 (Exe): Executes Song Arrange.
F6 (Exit): Exits Song Arrange mode.

---

7. When all the segments have been set, use the right cursor button to move the cursor to Destination Time. You'll want to set this to a place on the timeline that is after your current song.

❄ **SETTING THE DESTINATION TIME**

If you set the beginning time for the new playlist *before* the previous song end, the original playlist will be over written.
If you set the beginning time for the new playlist *after* the previous song end, a mark point is automatically set at the beginning of the new playlist.

8. Use the jogwheel to set the time location where the new song arrangement (or playlist) is to begin.

❄ **F KEY FUNCTIONS WHILE SETTING DESTINATION TIME**

F2 (Now): Locks in the time where the timeline is currently positioned.
F3 (Jump): Moves the timeline to the current value of Destination Time.
F4 (Arng): Moves the cursor back to Arrange.
F5 (Exec): Executes Song Arrange.
F6 (Exit): Exits the Song Arrange screen.

---

9. Press F5 (Exec). "Song Arrange Sure?" appears in the display.

10. Press YES. If you wish to cancel this procedure, press NO. When the Song Arrange operation is completed, the screen returns to the playlist display.

Song Split

Song Split allows you to make a copy of a song while specifying which virtual tracks you want to be carried over to the copy song. All markers, locators, Automix data, Tempo Maps, sync tracks, and system settings are also carried over to the new copy. The copy will have the same name as the original, except the last character will be replaced by the letter A.

Song Split will be cancelled if there is not enough memory on your hard drive to carry it out. Undo does not work on Song Split, but you can delete the newly created copy.

Song Split can be used for several different purposes. One is to use Song Split when you want to experiment with a different mix or version of your song. You can make a copy of the original song, do your remix, and then save the remixed copy under a different name so your original mix is preserved.

The procedure for using Song Split is as follows:

1. Hold SHIFT and press F1 (Song).

2. Press F1 (Split). If you don't see Split above the F1 key, press the PAGE button until you do.

3. Use the cursor keys and the jogwheel to select all the virtual tracks you want to be copied. Press F3 (Mark) or the YES button to mark the tracks for copying. All tracks with a checkmark next to them, as shown in Figure 10.8, will be copied.

Figure 10.8

The tracks with a checkmark next to them will be copied over.

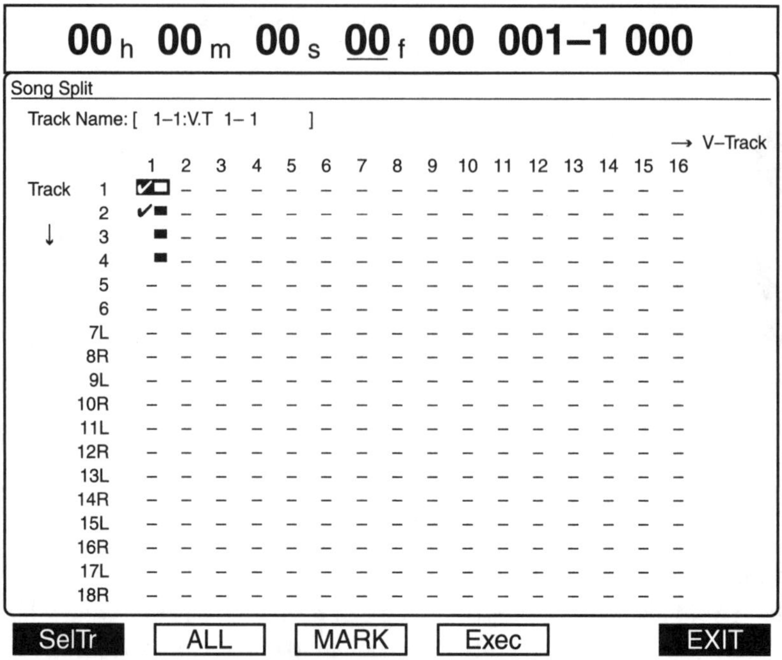

```
  00 h  00 m  00 s  00 f  00  001–1 000
┌─────────────────────────────────────────────────────┐
│ Song Split                                           │
│ Track Name: [  1–1:V.T 1– 1      ]                   │
│                                              → V–Track│
│            1  2  3  4  5  6  7  8  9 10 11 12 13 14 15 16│
│  Track  1  ☑▢ –  –  –  –  –  –  –  –  –  –  –  –  –  –  –│
│         2  ✔■ –  –  –  –  –  –  –  –  –  –  –  –  –  –  –│
│  ↓      3  ■  –  –  –  –  –  –  –  –  –  –  –  –  –  –  –│
│         4  ■  –  –  –  –  –  –  –  –  –  –  –  –  –  –  –│
│         5  –  –  –  –  –  –  –  –  –  –  –  –  –  –  –  –│
│         6  –  –  –  –  –  –  –  –  –  –  –  –  –  –  –  –│
│        7L  –  –  –  –  –  –  –  –  –  –  –  –  –  –  –  –│
│        8R  –  –  –  –  –  –  –  –  –  –  –  –  –  –  –  –│
│        9L  –  –  –  –  –  –  –  –  –  –  –  –  –  –  –  –│
│       10R  –  –  –  –  –  –  –  –  –  –  –  –  –  –  –  –│
│       11L  –  –  –  –  –  –  –  –  –  –  –  –  –  –  –  –│
│       12R  –  –  –  –  –  –  –  –  –  –  –  –  –  –  –  –│
│       13L  –  –  –  –  –  –  –  –  –  –  –  –  –  –  –  –│
│       14R  –  –  –  –  –  –  –  –  –  –  –  –  –  –  –  –│
│       15L  –  –  –  –  –  –  –  –  –  –  –  –  –  –  –  –│
│       16R  –  –  –  –  –  –  –  –  –  –  –  –  –  –  –  –│
│       17L  –  –  –  –  –  –  –  –  –  –  –  –  –  –  –  –│
│       18R  –  –  –  –  –  –  –  –  –  –  –  –  –  –  –  –│
└─────────────────────────────────────────────────────┘
  SelTr      ALL      MARK     Exec            EXIT
```

SHORTCUT FOR SELECTING TRACKS TO BE COPIED

You can quickly select all virtual tracks in a row by moving the cursor to the far left column of the appropriate track number and pressing YES or F3 (Mark).

Similarly, you can quickly select all virtual tracks in a column by moving the cursor to the top of the virtual track number column and pressing YES or F3 (Mark).

The F2 (All) button quickly selects all the virtual tracks in the song for copying.

4. You can check the track names of the virtual tracks by pressing F1 (SelTr). The Song Split (Select Track) screen appears, as shown in Figure 10.9. You can also choose tracks to be copied from this screen by pressing YES or F3 (Mark). You can press F1 (Back) to get back to the previous screen, but you don't have to. Song Split can be carried out from either screen.

5. Press F5 (Exec). The Song Split confirmation screen appears in the window.

6. Press YES to confirm Song Split or press NO if you wish to cancel. The "Store Current?" message appears.

7. Press YES if you wish to save changes made to the current song; otherwise press NO. The screen will return to the playlist display when Song Split is finished.

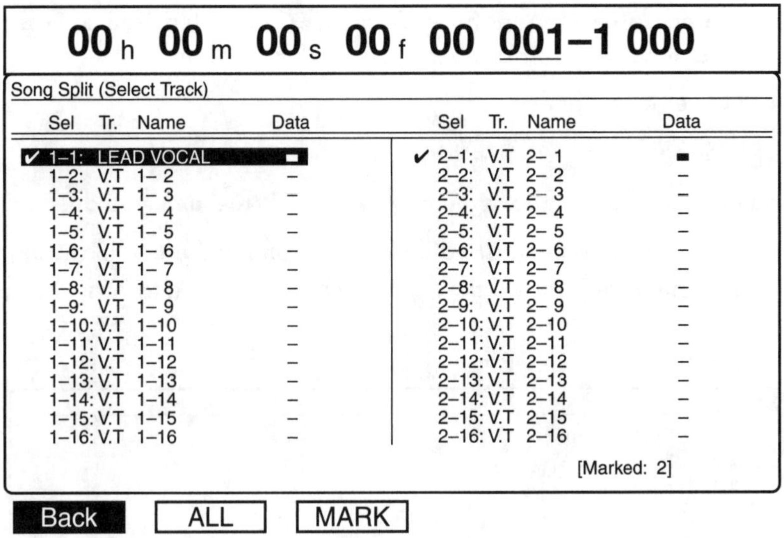

00 h **00** m **00** s **00** f **00** **001–1 000**

Song Split (Select Track)

Sel	Tr.	Name	Data		Sel	Tr.	Name	Data
✔ 1–1:		LEAD VOCAL	■		✔ 2–1:	V.T	2– 1	■
1–2:	V.T	1– 2	–		2–2:	V.T	2– 2	–
1–3:	V.T	1– 3	–		2–3:	V.T	2– 3	–
1–4:	V.T	1– 4	–		2–4:	V.T	2– 4	–
1–5:	V.T	1– 5	–		2–5:	V.T	2– 5	–
1–6:	V.T	1– 6	–		2–6:	V.T	2– 6	–
1–7:	V.T	1– 7	–		2–7:	V.T	2– 7	–
1–8:	V.T	1– 8	–		2–8:	V.T	2– 8	–
1–9:	V.T	1– 9	–		2–9:	V.T	2– 9	–
1–10:	V.T	1–10	–		2–10:	V.T	2–10	–
1–11:	V.T	1–11	–		2–11:	V.T	2–11	–
1–12:	V.T	1–12	–		2–12:	V.T	2–12	–
1–13:	V.T	1–13	–		2–13:	V.T	2–13	–
1–14:	V.T	1–14	–		2–14:	V.T	2–14	–
1–15:	V.T	1–15	–		2–15:	V.T	2–15	–
1–16:	V.T	1–16	–		2–16:	V.T	2–16	–

[Marked: 2]

| Back | | ALL | | MARK |

Figure 10.9
This is the Song Split (Select Track) screen. You may also use this screen to select tracks for copying.

Song Combine

Song Combine allows you to take two completely different songs and combine them into one song. When Song Combine is used, all the tracks from the second song (the source song) are moved to the current song (the destination song), and then the source song is deleted.

Undo does not work on Song Combine; therefore, it is a good idea to make backups of your source and destination songs to either CD-R or DAT.

Not everything is copied when you combine the two songs. The only things that are copied from the source song to the destination song are the performance data (audio) and the information that designates what track numbers the data is on.

Things that are not copied over are markers, locators, Automix data, Tempo Maps, sync tracks, and system settings. All these settings will be permanently lost when the source song is erased.

❄ **SAMPLE RATE AND RECORDING MODES**

To use Song Combine, the source song and the destination song must both share the same sample rate and recording mode.

When the two songs are combined, it is possible for tracks on the source song to overwrite tracks on the destination song. To prevent this from happening, you can use Track Exchange to move all of your source tracks to odd-numbered positions. Use Track Exchange again to move all your destination tracks to even-numbered positions. After Song Combine is completed, you can use Track Exchange one more time to move your tracks where you need them to be.

Use the following steps to complete Song Combine:

1. Hold SHIFT and press F1 (Song).

2. Press F2 (Comb). If you don't see Comb above the F2 key, press PAGE until you do.

3. Use the jogwheel to move the cursor to the desired destination song and press F3 (Mark) or YES to select it. The destination song should now have a checkmark next to it, as shown in Figure 10.10.

Figure 10.10

This is the Song Combine screen. Song number 6 has a checkmark next to it. That means it will be combined with the source song.

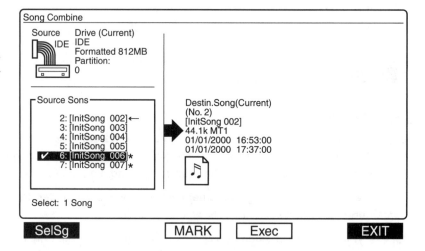

4. Press F1 (SelSg) and a list of songs will appear on the screen, as shown in Figure 10.11. Use the jogwheel to move to the desired source song and then press F3 (Mark) to select it.

5. Press F4 (Exec). The Song Combine confirmation message appears.

6. Press YES. If you would like to cancel this operation, press NO. "Store current?" appears in the display.

7. Press YES if you want to save any changes made to the current song. Otherwise, press NO. When Song Combine is finished, the screen will return to the playlist display.

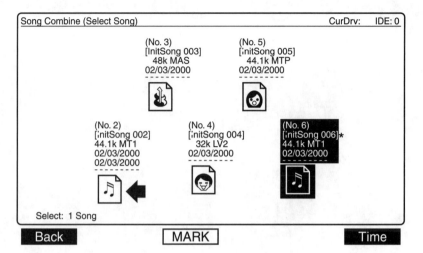

Figure 10.11
This is the Song menu screen. Use this screen to select the desired source song.

11 } Advances in Mixing with the VS-1680/1880

In a traditional mixing setting, you will usually have a dedicated multi-track recorder, a mixing console, and an effects rack. The VS-1680 eliminates the need for these separate external components. Everything you need is contained inside the box. It has its own multi-track recorder, mixing console, and effects rack built right in.

Mixing on the VS-1680 has been simplified in comparison to mixing on the VS-880 series. With the addition of the larger LCD screen, you can see most of your mixing tools on one screen. You can mix internally and keep everything "inside the box," eliminating the need for an external mixing board. You can also use the Direct Out function to send half of your tracks directly out of your VS-1680 and into a separate mixing board for external mixing.

Another great benefit of using the internal digital mixer is Automix. Automix allows you to play back predefined fader moves, pan moves, and effects setting changes in real time. Here are a few benefits of mixing with the VS-1680:

* Keeps everything in the digital domain.

* Using automation and scenes gives you more control over your mix.

* No need for an external mixer.

* You can compare several different mixes with the press of a button.

* You can save and re-load all your mixer and effects settings for every song.

* You can recall the levels and effects settings for bounced tracks and remix them.

Unlike the traditional recording setup, the VS-1680 gives you two totally independent digital mixers inside one box, as shown in Figure 11.1. It is key that you understand the position of these two mixers in relation to the recorder section.

Figure 11.1

The Input Mixer is positioned before the recorder section. The Track Mixer is positioned after the recorder section.

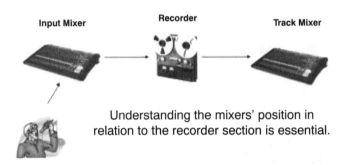

The VS1680 gives you two totally independent digital mixers inside one box.

Input Mixer   Recorder   Track Mixer

Understanding the mixers' position in relation to the recorder section is essential.

Any changes you make to the Input Mixer will affect all signals before they are recorded. Any changes you make to the Track Mixer will affect all audio that has already been recorded.

Channel Edit Screen

The channel edit screen will be your best friend when it comes time to mix your song. Roland put all the basic tools for mixing your tracks on this screen. Since you have two mixers in your VS-1680 (Input and Track), you also have two edit screens per channel. One is for the Input Mixer and the other is for the Track Mixer. When you are mixing your recorded tracks, you will want to use the channel edit screen for the Track Mixer. There will be times when you will use the channel edit screen on the Input Mixer, too (for example, if you are mixing not yet recorded MIDI tracks along with your recorded audio tracks). Use the Input Mixer's channel edit screen to control and edit the incoming virtual MIDI tracks.

The parameters that can be edited on the channel edit screen are:

❀ EQ

❀ Volume Level

❀ ATT (Attenuation)

❀ Phase

- ❄ Effects Inserts (Send and Return Levels)
- ❄ Effects Loop (Send Levels)
- ❄ Effects Pan
- ❄ Channel Pan
- ❄ Aux Send Levels
- ❄ Virtual Tracks (Track Mixer)
- ❄ Channel Link
- ❄ Group
- ❄ Solo
- ❄ Mute

Putting all these parameters on one screen makes mixing your tracks a breeze.

Channel Link

On a traditional mixing board, you usually have to use two faders to control a left and right stereo signal. If you want to make adjustments to the signal (such as EQ or effects changes), you have to change the settings on both channels. With channel link, you can make changes to both channels simultaneously. Channel Link pairs up adjacent, odd- and even-numbered channels, as shown in Figure 11.2. The settings of the odd-numbered channels will be the same as the settings of the adjacent, even-numbered channels.

LINKED CHANNELS ON THE VS-1824

The VS-1824 does not have any linked channels by default.

Unlinking the Defaulted Linked Channels

The defaulted linked channels can be unlinked at any time.

1. Go to the channel edit screen of a linked channel and use your cursor keys to select Link.

2. Use the jogwheel to change the setting to Off.

When the defaulted linked channels are unlinked, you will have to use the SHIFT button to get to the channel edit screen for the adjacent, even-numbered channels.

Figure 11.2

These are the adjacent channels that can be linked when Channel Link is enabled. In the VS-1680, channels 9/10, 11/12, 13/14, and 15/16 default as stereo linked channels. On the VS-1880, channels 7/8, 9/10, 11/12, 13/14, 15/16, and 17/18 default as stereo linked channels.

Track 1
2

Track 3
4

Track 5
6

Track 7
8

Track 9
10

Track 11
12

Track 13
14

Track 15
16

Adjusting the Volume Levels of Linked Channels

With Channel Link on, the overall volume balance of each channel is preserved. The odd-numbered fader now controls the overall volume for both channels. The even-numbered fader doesn't do anything. Using the following steps, you can change the volume balance of the two faders at any time, as shown in Figure 11.3.

1. Go to the channel edit screen of the linked channels you want to edit.

2. Press F5 (Fader). If you don't see "Fader" above F5, press PAGE until you do.

3. Press ENTER or F6 (PRM.V). The values of each fader appear in the display.

4. Use the cursor keys to select each fader value and use the jogwheel to adjust the setting.

5. Press PLAY/DISPLAY to exit.

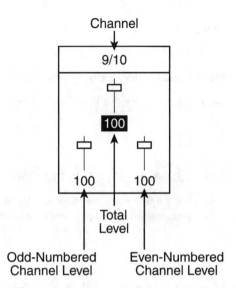

Figure 11.3
The individual level for each channel and the total level for both channels combined can be changed on this screen.

Adjusting the Panning of Linked Channels

With Channel Link on, you can adjust the linked channel's overall stereo image while preserving their pan position in relation to each other, as shown in Figure 11.4. Use the following steps to adjust the pan position for the linked channels.

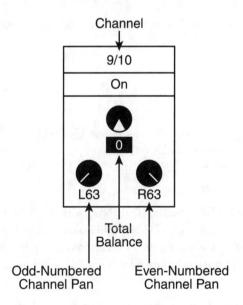

Figure 11.4
You can set individual pan settings for the even- and odd-numbered tracks, as well as the total balance of the two.

6. Go to the channel edit screen of the linked channels you want to edit.

7. Press F1 (Mix). If you don't see "Mix" above F1, press PAGE until you do.

8. Press ENTER or F6 (PRM.V). The values of each fader appear in the display.

9. Use the cursor keys to select each pan value, and use the jogwheel to adjust the setting.

10. Press PLAY/DISPLAY to exit.

 ADJUSTING CHANNEL LINK PAN SETTINGS WHILE SOUND IS PLAYING

You may notice "blips" in the sound while adjusting the pan when the sound is playing. This is perfectly normal and is not a malfunction. If you find this annoying, adjust the pan when the sound is not playing.

Attenuation

There may be times when you need to add more volume to a track that was recorded too low. Likewise, you may have a track that was recorded louder than all the other tracks. You can use the attenuation setting to raise or lower these problem tracks to match the other tracks. This makes mixing a lot easier. You can attenuate channels in the Track Mixer and the Input Mixer.

Phase

The VS-1680 features balanced TRS input jacks. The pin assignment of each input is configured as shown in Figure 11.5.

Figure 11.5

The pin assignment of the VS-1680's balanced TRS input jacks.

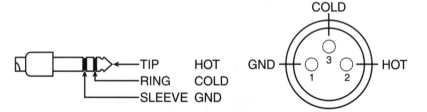

Some audio devices use the opposite HOT (TIP) and COLD (RING) wiring. Using such equipment "as is" may result in poor sound placement, loss of correct left-right balance, and loss of separation between left and right channels when using stereo inputs. In these cases, you need to reverse the phase of each channel. Another cause of phase misalignment is multiple mics picking up the same source (for example, drums).

To reverse the phase, select the Phase setting on the channel edit screen and use the jogwheel to change it. You have two choices on the Phase setting:

❋ NRM: Normal phase (same phase as input). Default setting.

❋ INV: Inverted (opposite) phase.

Grouped Faders

This option allows you to program one fader to control a group of faders. The VS-1680 gives you eight fader groups. You can assign any fader to any group. When you move any fader within a group, the volume level of all the faders within that group will move, while preserving each fader's individual volume in relation to the group. To set up a fader group, assign all the faders you want to be included in the group to the same group number in the channel edit screen under Group. For example, you can assign all your background vocal tracks to group 1.

Signal Buses

The VS-1680 has several different audio buses used for routing audio signals to specific places. The way you use these buses will depend on what you are trying to accomplish.

Recording Bus

The Recording bus is used to route signals for recording. There are eight channels to which signals can be routed from the Input Mixer, Track Mixer, and effects returns. Signals assigned to the Recording bus cannot be routed to the Mix bus at the same time.

Mix Bus

The Mix bus has two channels (left and right) and can take channels directly from the Input Mixer, the Track Mixer, and the effects returns. Signals assigned to the Mix bus are sent to the master outputs for monitoring. The signals sent to the Mix bus cannot be routed to the Recording bus at the same time.

Effects Bus

Signals routed to the Effects bus are sent to the optional effects board to have effects applied to them. The optional effects board has two stereo sides that allow the effects bus to have four channels (FX1 L/R and FX2 L/R). The Effects bus can be assigned signals from the Input Mixer and the Track Mixer. Signals routed to the Recording bus and the Mix bus can also be routed to the Effects bus. When two effects boards are installed, the Effects bus has a total of eight channels (FX1 L/R, FX2 L/R, FX3 L/R, and FX4 L/R).

Aux Bus

Signals assigned to the Aux bus are routed to the aux jack to allow the monitoring of additional mixes, such as headphone mixes. There are six channels on the Aux bus. (AUX1 L/R, AUX2 L/R, and AUX3 L/R) The Aux bus can take signals from the Input Mixer and the Track Mixer. Signals routed to the Recording bus and the Mix bus can also be routed to the Aux bus. This is convenient when you want to connect an external effects device or when you want an additional output that is independent from the master out jacks.

❄ **EFFECTS BOARDS AND AUX BUS**

When you have two optional effects boards installed, the Aux bus is reduced to two channels (AUX L/R). The other four aux channels are reassigned to the Effects bus (FX3 L/R and FX4 L/R). The Effects bus can be used as an Aux bus as well.

Mixing with Effects

There are two schools of thought for using effects. One is to add effects during recording. The other is to record your tracks dry (with no effects) and add effects later. The VS-1680 can accommodate either way. If you record your tracks with effects (printing or recording wet), you will not be able to change or edit the effects later. For most things, I highly recommend you record your tracks dry and add effects later, during the mixing stage. This allows you to experiment with different effects settings before deciding which is best for your tracks.

Each effects board is given its own control area. These areas are called EFFECT A and EFFECT B, as shown in Figure 11.6.

Figure 11.6
The first effects board is called EFFECT A and it controls FX1 and FX2. The second effects board is called EFFECT B and it controls FX3 and FX4.

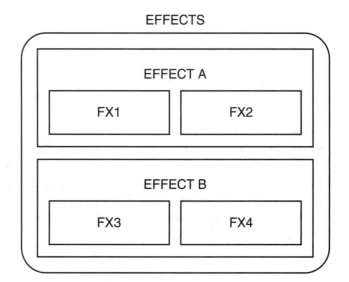

Follow these three general guidelines when using an effect:

1. Select the effect patch to use.

2. Determine if the effect should be used as an insert or loop effect.

3. Connect the effect to the appropriate mixer (track or insert).

Loop effects are generally reverb, delay, and chorus effects. These are also known as "time-based" effects. Insert effects are usually compressors, guitar processors, and voice transformer effects. These are also known as "dynamic-based" effects. If you are not sure whether an effect is a loop or insert effect, see the "Preset Patch List" in your Appendices booklet under "Type." The type of effect determines if it should be used as an insert or loop effect.

Assigning a Loop Effect

To assign a loop effect to a track using FX1, do the following:

1. Hold SHIFT and press F3 (FX A).

2. Press F1 (FX 1).

3. Press F2 (Sel). Use jogwheel to find the loop effect you wish to use.

4. Press F5 (Exec).

5. Press F6 (Exit). Press PLAY/DISPLAY.

6. Route the selected effect's return to the destination track.

7. Press the channel edit button for the track to which to add the effect.

8. Press the PAGE button until you see FX1 above F1. Press F1 (FX1).

9. Use the jogwheel to set the effect to PST. (Post Fader)

10. Use the down cursor to move to the send value.

11. Use the jogwheel to change the send value to the desired amount of effect.

12. Press PLAY/DISPLAY to exit.

Assigning an Insert Effect

To assign an insert effect to a track using FX1, do the following:

1. Hold SHIFT and press F3 (FX A).

2. Press F1 (FX 1).

3. Press F2 (Sel). Use the jogwheel to find the insert effect to use.

4. Press F5 (Exec).

5. Press F6 (Exit). Press PLAY/DISPLAY.

6. Press the channel edit button for the track to which to insert the effect.

7. Press the PAGE button until you see FX1In above F1. Press F1 (FX1In).

8. Press ENTER.

9. Use the jogwheel to select Ins, InsL, InsR, or InsS, as shown in Figure 11.7.

Figure 11.7

The insert effects screen allows you to insert a stereo or mono effect to a track. You can also adjust the insert send and return levels here.

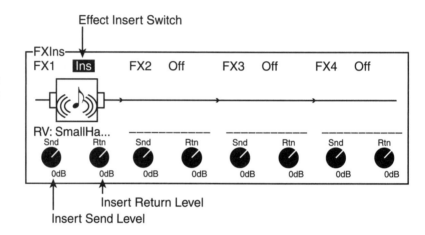

10. Use the cursor keys to move to the Send and Return levels, and use the jogwheel to change the settings. The default setting is 0db.

11. Press PLAY/DISPLAY to exit.

❉ **INSERTING EFFECTS**

If you don't need to use the insert effect in stereo, you can select either InsL or InsR. If you are using the insert effect in stereo, you can use either Ins or InsS.

When you select Ins or InsS, both sides (L and R) of the stereo effect are assigned to that track and cannot be used on any other track. "Ins" means the signal is routed to both sides of the effect simultaneously. "InsS" means the signal is routed to both sides of the effect in series. "InsS" means the signal goes through the left side first, then that affected signal is sent through the right side.

When you select InsL or InsR, only one side of the stereo effect is used. The other side is still free to be assigned to another track.

If you have two effects cards installed in your VS-1680, you can assign up to eight insert effects on eight different tracks at once using InsL and InsR on each channel.

User Effects

The VS-1680 allows you to create and save up to 200 customized effects patches. These are called user effects. You can create user effects by editing any of the preset effects and then saving them to any of the 200 user effects slots. If you do not save your newly created effects patch, it will be lost when you select another effects patch.

Creating a User Effect

The best way to create a user effect is to select a preset effect with a sound closest to what you wish to create, then alter the settings of that patch and save it.

Saving a User Effect

After you create your new user effect patch, you must save it before you select another effects patch or you will lose everything you just created. To save the user effect, do the following from the effect's edit screen:

1. Press F4 (Save). The Effect Name screen appears in the display.

2. Use the jogwheel to select the destination patch number (U000-U199).

3. Use the cursor keys and the jogwheel to create the name of the user patch. The F keys work as follows:

    ❋ F1 (Hist): Takes you through a list of the last 20 user patch names entered, one at a time.

    ❋ F2 (Clr): Clears all the characters in the window.

    ❋ F3 (Del): Deletes the character where the cursor is positioned.

    ❋ F4 (Ins): Inserts a space where the cursor is positioned.

    ❋ F5 (Write): Stores the user patch and exits the screen.

    ❋ F6 (Exit): Exits the screen without storing the user patch

> ❋ **ENTERING CHARACTERS**
> If you press and light the [NUMERICS/ASCII] button, you can use the SELECT button to enter characters in a manner similar to a computer keyboard.

4. After entering the name of the new effects patch, press F5 (Write).

5. Press PLAY/DISPLAY to exit.

Important Reminders About Using Effects

Using effects properly seems to be the hardest concept to grasp for the new VS user. Once you understand the basics of how effects are routed, the difficulty disappears. There are many different ways to use effects in your VS-1680; however, there are some basic guidelines that you should always remember:

❄ If you insert an effect anywhere in the VS-1680 (Track Mixer, Input Mixer, or Master Block), that effect cannot be used on any other tracks or inputs. The exception is when you only use one side of the effect (InsL or InsR). If you have already inserted an effect on another channel or in the Master Block, the display will tell you so.

❄ If you've assigned an effect return to a track in order to print the effect, you must unassign the effect return from the track in order to have it return to the main stereo mix.

❄ To print an effect, make sure it is routed through the Input Mixer and not the Track Mixer. To listen to an effect while recording without printing it, make sure the effect is routed through the Track Mixer and not the Input Mixer.

Using EQ

The VS-1680 allows you to choose between a two-band (High, Low) and a three-band (High, Mid, Low) parametric EQ for each channel in the Track and Input Mixers, as shown in Figure 11.8. You can adjust these parameters in real time while your song is playing. There are different ways to use the onboard EQ. One way is to increase the gain of the frequency to get a desired result. Another way is to decrease the gain. Decreasing the gain is referred to as using "subtractive" EQ. Increasing the EQ gain always adds some noise, hence, the higher the gain, the louder the noise. This is why many engineers prefer to use subtractive EQ whenever possible.

EQ can be used during the recording, mixing, and mastering stages or your recording process. I have always found that I get the best results when I use EQ sparingly. I use it to help my tracks blend together. With that said, I tend to use EQ the most in the mixing stage, and only if needed.

To adjust a track's EQ, do the following:

1. Go to the channel edit screen for the track you want to adjust EQ on.

2. Use the cursor keys to move to the EQ section of the display, or press F2 (Low). If "Low" doesn't appear above F2, press PAGE until it does.

3. Press ENTER/YES. The EQ curve display appears.

4. Use the cursor keys to highlight SW and use the jogwheel to turn it to On.

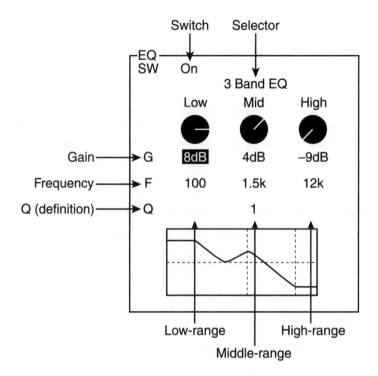

Figure 11.8
The EQ display allows you to choose between a two- or three-band parametric EQ for each channel of the Track and Input Mixers.

5. Use the cursor keys to move to the desired EQ parameter. Use the jogwheel to select the desired value.

6. Press PLAY/DISPLAY to exit.

The settings on the EQ display are as follows:

SW (Equalizer Switch): Turns the EQ on and off.

(Equalizer Selector): Selects how many bands of EQ you would like to use.

❅ **Two-band EQ:** Low and High bands are available for all 26 inputs and/or track channels at once (28 for the VS-1880 and VS-1824).

❅ **Three-band EQ:** Low, Mid, and High bands are available for 16 inputs and/or 16 track channels at once.

Low: This adjusts the gain (–12db to +12db) and the shelving frequency (40 Hz - 1.5 kHz) of the low-band EQ.

Mid: This adjusts the gain (–12db to +12db), the center frequency (200 Hz - 8 kHz), and the Q (0.5 - 16) of the mid-band EQ. The mid-band EQ is not available when the two-band EQ is selected.

High: This adjusts the gain (–12db to +12db) and the shelving frequency (500 Hz - 18 kHz) of the high-band EQ.

Scenes

A scene stores all EQ, routing, fader-position, pan-position, effects, V-Track selection, and master-level settings. Scenes are very useful at mixing time. They allow you to experiment with different mixes of your song and then save the mixes with the song. You can store up to eight different scenes per song. You can only change scenes when the VS-1680 is not playing.

Saving a Mixer Scene

After you adjust all your mixer settings the way you want, you should save your mix as a scene:

1. Press SCENE. The button indicator will light. Whenever the SCENE indicator is lit, the locator buttons are ready to store and recall scenes. Any locator buttons that are blinking have a scene stored on them. The locator buttons that are unlit are available to store a scene.

2. Press any locator button that is not lit.

Recalling a Mixer Scene

To recall a mixer scene, make sure the song is not in Play mode, then do the following:

1. Press SCENE. All locator buttons that have scenes on them will be lit.

2. Press the appropriate locator button for the scene you wish to use.

Deleting a Mixer Scene

You can delete scenes while the song is not playing by doing the following:

1. Press SCENE. All locator buttons that have scenes on them will be lit.

2. Hold CLEAR and press the locator button for the scene you want to delete.

Updating a Mixer Scene

You can make changes to a saved scene. This is done by recalling than deleting a scene. Make your desired changes to the mixer settings and then restore the scene. Follow the steps below to update a mixer scene:

1. Press SCENE.

2. Press the locator button for the scene you wish to update. After the scene is recalled, the scene returns to the playlist display and the scene indicator goes off.

3. Press SCENE again.

4. Hold CLEAR and press the locator for the scene you wish to update.

5. Make the desired changes to the mixer. You don't have to make changes to every mixer setting. You only need to make adjustments to the mixer settings you wanted to update from the previous scene.

6. Press SCENE.

7. Press the locator button to save the scene again.

Vari Pitch

Vari Pitch allows you to change the tune or pitch of your recorded tracks by adjusting the playback speed. This can come in handy if you want to record an instrument alongside existing recorded tracks, but the instrument is not in tune with the tracks. If the instrument is difficult to tune to the tracks, like an acoustic piano, you may find it is easier to use Vari Pitch to tune the tracks to the piano.

You can also use Vari Pitch to create certain special effects. The limits of its use are really up to your imagination. To use Vari Pitch, do the following:

1. Hold SHIFT and press F5 (SYSTEM).

2. Press F3 (Play). If you don't see "Play" above F3, press PAGE until you do.

3. Use the cursor keys to move to VariPitchSw.

4. Use the jogwheel to select On.

5. Use the cursor keys to move to Vari Pitch.

6. Use the jogwheel to change the value for the sample rate, which will change the playback speed. Listen during playback to see how the pitch changes.

7. When you are done, press F6 (Exit) to exit.

8. To return to normal playback speed, turn the VariPitchSw switch to Off.

VARI PITCH INDICATOR

A small "V" appears next to the current time in the upper part of the display when Vari Pitch is active.

Automix

One of the most powerful features of the VS recorders is Automix. Automix allows the VS-1680 to remember such instances as complex fader moves, pan moves, and effects settings and play them back automatically. This is a great tool for getting your mix to sound exactly how you want it. You can save the Automix and then recall it to tweak your mix until it is perfect. Every Automix setting is editable and can be changed at any time. The following items can be automated:

Input Channel/Track Channel:

* ❋ Faders
* ❋ Panning
* ❋ FX1,2,3, and 4 Lev (Effect 1,2,3, and 4 Send Levels)
* ❋ FX1,2,3, and 4 Pan (Effect 1,2,3, and 4 Send Pan)
* ❋ AUX Lev (AUX Send Level)
* ❋ AUX Pan

Stereo In:

* ❋ Fader - Balance

Effect Return:

* ❋ Effect 1,2,3, and 4 Return Levels
* ❋ Effect 1,2,3, and 4 Return Balance

Master Block:

* ❋ Master Level
* ❋ Master Balance
* ❋ Monitor Level
* ❋ Monitor Balance
* ❋ Master Effects 1,2,3, and 4 Send Levels
* ❋ Master Effects 1,2,3, and 4 Send Balance

Effects:

* ❋ FX1,2,3, and 4 Program Numbers for Patch Changes.

To begin using Automix, press AUTOMIX. The button indicator will light, indicating Automix mode is on. In a new song, all the SELECT buttons and the EDIT/SOLO button will begin to blink. Automix record is turned on for all inputs, tracks, effects returns, and the master fader.

It is important to understand the status of the indicator lights, as shown in Figure 11.9.

One of the biggest reasons why people have problems using Automix is improper setting of lights. It is not necessary to leave all the lights blinking. This can lead to undesired changes if a fader or knob is accidentally changed. You only need blinking lights for tracks or channels you want to

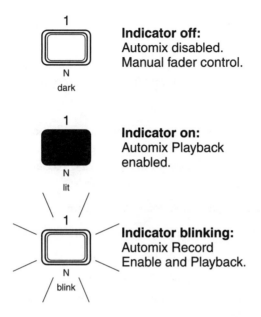

Indicator off:
Automix disabled.
Manual fader control.

Indicator on:
Automix Playback
enabled.

Indicator blinking:
Automix Record
Enable and Playback.

Figure 11.9
The status of the indicator lights tells you what track or tracks are ready to be Automixed. The lights can be off, on, or blinking. You need to set the lights appropriately to get the desired Automix effect.

Automix. For example, if you are only trying to automate track 1, you can turn the indicator lights for all other tracks and channels to the off or non-blinking status.

❊ **CHANGING THE BLINKING LIGHT STATUS**

To change the status of any blinking light during Automix, HOLD the Automix button and press the blinking light until it changes to the status you need.

Adjusting the Automix Display

You can change the display so that it shows the fader and pan settings instead of the meter positions. Some people find this very handy when working with Automix, though it's by no means necessary. If you want to change the display to view the fader and pan positions, do the following:

1. Press PLAY/DISPLAY.

2. Press PAGE until you see "F/P" above F5.

3. Press F5. The Fader/Pan display appears.

4. Press F1 (LMTrk) to view fader and panning positions for the Track Mixer.

5. Press F2 (LM In) to view fader and panning positions for the Input Mixer.

6. Press F3 (LMAux) to view fader and panning positions for the effects sends and aux send.

When you are done viewing the fader pan display, press F5 (Metr) to view the meter positions again.

There are three types of Automix: Realtime, Snapshot, and Gradation. Each type of Automix has been created for specific uses, but how you use each one is totally up to you.

Realtime

Realtime Automix allows you to record fader movements in real time while your song is playing. This type of Automixing is useful when you do a lot of "fader riding." Automix can remember every movement you make with each fader and play it back perfectly. To perform a realtime Automix of track faders, do the following:

1. Press AUTOMIX. It should light up, indicating Automix mode is on.

2. Locate the point in the song where you wish to begin recording realtime Automix.

3. Hold AUTOMIX and press the TRACK SELECT button for the track(s) you want to Automix so that it is blinking. If it is already blinking, you can skip this step.

4. Hold SCENE and press the REC button. The "Automix Record" message starts to flash in the upper right-hand corner of the display.

❋ **RECORD BUTTON INDICATOR**

The REC button does not light up at this stage. Do not let this confuse you.

---

5. Make sure the FADER/MUTE indicator is set to TR for tracks.

6. Adjust the track fader for the beginning fader level as desired.

❋ **FADER MATCH**

If fader match (under System Parameters) is set to Null instead of Jump, and the current physical fader position does not match the actual volume level, you must first move the physical fader to match the position of the recorded fader. This is referred to as "crossing the null point."
When the display is set to view faders and panning, the position of each physical fader is represented by a black dot and the actual level that is recorded using Automix is represented by a white circle. Before beginning Automix, slide the physical faders all the way up and then all the way down so the black dot disappears. Make sure that the FADER/MUTE is set appropriately (IN or TR), depending on whether you are trying to control the input channels or the track channels.

---

7. Press PLAY to begin recording Automix data.

8. While the song is playing, move the faders to adjust the mix of your song as you like. New Automix data will only be recorded for those faders that are moved during this step.

9. Press STOP when you are finished making your fader moves. Automix markers (markers with an "A" after the marker number) will appear in the playlist display where Automix data was created.

10. Rewind to the beginning of your song and press PLAY. Your song will play back all of your recorded fader moves.

❋ **!!! LACK OF EVENT !!! WARNING MESSAGE**

The smallest unit of memory that the VS-1680 uses to store recorded information is called an "event." Each newly created song is given approximately 18,000 events. The number of events that are used will change depending on what you are doing. For example, Automix markers use six events each. If you see the "!! Lack of EVENT!!" warning message appear while using Automix, the available number of events has dropped to 1000 or below and you will not be able to continue using realtime Automix. If you do a lot of editing along with a lot of realtime Automix moves, you can periodically check the remaining amount of events by doing the following:

SHIFT → SYSTEM → SYSTEM PARAMETERS → Prm 2 → Change remaining display to Event → EXIT → PAGE/DISPLAY.

Hold SHIFT and press PAGE/DISPLAY until you see the remaining number of events in the upper left-hand corner.

Snapshot

You can take a picture or "snapshot" of your mixer, fader, pan, and other Automixable parameter settings and have them recalled in an instant at any point in your song. The way a snapshot works is very similar to a camera, like the one shown in Figure 11.10.

Snapshot Automix is very convenient when you need to make instantaneous level changes in the middle of a song. You can also use it for such things as changing effects on a guitar for a solo. If your mix requires your fader levels to move instantaneously, using snapshot may be easier than using realtime. To use snapshot, do the following:

1. Press AUTOMIX. It should light up, indicating Automix mode is on.

2. Locate the point in the song where you want the snapshot to occur.

3. Select the mixer channels with the settings you want to be recorded in the snapshot. All channels with blinking SELECT buttons will be recorded.

4. Make all the mixer settings you wish to be recorded in the snapshot.

Figure 11.10

Just like the camera in this picture, the VS-1680 can take pictures or "snapshots" of all your mixer, fader, and pan settings.

5. Hold SCENE and press TAP. A marker is placed at the current time location. A snapshot of all mixer settings is recorded and stored with that marker. Any marker that stores Automix data will appear with an "A" after it.

> ❄ **NOTE ABOUT SNAPSHOT MARKERS**
>
> If there is a marker within 0.1 seconds before or after the location of the new snapshot, the snapshot information will be stored at the previously existing marker location. A new snapshot marker will not be created.

Using Snap Mode

There may be times when you don't want the fader levels recorded to your snapshot. For instance, if you were trying to automate an effects change for a guitar solo, the only thing you would want to change would be the effects settings. Snap mode allows you to specify whether or not the fader levels will be recorded to the snapshot. Use the following procedure to set the Snap mode accordingly.

1. Hold SHIFT and press F6 (Utility).

2. Press F5 (A.mix). If A.mix does not appear above F5, press PAGE until it does.

3. Use the jogwheel to select the desired Snap mode setting.

   ❄ **ALL:** All settings are recorded to the snapshot.

   ❄ **MaskFader:** Fader settings are ignored.

4. Press PLAY/DISPLAY to exit.

Using Snapshot to Automate Effects Changes

You can tell the VS-1680 to automatically switch effects patches anywhere in your song. Use Snapshot Automix to accomplish this. Let's say you want to switch FX1 from a reverb to a delay in the middle of your song. Use the following steps to automate the effects changes:

1. Press AUTOMIX. It should light up, indicating Automix mode is on.

2. Make sure the effects return button for FX1 is blinking.

3. Assign a reverb patch to FX1.

4. Go to the beginning of the song, hold SCENE, and press TAP.

5. Locate the point in the song where you want the effects to change to a delay.

6. Change FX1 to a delay effects patch.

7. Hold SCENE and press TAP.

8. Rewind to the beginning of the song and press PLAY. You will hear reverb at the beginning of the song. When you get to the second Automix marker, you will hear the effect change from reverb to delay.

This procedure automates effect patch changes only.

❋ **AUTOMATING EFFECTS PARAMETERS**

You can automate effects parameter changes, too. This is done by creating multiple versions of your effect with different settings and then saving them as user effects. You can then use a snapshot to recall the different versions at any point in your song.

For example, let's say you are using a short delay on a vocal track, but you want the delay to have a longer decay at a breakdown part of the song. You would just create two versions of the delay patch. Make one with a short decay and the other one with a long decay, and save the patches to two user banks. You can then use Snapshot Automix to create a snapshot at the beginning of the song with the short decay version of the delay effect. Advance the song to the breakdown. Select the long decay version of the delay and create another snapshot at that point. Lastly, move to the end of the breakdown, select the short decay version, and create a third snapshot. When you play back the song, the vocal track will only have a long delay effect on the breakdown.

Gradation

Now that you understand realtime and snapshot automation, we can cover gradation. Gradation Automix is used to automate such things as panning, fade-ins, and fade-outs. You have to understand snapshots before you can perform gradation because snapshots are also used to make a successful Gradation Automix.

The principle of gradation is simple. You take two snapshot markers and use gradation to make a smooth cross-sweep between the two. Let's say you wanted to automate a pan movement from hard left to hard right. Perform the following procedures to do so.

1. Locate the point in the song where you want the pan to start as hard left.

2. Set the pan to hard left and place a snapshot marker there.

3. Locate the point in the song where you want the pan to end up as hard right.

4. Set the pan to hard right and place a snapshot marker there.

5. From the position of the second of the two snapshots (hard right pan), hold SCENE and press PREVIOUS.

6. Gradation Sure? appears. Press YES.

7. Rewind to a point before the first marker and press PLAY. You will hear your track smoothly transition from a hard left pan to a hard right pan in real time.

Where your timeline is positioned in relation to the snapshots will determine how the gradation is executed. Look at the following examples:

When the timeline is positioned between two snapshot markers, as shown in Figure 11.11, the gradation will take place between the two adjacent snapshot markers. When you press SCENE and NEXT or SCENE and PREVIOUS, the results will be the same.

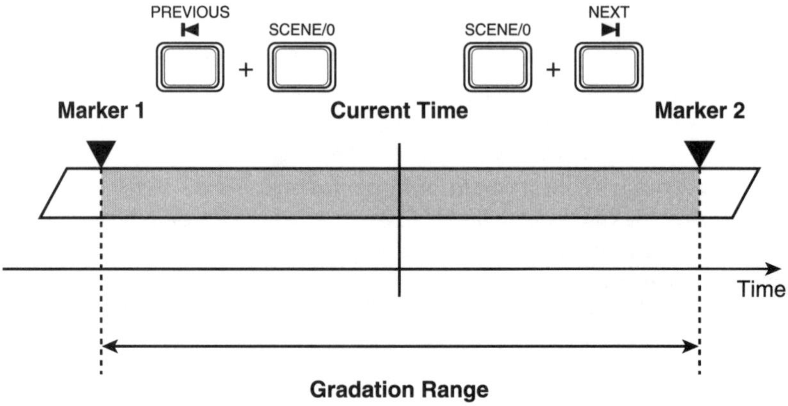

Figure 11.11

When you place the timeline between two snapshot markers, the gradation will take place between the two.

When the timeline is positioned at a marker (not between), pressing SCENE and NEXT will be different from pressing SCENE and PREVIOUS, as shown in Figure 11.12.

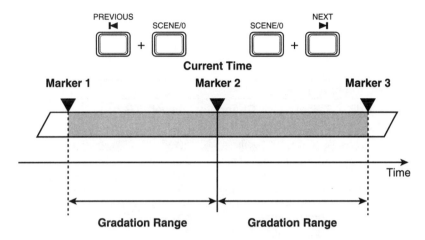

Figure 11.12
Placing the timeline at a snapshot marker that is between two snapshot markers will have a different effect when pressing the SCENE/NEXT and SCENE/PREVIOUS buttons.

Pressing SCENE and NEXT when the timeline is placed on a snapshot marker that is between two snapshot markers will cause the gradation to occur between the current snapshot marker and the next one.

If you press SCENE and PREVIOUS, the gradation will occur between the current snapshot marker and the previous one.

Micro Edit

The most powerful feature of the VS-1680's automation is Micro Edit. Every parameter you automate can be edited or deleted using Micro Edit. Once you become familiar with using Micro Edit, you can use it to carefully tweak your Automix to perfection.

The general method for tweaking your Automix in Micro Edit is as follows:

1. Hold SHIFT and press F6 (UTIL).

2. Press F5 (A.Mix). If A.Mix does not appear above F5, press PAGE until it does.

3. Press F2 (Micro). The Micro Edit screen appears, as shown in Figure 11.13.

4. The left cursor moves to Edit Target. Use the jogwheel to select the Automix parameter you wish to edit.

5. Use the up and down cursors to move to the marker setting you wish to edit.

6. Use the jogwheel to make changes to each value.

7. Repeat steps 4, 5, and 6 for each Automix setting you wish to change.

8. When you are done, press PLAY/DISPLAY to exit.

Figure 11.13

This is the Micro Edit screen, where most of your micro editing will take place.

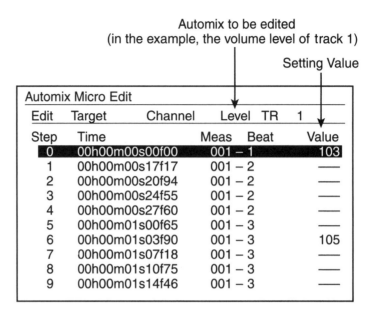

Automix to be edited
(in the example, the volume level of track 1)

Setting Value

Automix Micro Edit

Edit	Target	Channel	Level	TR	1	
Step	Time		Meas	Beat		Value
0	00h00m00s00f00		001	– 1		103
1	00h00m00s17f17		001	– 2		——
2	00h00m00s20f94		001	– 2		——
3	00h00m00s24f55		001	– 2		——
4	00h00m00s27f60		001	– 2		——
5	00h00m01s00f65		001	– 3		——
6	00h00m01s03f90		001	– 3		105
7	00h00m01s07f18		001	– 3		——
8	00h00m01s10f75		001	– 3		——
9	00h00m01s14f46		001	– 3		——

Adding an External Mixer

For those of you who don't want to give up mixing on your external analog mixer, it is possible to send half of your VS-1680's 16 recorded tracks to an external mixer for external processing. Use the Direct Out function to accomplish this. The Direct Out function allows you to choose between tracks 1-8 or tracks 9-16 to be sent directly out of the eight analog outputs. To enable the Direct Out function, do the following:

1. Press EDIT/SOLO. The Master Block is displayed.

2. Press F5 (DIR). If "DIR" does not appear above F5, press PAGE until it does.

3. Use the jogwheel to change the setting for DIRECT OUT.

   ❋ **DIR OUT (DIRECT OUT):** Select tracks to be assigned as Direct Out.

   ❋ **Off:** Direct Out is not used.

   ❋ **1-8:** Tracks 1-8 are output from the eight analog output jacks.

   ❋ **9-16:** Tracks 9-16 are output from the eight analog output jacks.

❋ **DIRECT OUT ASSIGNMENTS**

When tracks 1-8 are selected, the Direct Out assignments are:
Track 1: MASTER jack (L)
Track 2: MASTER jack (R)

Track 3: AUX A jack (L)
Track 4: AUX A jack (R)
Track 5: AUX B jack (L)
Track 6: AUX B jack (R)
Track 7: MONITOR jack (L)
Track 8: MONITOR jack (R)
When tracks 9-16 are selected, the Direct Out assignments are:
Track 9: MASTER jack (L)
Track 10: MASTER jack (R)
Track 11: AUX A jack (L)
Track 12: AUX A jack (R)
Track 13: AUX B jack (L)
Track 14: AUX B jack (R)
Track 15: MONITOR jack (L)
Track 16: MONITOR jack (R)

Initializing the Mixer Settings

There may come a time when you are dissatisfied with your mix and want to start over from scratch. This is a good time to initialize the mixer settings. This feature will restore all the mixer's parameters to the default settings. This gives you a chance to wipe the slate clean and start anew. Initializing the mixer does not erase your song or your song data. To initialize the mixer, do the following:

1. Hold SHIFT and press F5 (System).

2. Press PAGE until INIT appears above F1.

3. Press F1 (INIT). Init Mix/Sys Prm Sure? will be displayed.

4. Press YES.

5. Press PLAY/DISPLAY to exit.

12 } Advances in Mastering with the VS-1680/1880

Mastering is the process of preparing your two-track stereo mix for final playback on a separate medium. In this day and age, that medium is usually a CD (compact disc). You always have the option to take your finished mix to a professional mastering lab or send your tracks out to a computer or external mastering unit (as shown in Figure 12.1) for external mastering. However, you can also achieve great results with the tools that are already provided inside the VS-1680.

Figure 12.1
The Alesis Masterlink is an example of an external mastering device you can send your tracks to for external mastering. The VS-1680 has mastering tools similar to those found inside the Master-link. With patience and practice, you can create quality-mastered tracks inside the VS-1680 without the use of an external mastering device.

❋ **VS-1680 V-XPANDED OPTION**

The original VS-1680 did not have any mastering capabilities. These features were added later in an operating system update and were given the name "V-Xpanded." If you have an original VS-1680 that does not have the V-Xpanded functions, you can download any version (v2.0 or higher) of the VS-1680 operating system from the Roland Web site to get the V-Xpanded features.

The mastering section of the VS-1880 has some improvements over the VS-1680. With a dedicated Mastering button on the VS-1880, all the tools you need to do a quality-mastering job are just one button-push away.

Mastering Room

The Mastering Room contains everything you need to turn your 16 tracks into a final master that is ready for CD burning. On the VS-1680 V-Xpanded, entering the Mastering Room is different from entering on the VS-1880. On the VS-1680, do the following to enter the Mastering Room:

1. Press MASTER.

2. Press PAGE until you see M.Tr above F6.

3. Press F6.

4. Press ENTER.

ENTERING MASTERING ROOM ON VS-1880 AND VS-1824

Press the CD-RW MASTERING button in the upper right-hand corner of the VS-1880 and VS-1824, then press F1 (MstRm) to access the Mastering Room.

Mixing Down to the Master Tracks

You can record data on all 16 tracks and then master them down to a two-track stereo pair using the Mastering Room. On the VS-1680, you can mix down to any open V-Tracks you wish using the Mastering Room.

1. Enter the Mastering Room as described earlier in this chapter.

2. Adjust your faders and mixer settings to how you want them for your mixdown. You can practice your mix while the SW switch is set to OFF.

3. Press PLAY to hear your mix. Use the master level fader to push the overall level in the OUT meter as close to 0db as possible without clipping. (Clipping means hitting 0db.) When you are happy with the mix and the output level, press STOP and rewind to the beginning of the song.

4. Use the cursor keys to select SW. Use the jogwheel to change it to On.

5. Use the cursor keys to move to the STATUS setting.

6. Use the jogwheel to change it to REC.

7. Press REC and PLAY on the transport controls.

8. When you reach the end of the song, press STOP.

9. To hear your newly mastered tracks, follow the instructions under "Playing Back the Master Tracks."

10. If you are unhappy with the mixdown, press UNDO to cancel it. Then go back to the Mastering Room and repeat steps 4-9.

Playing Back the Master Tracks

After you have completed mixing down to the master tracks, you will have to turn them on to hear them play back. When the mastering tracks are turned on, you will not be able to hear the original 16 tracks. Do the following to play back the mastering tracks:

1. Press PLAY/DISPLAY.

2. Press PAGE until you see "M→***" (*** is either Rec, Ply, or Off) above F6.

3. Press F6 until "M→Ply" (Master Play) appears.

4. Press F6 again to select this setting.

❆ **MASTER TRACKS STATUS DISPLAY**

After you press F6 to select M→Ply, the display will change. It will no longer display "M→Ply" even though you are in the master track play status. This is very confusing to many new users of VS studios. Just remember that the status on the display is telling you what status it will be in *after you press it.* *The background of the Master Level L/R indicators will change accordingly.*

❆ Clear or no background = 16 track recording mode

❆ Normal or darkened background = Master track recording mode

❆ Square box surrounding L/R indicators = Master track playback mode

5. Rewind to the location where you began the mixdown.

6. Press PLAY. The master tracks start to play while all the other tracks are muted. At this time, the master volume fader controls the master tracks.

Understanding the MTK

MTK stands for Mastering Tool Kit. If you have one or two of the VS8F-2 effects cards installed inside your VS studio, you will have access to nineteen MTK effects patches. These patches are numbered on the card from 210-228 and they will have "MTK" after the patch number, followed by a specific patch name.

The MTK effects patch is not just one effect, but a powerful multiprocessor that combines several different effects processors. The different effects processors that make up an MTK patch are:

* Four-Band EQ
* Bass Cut Filter
* Stereo Enhancer
* Multiband Stereo Expander
* Multiband Stereo Compressor
* Stereo Limiter
* Soft Clip Processor

Tone-Shaping Processors

The MTK gives you three different tone-shaping processors to manipulate the overall tonality or "spectral balance" of the signal.

Four-Band EQ

The first tone-shaping processor in the MTK chain is the Four-Band EQ. Each band (or part) of the EQ can be designated as one of two types of EQ. The two types of EQ are Peak and Shelving:

* **Peak EQ:** This type of EQ allows you to target a specific frequency and then raise or lower its volume.
* **Shelving EQ:** This type of EQ allows you to raise or lower all the frequencies above (high shelf) or below (low shelf) a specified frequency.

Use the four-band EQ to help clean up your mix. Use it to reduce unwanted frequencies while trying to boost weak frequencies.

Bass Cut Filter

Bass Cut is the next tone-shaping processor in the chain. This is basically a high pass filter with a very deep slope. In mastering, this is mostly used to reduce or remove "subsonic" frequencies. These are sounds that are not detectable by the human ear.

The Bass Cut filter is very simple to use. There are only two controls for it:

❄ **ON/OFF:** Turns the Bass Cut filter on or off.

❄ **FREQ:** Sets the cutoff frequency (where all frequencies are removed). For most types of music, the default setting of 20 Hz is fine.

Stereo Enhancer

The final tone-shaping processor in the chain is the Enhancer. It works by adding musical harmonics at and above a selected frequency. Depending on the setting, the enhancer adds brilliance, edge, or "air" to the sound. There are four controls in the Enhancer:

❄ **SW:** The on/off switch. It turns the Enhancer on or off.

❄ **Sens:** Sets the intensity of harmonics added to the signal.

❄ **Freq:** Sets the frequency where the Enhancer begins to act. This can be set from 1 kHz to 10 kHz.

❄ **MixLv1:** Sets the amount of the Enhancer effect that is blended with the mix.

Dynamic Processors

Many mixes are made up of instruments and sounds that are loud and soft. These variations are referred to as musical dynamics. A dynamic processor is basically an automatic volume control. Changes in the signal's level trigger the processor to act, adjusting the volume according to the processor's settings. There are four powerful dynamic processors in the MTK chain to control them.

Expander

The first multi-band dynamic processor in the chain is the Expander. The Expander works by reducing the volume of signals that fall below a specified threshold. The Expander contains the following controls:

❄ **SW:** The on/off switch. It turns the Expander on or off.

❄ **Lo, Mid, and Hi:** Selects the desired band for editing.

❄ **Thre:** Sets the threshold for the selected band.

❄ **Ratio:** Sets the ratio of volume reduction applied to the selected band once the signal falls below the threshold.

❄ **Atk:** Sets the attack time for the selected band.

❄ **Rel:** Sets the release time for the selected band.

Compressor

The second dynamic processor in the MTK chain is the Compressor. The Compressor works in the exact opposite way as the Expander. The Compressor works by reducing signal volume levels that rise above a specified threshold. The Compressor has the same controls as the Expander.

Limiter

The Limiter is the third dynamic processor in the MTK chain. You can use this to maximize the overall volume and impact of your mix. There are four controls to the Limiter:

* **SW:** The on/off switch. This turns the Limiter on or off.
* **Thresh:** Sets the Limiter's threshold.
* **Attack:** Sets the Limiter's attack time.
* **Release:** Sets the Limiter's release time.

Soft Clip

Soft Clip is the final dynamic processor in the MTK chain. This is basically a limiter that kicks in at the last minute to reduce high signal levels that might overload the MTK's output section. Soft Clip rounds off the "knee" or point when the limiter attacks the audio signal as it surpasses the threshold setting to make the limiting effect "softer" or less harsh to the ear. The Soft Clip also adds a bit of warmth to the sound that is similar to vintage tube-type processors.

There is only one setting in Soft Clip, the on/off switch. Once on, it does all the processing automatically.

Dynamics Mixer

There is one more part to the MTK. It is called the Dynamics Mixer. This allows you to adjust the volume of each frequency band after processing. The Dynamics Mixer is positioned right after the compressor in the MTK chain. There are only three settings in the Dynamics Mixer:

* **Low:** Adjusts the volume of the low frequency band.
* **Mid:** Adjusts the volume of the mid frequency band.
* **High:** Adjusts the volume of the high frequency band.

Mixing Down with the MTK

There are two methods for mixing down your tracks to the Mastering Room. One way is to mix your tracks down to a two-track stereo master without MTK, then run the two-track stereo pair through the Mastering Room with an MTK patch applied. The other way is to mix down all your tracks in the Mastering Room while applying an MTK effects patch at the same time. Either way is fine, and the method you choose will basically depend on how many effects you need to use simultaneously.

A single MTK effect takes up an entire effects card. If you have two effects cards installed, you can use one for the MTK and the other for two stereo effects. If you need to use more than two stereo effects for your stereo bounce, you will want to add the MTK after you mix down to two tracks. If you don't need to use more than two stereo effects for your bounce, then you can apply an MTK patch to the Mastering Room while performing the stereo bounce. To mix down to two tracks while adding an MTK patch, do the following:

1. Enter the Mastering Room as described earlier in this chapter.

2. Set your faders and mixer settings how you want them for your mixdown. You can practice your mix while the SW switch is set to OFF.

3. Use the cursor keys to move to FXIns.

4. Press ENTER.

5. Use the cursor keys to select either FX1 or FX3. These are the only ones you can use for an MTK patch.

6. Use the jogwheel to change the setting to Ins.

7. If you selected FX1, press F1 (FX1). If you selected FX3, press F3 (FX3).

8. Press F2 (Sel).

9. Use the jogwheel to find the MTK patch you want to use.

10. Press F4 (Exec).

11. Press F6 (Exit).

12. Press PLAY to hear how your newly selected MTK effect patch sounds on your mix. Use the master level fader to push the overall level in the OUT meter as close to 0db as possible without clipping. (Clipping means hitting 0db.) When you are happy with the mix and the output level, press STOP and rewind to the beginning of the song.

13. Use the cursor keys to select SW. Use the jogwheel to change it to On.

14. Use the cursor keys to move to the STATUS setting. Use the jogwheel to change it to REC.

15. Press REC and PLAY on the transport controls.

16. When you reach the end of the song, press STOP.

17. To hear your newly mastered tracks, follow the instructions under "Playing Back the Master Tracks."

18. If you are unhappy with the mixdown, press UNDO to cancel it. Then go back to the Mastering Room and repeat steps 13–17.

Getting the Best from the MTK Presets

Major record labels and professional recording studios spend thousands of dollars to have their final mixes mastered in expensive mastering labs. Mastering is an art in itself. It can take years of practice, patience, and experience to learn how to do it properly.

One great thing about the VS-1680 is the MTK presets. These presets have been pre-configured by Roland engineers and professional soundmen to help you put a high-quality mastered finish on your mix. There are 19 preset MTK patches that are all configured for a different type of mix. The MTK patches are as follows:

* P210: Mixdown
* P211: PreMaster
* P212: LiveMix
* P213: PopMix
* P214: DanceMix
* P215: JingleMix
* P216: HardComp
* P217: SoftComp
* P218: CleanComp
* P219: DanceComp
* P220: OrchComp
* P221: VocalComp
* P222: Acoustic
* P223: RockBand
* P224: Orchestra
* P225: LoBoost
* P226: Brighten
* P227: DjsVoice
* P228: PhoneVox

The best way to use the MTK presets is to finish mixing your song first and then run the tracks through the Mastering Room. While your song is playing through the Mastering Room, insert different MTK patches to the Mastering Room's Effects bus. The cool thing about this process is that the VS-1680 allows you to do all this in real time.

While the song is playing, you can audition all of the MTK presets and then decide later which one you want to use. You may find that you are able to use many of the MTK presets "as is."

Sometimes, you can start with a good-sounding preset and then tweak it by going into the preset's editing functions. This way, you can customize the preset to fit your song's specific needs.

❋ **MTK PRESET TWEAKING CAUTION**

Be careful when you are tweaking the MTK presets. The processors in the MTK are very powerful and can drastically alter the sound of your mix. If you are not careful, you can potentially tweak your mix to the point where the end result is much worse than the original.

If that happens, you can select another MTK preset, then go back to the original preset. This restores the original preset back to its default settings, giving you a chance to start over.

Recording Your Mastered Tracks

When you are finished mastering your tracks, you have several options for recording them to CD. If you have an optional Roland CD-R/W burner connected to your VS-1680, you can burn a copy of your mix directly to the CD burner. If you don't have the optional burner, you can run the two tracks out of the VS-1680 and into a computer or standalone CD burner. You can use the analog outs or the digital outs to accomplish this.

When preparing the tracks to be recorded to the optional CD burner, you must adhere to the following rules:

1. **Sample Rate and Recording Mode:** Only tracks recorded with a sample rate of 44.1kHz can be written to CD-R discs. Make sure you select the 44.1kHz sample rate when you create a new song if you plan on recording it to CD. You may use any of the recording modes, but the recommended ones are MTP, CDR (VS-1880, VS-1824 ONLY), MAS, or MT1.

2. **Levels and Mixer Settings:** When recording an audio CD, only the actual audio will be recorded. Mixer, EQ, effects settings, and Automix data will not be transferred. Any desired level settings, panning, EQ, and effects settings must be recorded and performed on the source tracks during bouncing.

3. **Track Bouncing:** You can select any two V-Tracks to be recorded to the CD. If your song exists in a multi-track format, it must be mixed and then bounced down to two tracks before it can be recorded as a CD audio track to the optional Roland CD burner.

4. **Deleting Silence:** The two tracks will be written from the beginning of the tracks, normally "00h00m00s00" to the end of the tracks. Any blank space or silence on the track before the actual performance will be recorded as silence on the CD. To avoid this, use Track Cut to remove any unwanted silence at the beginning and end of the tracks.

13 } Roland VS-2480

Welcome to the Big Boy. Seventeen motorized faders, 16 mic pres, two R-BUS ports, coax and optical SP/DIF I/O, 24-track playback, 48-channel automated mixing with EQ, and dynamics on every channel. Comprehensive, non-destructive editing capabilities. As many as eight professional-quality effects processors. SCSI bus for external storage. CD and DVD archival for projects. Phrase pads for triggering samples. VGA output and mouse/keyboard support. All in a box you can easily fit on your desk or take to a gig.

While working in a recording studio in 1978, we could hardly dream of such a system. All the equipment required to assemble a comparable system would have taken up a very good-sized room and easily cost 10, 50, or even 100 times as much as the VS-2480.

I hope to illustrate for you how you can achieve good results quickly with your VS-2480. There is no substitute for practice and experience. The VS-2480 is both capable and complex. Just believe in yourself and your equipment, and there won't be much that you cannot accomplish!

Let's take a quick look around.

Hooking Up

Here's how the VS-2480 interfaces with the rest of the world.

ANALOG I/O

XLR/TRS Inputs

The XLR and TRS inputs are the connections to the 16 mic preamps. The XLR connectors also have the ability to provide phantom power for condenser mics. Avoid using both the XLR and the TRS inputs for the same channel (see Figure 13.1). I once had an SM57 plugged into channel 1 XLR and also had a tone generator plugged into channel 1 TRS. I noticed a faint tone in the studio, and sure enough, the tone was coming from the SM57!

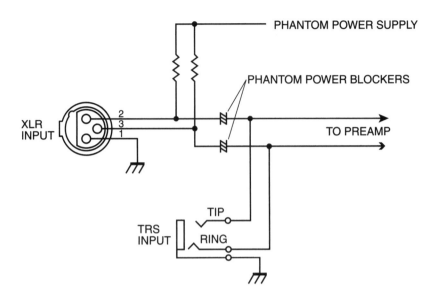

Figure 13.1
Both the XLR and the TRS inputs pass through the VS-2480's preamps. The only way to bypass the VS-2480's onboard preamps is with a digital signal.

HI-Z

The HI-Z input is for your guitar, bass, or any other instrument with a standard ¼" guitar cable connection. The pushbutton next to the HI-Z input must be pressed in to connect the HI-Z input to input channel 16. While the HI-Z input is enabled, the TRS input for channel 16 is disabled.

 HINT: TALKBACK MIC

If you are not using the actual HI-Z input, you can utilize the HI-Z switch as a talk-back mic control. Just connect a mic to the channel 16 TRS input, and use the HI-Z Switch to mute or enable the mic.

TRS Outputs

There are eight analog balanced line level outputs available on the VS-2480. Normally, outputs 1 and 2 are master outputs, and outputs 7 and 8 are Monitor outputs. The remaining four outputs may be assigned in pairs to aux busses or direct outputs.

DIGITAL I/O

R-BUS

Each of the two R-BUS connectors can send and receive eight channels of digital audio to and from an R-BUS–enabled system. Roland has produced several devices that transfer audio via R-BUS, such as other digital recorders and digital mixers, input expanders, keyboard modules, and digital interfaces such as the DIF-AT24 ADAT interface device.

SPDIF

Coax and optical SPDIF connectors will send and receive digital audio to and from any device that supports SPDIF, from CD and MD players to high-end mic preamps and effects processors.

Digital Connection Considerations

Master Clock

The Master Clock selection is found in the UTILITY → PROJECT PARAMETER menu item, as shown in Figure 13.2.

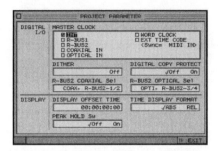

Figure 13.2
Project parameters.

Improperly setting the Master Clock will result in loud clicks and pops on the digital input channels. Normally, the VS-2480's internal clock (INT) is the Master Clock source, but when recording from either of the two SPDIF connections, set the Master Clock source to your audio source. Many R-BUS devices have the ability to receive Master Clock signals from the VS-2480, or you may choose to clock the VS-2480 from the R-BUS device.

Sync Parameters

Sync refers to keeping several machines synchronized during record, play, and transport functions. Many input devices, such as preamps or compressors, do not require synchronization at all. Other devices, such as sequencers, drum machines, and other multitrack recorders, need to stay synchronized to the timeline to be useful. The Sync settings are found in the UTILITY → SYNC PARAMETER menu item, as shown in Figure 13.3.

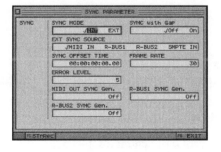

Figure 13.3
Sync parameters.

The VS-2480 may receive MTC sync signals from R-BUS source, MIDI IN, or the SMPTE input connection. The VS-2480 may provide its sync signal on either R-BUS port or the MIDI OUT port.

MIDI Machine Code

MIDI Machine Code (MMC) is a set of messages that control transport functions. The MIDI settings are found in the UTILITY → MIDI PARAMETER menu item, shown in Figure 13.4.

Figure 13.4
MIDI parameters.

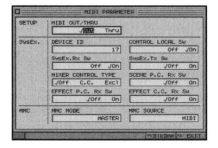

The VS-2480 may be set to send, receive, or ignore MMC commands. If you wish to send MMC commands, be sure to set the SysEx.Tx Sw (SystemExclusive Transmit Switch) to ON.

Other Connections

MIDI IN/OUT

MIDI can be used to synchronize drum machines and other MIDI sequencers to the VS-2480. MIDI IN allows the 2480 to sync to other devices via MTC timecode.

Word Clock and SMPTE

These connectors allow the VS-2480 to be synchronized to a common timing clock, as utilized in many professional recording and editing facilities for both audio and video.

SCSI

The SCSI connector allows the VS-2480 to exchange data with external storage devices, such as the Roland VS-CDRII/III or external SCSI hard drives.

Inside the Box

Sixteen Faders in Four Groups

The 16 channel faders control the levels of all inputs, tracks, AUX sends, and effects returns. However, there are 64 items to control and only 16 faders. To accommodate this, there are four buttons that select what the faders currently represent. The selections are:

 ❋ IN 1-16: The faders represent and control input channels 1–16.

- ❋ **IN 17-24/AUX MST:** The faders represent and control input channels 17–24 and AUX Master send levels.
- ❋ **TR 1-16:** The faders represent and control track channels 1–16.
- ❋ **TR 17-24/FX RTN:** The faders represent and control track channels 17–24 and effects return levels.

Input Channels

The input channels control audio that is coming into the VS-2480 before the audio is recorded. Any dynamics, EQ, or inserted effects applied to the input channel will be recorded.

Track Channels

The track channels control audio that is coming from the VS-2480's track recorder section. Any dynamics, EQ, or effects applied to the track channel will not be recorded to the track, but will simply change the way the track is heard.

AUX MSTR Channels

These faders control the level of the AUX busses. The AUX busses can supply signals to either the effects boards or the TRS output jacks.

FX RTN Channels

These faders control the amount of effects that are being supplied or returned to the Master bus. (The Master bus is where the main mix happens.)

Routing

Think of routing as the VS-2480's internal patch bay. This is where you connect the INs and OUTs and assign who is listening to what...all staying within the digital domain.

Patch Bay

There are a number of important features to be found in the patch bay section, shown in Figure 13.5.

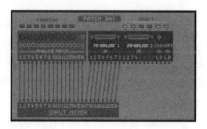

Figure 13.5
Patch bay routing.

Phantom Power

Phantom power for each of the eight XLR connectors may be individually turned on or off by the controls at the top of the screen.

Input Mixer Source Assignment

The lines connecting the analog and digital inputs to the Input Mixer move in pairs. Any pair of the 16 analog inputs, any pair of inputs from either R-BUS, or from either of the SPDIF stereo channels may be connected to each pair of Input Mixer channels.

RBus2/SPDIF Select

A total of up to 16 digital inputs can be used at one time on the VS-2480, though there are 20 digital inputs available. Due to this hardware, the digital inputs from R-BUS 2 and the two stereo SPDIF input channels are configured to share eight digital inputs. The SELECT buttons let you select from among the available inputs.

Track Assign

Figure 13.6

Track assignment routing.

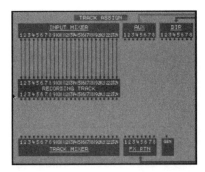

Here you can select the sources for the 24 recording tracks. Available sources include:

* **Input Mixer:** Any of the 24 Input Mixer channels.
* **AUX:** Any of the 8 AUX busses.
* **DIR:** Any of the 8 DIR busses.
* **Track Mixer:** Any of the 24 Track Mixer channels. Routing track A to recording track B removes track A from the Master bus.
* **FX RTN:** Any of the eight effects returns. This allows you to print effects. Only effects channels that actually have effects boards installed are available. Routing a loop effect to a recording track removes the effects from the Master bus.
* **GEN:** The output of the oscillator/noise generator/metronome is available here. This provides a quick way to print a click track assigned to a track channel, providing greater control.

Output Assign

All the VS-2480's output connections are listed across the top of the screen, as shown in Figure 13.7. Select a pair of outputs and drag with the mouse or spin the jogwheel to assign what is going where. The Track Direct Out control allows individual pairs of tracks to be connected to any output connection.

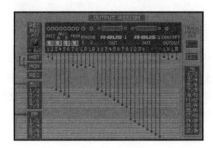

Figure 13.7
Output assignment routing.

¼" TRS Outputs

The MST (Master) bus is always present at TRS outputs 1 and 2, and the MON (monitor) bus is always present at outputs 7 and 8. Outputs 3 and 4 (AUX A) and outputs 5 and 6 (AUX B) may be fed from any AUX or DIR pair. (Again, ALL outputs can have various sources.)

Digital Outputs

The R-BUS outputs may be fed from the Master bus, the Monitor bus, or any AUX or DIR pair. The R-BUS 2 and SPDIF output availability depends on the settings of the SELECT buttons in the patch bay routing section.

Monitor Bus Select

The source for the Monitor bus is normally the Master bus, but you can select the Record bus, or any AUX or DIR pair, to feed the Monitor bus. If the Record bus is selected as the source for the Monitor bus, the REC BUS ATT button controls the level of the Record bus as supplied to the Monitor bus.

Track Direct Out

If the TRACK DIRECT OUT button is engaged, any track pair may be assigned to any output pair of connectors. The PRE/POST button controls if the direct signals are provided before (PRE) or after (POST) the track faders.

Loop Effects Assignment

The loop effects assign screen is shown in Figure 13.8. Here is where you choose input sources for the internal effects processors.

Figure 13.8
Connect any of the eight available effects processors to any AUX or DIR pair.

FKey Options

You can save commonly used routings and load them from memory (EZ Routing). You can also reset or completely clear either the patch bay or the track assignments with the touch of a button, much faster than resetting all the connections manually.

Making Connections

In the routing screens, all connections have one end that is fixed (that is, cannot be moved) and one that may be attached to many destinations. Track connections are represented by single lines. Input, output, and effects connections are represented by dual lines. These representations are indicative of the hardware they represent. Typically, converter chips, both A/D and D/A, are stereo units.

With the Mouse

Making connections with your mouse is very simple, as shown in Figures 13.9 thru 13.11.

Figure 13.9
Grab the connection with the mouse.

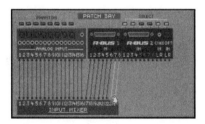

You can grab the connection at either end. When you grab the connection, it turns white.

Figure 13.10
Drag the connection.

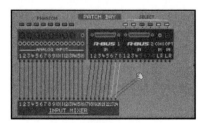

Patch bay and track assignments are adjusted horizontally, while output and effects assignments are adjusted vertically.

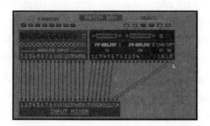

Figure 13.11
Drop the connection.

Each of the possible connection points for the selected connection will be highlighted as you drag over them. The mouse pointer turns into a pointing finger when you hover above one.

With the Cursor Buttons and Time/Value Dial
Use the PAGE key if necessary to select page 1 of 2 for the F-Keys. Use the F1, F2, F3, and F4 buttons to select one of the four main routing areas.

Use the cursor keys to select the fixed end of the desired connection.

Use the Time/Value dial to select the desired destination.

Using the Quick Routing screen
Press and hold any of the TRACK STATUS buttons to invoke the Quick Routing screen.

Tracks, V-Tracks, and Master Tracks

> ❋ **Talking about Tracks**
>
> Throughout this section, when I mention tracks by number, I'll use the following nomenclature:
> Track #.V-Track # for single tracks. (i.e., V-Track 6.1)
> Track #/#.V-Track # for linked tracks. (i.e., V-Track 23/24.16)

There are 24 tracks that can play simultaneously, and each of the 24 tracks has 16 V-Tracks from which to choose. The Master tracks actually consume some of tracks 23 and 24's V-Track allotments.

The Master tracks may be in either the "native" format of the project or in 16-bit CDR audio format. 16-bit CDR format tracks are identified with an asterisk (*) next to the V-Track number. Once a Master track has been recorded on, its mode (native or CDR) cannot be changed, even if the data on the tracks has been deleted. After deleting the Master tracks with the undesired mode, optimizing the project will allow the mode change to occur.

Master tracks in the native project format may be played along with any other tracks in the project, making them useful for sub-mixes. For example, you could create a mix of three background vocals with effects to V-Tracks 23/24.16, then phrase move the stereo pair to another linked pair of channels for inclusion in the mix, freeing up V-Tracks 23/24.16 for future mastering use.

Even though the Master tracks consume V-Tracks from tracks 23 and 24, any V-Track not currently designated as the Master tracks may be included in your mix. You can have a stereo drum mix on V-Tracks 23/24.1 and still use V-Tracks 23/24.16 as your Master tracks.

14 } The Channel Strip

The channel strips are the same for both the Input Mixer and the Track Mixer. This section presents the channel strip in the order in which it processes an audio signal.

By the time your signal hits the channel strip, it is already in a digital format.

Changing Data

With the Mouse

When you click on a data value to change it, you may be presented with a pop-up list of available choices, as shown in Figure 14.1. If the data is numeric, you can drag the mouse up or down to change the data's value. You can quickly change most settings on the VS-2480 with your mouse.

Figure 14.1
Select a parameter.

When you roll the mouse pointer over a field that it can modify, the pointer displays a hand. What happens next depends on the type of data to be changed.

Several parameters present a list of available choices, such as V-Track and filter mode, as seen in Figure 14.2.

Figure 14.2

A pop-up list of choices for V-Track.

For numeric data, the mouse pointer assumes the shape of an up and down arrow, as seen in Figure 14.3. To change the data value, drag the mouse up and down while the dual arrow is displayed.

Figure 14.3

The mouse pointer becomes an up/down arrow to adjust numeric entries.

With the Cursor Buttons and Time/Value Dial

You can navigate the various data fields using the cursor buttons and use the Time/Value dial to edit the data.

 When using the Time/Value dial to edit data, press SHIFT to change the value in an alternate increment. Depending on the value being adjusted, the alternate increment may be larger or smaller than the normally available increment.

Track Selection and Control

Patch Bay (Input Mixer Channels Only)

Choose any of the available input sources. Selection is the same for pairs of adjacent channels.

Phantom Power (Analog Input Channels 1–8 Only)

Toggles phantom power for these input channels.

Status (Track Mixer Channels Only)

Choose PLAY, RECORD, or OFF.

V-Track (Track Mixer Channels Only)

Choose V-Tracks 1–16. Each V-Track can be named. A list of named V-Tracks can be navigated with the mouse. Taking the time to name your V-Tracks as you go will help you stay on top of your project.

Phase

The Phase switch literally turns your audio upside down! The choices are Normal or Inverted. If you have several mics on one source, experimenting with the Phase switch's settings on the several channels will yield different results.

Channel Group

When you create a group of channels, they will all react proportionally to the motion of any fader within the group. By grouping all the faders that control your drum tracks, for example, you can raise or lower the entire drum mix with one fader. You should get the individual levels set first, then group the channels.

Channel Link and Fader Link

When you are dealing with a stereo source, you may Channel Link adjacent channels to share adjustments of dynamics and EQ. By selecting the SUB DISP button under the VGA fader of linked channels, the individual channels may be panned and leveled. The main track faders then control how much of the custom pan and leveled signal reaches the mix.

If you wish to maintain control over each channel separately, Fader Link allows you to link only the faders.

> ❀ **Faders Fight Back**
>
> When adjacent channels are linked remember to adjust only one of the faders manually and let the VS-2480 move the other one for you. You will notice the VS-2480 fighting back if you attempt to move both faders.

Phrase Pads

In the Phrase Pad mode, each channel (or channel pair) becomes a sample player. Each track designated as a phrase pad will play the first phrase that occurs on the track. That phase does not need to be located at Zero; it can be anywhere on the track.

While the VS-2480 is in Phrase Sequence mode, the TRACK STATUS buttons are the triggers for the samples. The manner in which the playback occurs is governed by the Phrase mode switch.

Mode	Playback
GATE	The sample will only play as long as its associated PHRASE PAD button is depressed.
TRIGGER	Pressing the PHRASE PAD button once will start the phrase, and pressing it again will stop the phrase.
ONE SHOT	The entire sample plays each time the PHRASE PAD button is pressed.

Dynamics

The VS-2480 offers a number of very powerful dynamics processors.

Compression

Use the Compressor, shown in Figure 14.4, to help tame the peaks of a signal. A compressor reduces the output signal automatically whenever the input signal exceeds a certain level. This allows you to hear more of the "meat" of the signal. The Threshold setting determines at what level the Compressor kicks in. Levels below the threshold are not affected. The Ratio setting controls how much compression is applied once the signal level exceeds the threshold. The Attack and Release settings control the speeds of change of the compression effect.

Figure 14.4

The Compressor controls.

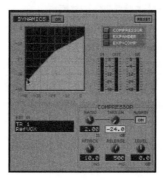

Expander

Use the Expander effect, shown in Figure 14.5, to reduce the level of background noise in your signal. From gentle background reduction to extreme gating, expansion can clean up your mix in an automatic way. The Threshold setting determines at what level the Expander kicks in. Levels above the Threshold are not affected. The Ratio setting controls how much attenuation occurs when the level is below the threshold. The Attack and Release settings control the speeds of change of the Expander effect.

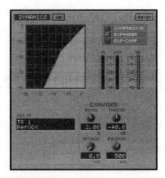

Figure 14.5
The Expander controls.

Combined Compressor and Expander

Figure 14.6 shows the Compressor and Expander combined. Combine the two sections to treat particularly unruly signals, such as a loud guitar amp with a lot of "buzzing" noise when the performer is not playing and a lot of peaks in the signal when he is playing.

Figure 14.6
The combined controls.

> ❋ **Limitations of Dynamics Processors**
>
> While the VS-2480 is powerful, its power is limited. One such limitation applies to the Dynamics processors: If any track uses combined Compression and Expansion, no input channel may use ANY dynamics processing at all. The reverse is also true.
> One other limitation is that the dynamics settings are not included in the list of things that may be Automixed.

Dynamics Key Source

The process of reacting to a signal is referred to as keying off of that signal. Hence the designation of the Key In signal track. Normally, the dynamics react to changes in the signal that they are processing. Sometimes, it is useful to have the dynamics react to a different signal than the one they are processing. The Key In data area lets you choose any of the 24 Track Mixer channels as a key source.

Dynamics Metering

The VU meters within the Dynamics processor are good indicators of your signal's current level. The GR (Gain Reduction) meters show how much the Dynamics processor is changing your signal.

Effects Inserts

When you want to pass a channel's audio through an effect and have that effect only applied to that channel, use the Effects Inserts. Examples of traditional insert patches are guitar amp simulators, microphone modelers, or custom EQ patches.

The small horizontal blue bars next to each effects block control the FX SEND (upper blue bar) and FX RETURN (lower blue bar), as shown in Figure 14.7. Grab the blue bar and drag the mouse up or down to adjust these values.

Figure 14.7
FX3 inserted. Note the horizontal bars directly above the cursor.

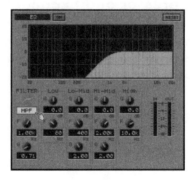

Attenuator

Sometimes, after dynamics and effects processing, the signal is just too hot for the EQ stage, as evidenced by the IN/OUT VU meters in the EQ section. You can use the ATTEN control to bring these signals down to a usable level. You may also dial in 6dB of gain to boost a weak signal, but remember that the ATTEN control is the signal after the dynamics and effects processing.

EQ

The VS-2480 offers a number of EQ filters for you to use on your tracks.

Filter

Use the High Pass Filter (HPF) to control bass build-up in your mixes. Using the HPF on nearly all of your input and track channels will make mixing easier by preventing a lot of bass build-up. Low E on a bass is right around 40Hz, and low E on a guitar around 80Hz. Using the HPF at 120Hz on vocals helps cut down room noises and outside noises. While there are often good reasons to set them lower, these are easily remembered guidelines.

The Q of the HPF controls the sharpness of the filter, but it also boosts the filter frequency. This fact can be used to fatten up kick drums and toms. Here's how:

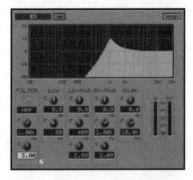

Figure 14.8
Select the HPF.

Invoke the HPF Filter setting. Initially, the cutoff frequency will be 1000Hz.

Set the Q fairly high and tune the filter to the drum on the track. Bass drum fundamentals are usually found between 30 and 60 Hz, floor toms 60 to 80 Hz, and rack toms 80 to 120Hz.

Observe the EQ's IN and OUT meters while tuning the filter. Keep the IN level moderate, and look for a peak on the OUT meter when the filter frequency matches the intonation of the drum.

Figure 14.9
Tuning the filter.

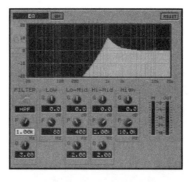

Figure 14.10
Observe the output level.

Figure 14.11
Moderate the effect.

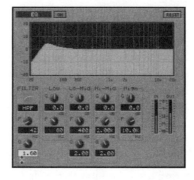

Once you find the fundamental tone of the drum, lower the Q so the effect is subtle. A little goes a long way. It is easy to let this trick become too "boom-y."

The other filter modes—LPF (Low Pass), BPF (Band Pass), and BEF (Band Eliminate)—are useful for correcting various signal faults or for special effects.

4-Band EQ

The 4-Band EQ offers a low shelf filter, two parametric mid-band filters, and a high shelf filter for shaping your sound. It is generally recommended to reduce frequencies via EQ rather than boost them. If you do a lot of boosting, make sure to watch the VU meters so that you don't overdrive the signal before it hits the fader.

EQ with Your Mouse

You may also adjust the EQ with your mouse. The four small red arrows correspond to the four EQ sections. Just grab the red arrows and go. This is good for a quick start, but since you can't change the Q of the filter sections this way, you'll want to go in and fine-tune the settings.

AUX Sends and DIR Assignments

The AUX Sends and DIR Assignment buttons let you create sub-mixes and send your signal to internal or external effects processors. You can mix signals from many channels on the AUX busses, but only one channel may occupy a direct output at any time.

Mono versus Linked AUX Operation

Normally, each AUX bus is its own entity. However, adjacent pairs of AUX channels may be linked, and track signals may then be panned across the linked pair, as shown in Figure 14.12.

Figure 14.12
Linked and unlinked AUX control layout.

Access the AUX LINK function by holding SHIFT and pressing the MASTER EDIT button, or by using the Mixer dropdown menu's Input Mixer/Master Block item.

PRE/POST Sends

If PST is selected, the audio being supplied to the AUX channel is controlled by the track's fader as well as the AUX send level. If PRE is selected, the AUX send level is independent of the track fader level. Selection of PRE or PST for any AUX send applies to all tracks.

DIR Sends

The Direct Outs are eight more possible paths you can use to send audio to an effects board or another of the VS-2480's outputs. The DIR OUTs are not busses—there are no mixing facilities for the DIR OUTs, and only one source may utilize any Direct Out at any one time. The DIR OUTs can be prefader or postfader.

Mix, Mute, and Solo Buttons

The MIX button must be illuminated to allow the track's audio to be presented to the Master bus. AUX sends, however, continue to work even if the MIX button is turned off.

The MUTE button prevents any audio from being presented to the Master bus, AUX busses, or DIR busses.

The SOLO button stops everything but the soloed signal from playing. Never push SOLO when you are recording!

15 } Project Basics

There are some basics that are common to most projects.

Project Management

Project management is largely a matter of developing a method of describing your projects and having the discipline to stick to it. Your method will evolve as you become more familiar with the VS-2480 and its disk operations.

The Project List Dialog

The Project List dialog, shown in Figure 15.1, displays a list of all partitions on any connected drives, as well as any optical drives that are attached.

The current drive is denoted by a black square with the letter C in it. The files on the current drive are also listed.

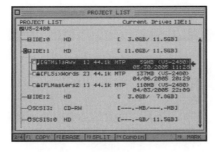

Figure 15.1
The Project List dialog.

The IDE: partitions are on the VS-2480's internal hard drive. The SCSI3: drive is an external SCSI CD–RW drive set to SCSI address 3. The SCSI5:0 drive is the first partition on an external SCSI hard drive set to SCSI address 5. Other partitions on that drive are denoted as SCSI5:1, SCSI5:2, and so on.

Creating a New Project

You may only create a new project in the current partition. There are several choices you must make when you create a new project.

Project Name

The project name is limited to 12 characters. Adopting a naming standard early will help you keep track of your projects down the road. Here's my method:

Reserve the first two characters for the initials of the artist.

and

Reserve the last two characters for an incrementing version number.

Use the remaining space to approximate a title. It is common to simply use the first letter of each word, with a few letters of the last word if there is enough room to do so.

Copying Parameters

You may choose to make your new project a copy of the current project's settings. Choose Copy Utility Prm to copy all the info in the Utility menu to the new project. You may also choose Copy Mixer/Scene Prm to copy the mixer and scene settings.

Project Type

When you start a new project on the VS-2480, you may choose from several sample rate and recording mode options. The decisions you make at this point will determine sound quality and storage size. The more hi-fidelity your choice, the larger the files created. Some of the more hi-fidelity choices may result in reduced channel capacity for both recording and playback. I choose to work primarily in 44.1k sample rate and MTP recording mode, allowing 16-track recording and 24-track playback with 24-bit data. Table 15.1 lists the recording modes and their limitations.

Table 15.1　Recording Modes and Number of Available Tracks at Different Sample Rates

Recording Mode	Up to 48kHz, Play/Record	64kHz and over, Play/Record
M24	16/16	8/8
MTP	24/16	12/8
CDR	16/16	(44.1 only)
M16	16/16	8/8
MT1	24/16	12/8
MT2	24/16	12/8
LIV	24/16	12/8
LV2	24/16	12/8

Saving and Protecting Projects

You just can't save your project too many times. Save after good takes, large edits, when you define a new scene, or just about any time at all.

The VS-2480 will ask if you want to save your project before many disk-based activities. Usually, you'll want to go ahead and save it again. If you don't save it, the VS-2480 reloads the most recent copy of the project from disk.

If you protect your project, the VS-2480 knows not to prompt you to save over it. Protecting projects saves time by eliminating this prompt. Protected projects also generate a warning if you ask the VS-2480 to erase them, just to be sure.

Copying and Backing Up Projects

At some point in the life of your project, you will want to make a copy of it. You may decide to make a copy after each session or only now and then. Backup copies of projects can be a life-saver for those "just in case" and "oops" scenarios that are bound to crop up now and then.

Before you may copy or back up projects, you must "mark" them in the Project List dialog. The Project Copy dialog, shown in Figure 15.2, shows the project(s) you have selected to copy and combined file size.

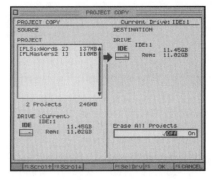

Figure 15.2
The Project Copy dialog.

When you copy a project or a group of projects, you must select the destination drive. Click on SelDrv or press F4 to display a list of all available partitions, their sizes, and remaining capacity. Make sure that the destination drive has sufficient capacity for the project(s) to be copied. Always try to leave a little breathing room of a few hundred empty MB on a partition. To provide more security, projects should be copied either to another partition on the internal hard drive or to a partition on an external SCSI drive. Projects cannot be copied to CDR or DVD. The copy process can be started and then left unattended. It will either succeed or fail with no further user intervention.

An image of a project may be stored as data to a CDR or DVD. This process is referred to as backing up. A backup of a project may only be restored. If a backup cannot fit entirely on one CDR, you will be prompted to enter additional CDRs as required. For larger projects, this can become quite tedious.

Backups are not copies, and copies are not backups, although both methods retain all the data for a project. There is an old saying about digital data: If it is not stored in at least two places, it's not safe. The VS-2480 data is no exception. If the data is important, make two copies or backups on different devices and physically store them in different places.

Sharing Data

Complete tracks from the current project may be split into their own project. The split process actually creates copies of the track data, leaving the original project intact.

You can export tracks or phrases as .WAV data for use in most professional digital audio environments. You can also import .WAV data from a CD or capture a stereo audio track from a CD.

> ❋ **.WAV Format Conversion**
>
> Any audio data that you import into your project will be converted to the sample rate and recording mode defined by the project during the import process.
> When you capture a track from a CD, you also have the option to capture it as 16-bit CD audio data to the mastering tracks.

You can combine two projects into one. To combine two projects, they must both reside in the same partition. You must mark the two projects in the Project List dialog, one of them being the current project and the other being any project of the same type. The second project will be absorbed by the current project and will no longer be available as an individual project.

The VS-2480 can use data from or format data for other digital recorders. You can export the project in a format that is compatible with other Roland VS workstations or import projects created on those workstations.

Moving Around Within Your Project

One of the keys to working efficiently is the ability to navigate quickly to various edit points. As with many things on the VS-2480, there is more than one way to accomplish this.

Cursor Buttons and Time/Value Dial

While viewing the Home screen, the cursor buttons, shown in Figure 15.3, will shift the focus of the Time/Value dial along the values in the upper left of the display. This makes it very easy to move in large or small steps by selecting the proper increment and dialing away.

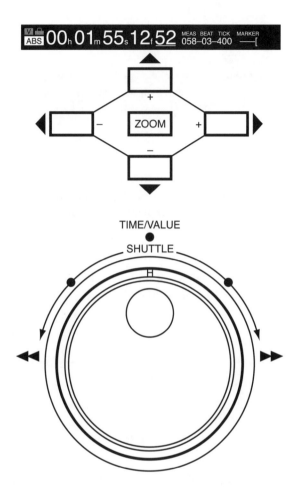

Figure 15.3
The left/right cursor keys
select which value to edit.

Select hours, minutes, seconds, frames, sub-frames, measure, beat, tick, or marker with the left/right cursor keys. Use the Time/Value dial to move the project forward or backward by the selected increment.

For very small movements, set the focus to the sub-frames value and hold down the SHIFT button while adjusting the Time/Value dial. If you have placed markers throughout your project, you can scroll to any marker number. If your project has been recorded to a VS-2480-provided Tempo Map, you can scroll by measures, beats, and ticks.

> ✳ **Quick Scrolling**
>
> You can also scroll through the values displayed in the upper left with your mouse. Just click the mouse on the desired increment and drag the mouse up or down to change the data. If the project is playing, it will continue to play normally until you release the mouse, then snap directly to the new point and continue playing from there.

Shuttle Ring

Just twist the Shuttle ring to move your project forward or backward. The further you twist, the faster the project moves. If the project is playing when you use the Shuttle ring, the audio will be muted except for small bursts, making it difficult to know exactly where you are just by listening, especially at greater speeds.

Previous and Next

These controls move you to the previous or next "edge" of a phrase on the currently selected track. Any start or end of a phrase is considered an edge. If no edge exists in the requested direction, the project just will stay where it is.

Locators

A locator is simply a numbered point in time. There are 100 available locators for any one project. Naming your locators as you go will help you keep track of your project.

Locators are organized as 10 banks of 10 locations. To access the different banks, hold SHIFT and press the LOC button. Nine of the 10 numeric buttons will flash. The button that is solidly illuminated is the current bank. Press any of the numeric buttons to select the corresponding bank. Bank 0 is selected by default.

Once you select the desired bank, and the LOCATOR button is solidly illuminated, pressing any non-illuminated numeric button will save the current location, and pressing any illuminated numeric button will recall the corresponding saved location and jump to that point in time within the project.

To undefine a locator, hold the CLEAR button and press the illuminated numeric button that corresponds to the locator to be undefined.

> ✳ **Locator Scratchpad**
>
> I like to use locator bank 9 as a scratchpad while editing. Select bank 9 and use its locators while working on a specific item. If you always use bank 9 for temporary workspace, you can feel pretty safe about clearing any defined locators you may find there when you start your next editing task.

Naming Locators

Click on the LOC button near the upper-right corner of the VGA display to access the Locator dialog, as shown in Figure 15.4.

Figure 15.4
Click on the LOC button to open the Locator dialog box.

Here you can assign names to your locators and view their information, in addition to setting or clearing them.

Markers

Dropping a marker is a quick way to note a particular point in your project. Markers cannot be named.

* To drop a marker, just press the TAP button.

* Hold SHIFT and press the PREVIOUS or NEXT button to move adjacent markers.

* To remove a marker, move directly to it, hold the CLEAR button, and press the TAP button.

* CDR markers are special markers that denote the start of a new track on an audio CD (more on that later).

Jump Button

Press the JUMP button and enter any time or measure/beat desired, and the VS-2480 will locate to the desired point immediately.

Viewing Your Project

The VS-2480 provides many different ways to view the parameters of your project.

Home Screen View

The Home screen, shown in Figure 15.5, is your all-around display area. Press the HOME button next to the F6 button under the LCD display, or click on the HOME button in the top right of the VGA display, to access the Home screen.

Figure 15.5

The Home screen.

The Home screen is divided into several distinct areas.

The Time/Transport display area, shown in Figure 15.6, shows actual project time in several different formats and has clickable buttons to emulate the physical Transport Control buttons.

Figure 15.6

The Time/Transport display area.

A lot of control is packed into the project information area, as shown in Figure 15.7. Left to right on the top row are the Mastering mode controls (On/Off, Play/Record), the Phrase Pad mode controls (On/Off, Play/Record, Undo/Redo), the Automix controls (On/Off, Play/Record, Undo/Redo, Snapshot), and the main editing controls (Undo/Redo).

On the second row we find the external SYNC On/Off control, the metronome control (Off/Internal/MIDI), Auto Punch and loop On/Off Controls, and project information.

Figure 15.7
Project information and controls display area.

Previous and next controls (Transport), marker controls, and buttons providing access to locator and scene dialogs are found on the third row.

The Fader display area actually displays the values of the knobs associated with the currently selected bank of faders. These could be pan settings, AUX send settings, or dynamics/EQ settings, as determined by a few buttons on the VS-2480. Pressing the button immediately to the right of the row of knobs will allow the knobs to function as dynamics/EQ controls. The control button glows red in this mode. If the Global Knob/Fader Assign switch is set to Knobs, these knobs may also represent the AUX 1-8 send levels when the KNOB/FADER ASSIGN button is illuminated.

To the right of the Fader display area are the input clip indicators. These warn you of overloaded input channels.

The Playlist area, shown in Figure 15.8, shows all the phrases on the currently selected V-Tracks. The vertical red line in the Playlist area is the timeline, and it represents the current project time. From left to right, each track's number, V-Track selection, name, mute, solo, Automix, and phrase pad status are displayed, as is the overall channel status. You can change most of these parameters by clicking on the status indicators with the mouse.

Figure 15.8
The Playlist area, zoomed out to display the entire project.

You can zoom in on tracks or time regions by holding the SHIFT button and using the cursor keys to zoom in or out, both horizontally and vertically. Figure 15.9 shows the same timeline as Figure 15.8, but zoomed in horizontally to show more timing detail.

Figure 15.9
The same timeline, zoomed in horizontally.

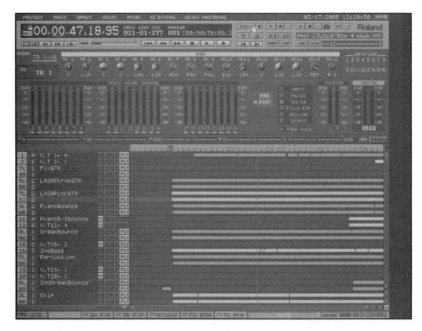

Zooming in on tracks makes it easier to edit them with a mouse. If you zoom in close enough, a visual representation of the audio data on the track will be displayed. Figure 15.10 shows two tracks zoomed in to the maximum magnification.

Figure 15.10
Zooming in vertically displays more information per track.

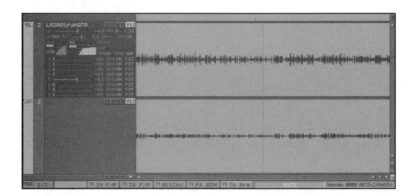

Most of the track parameter representations in the Close Zoom mode actually work with the mouse. For example, you can adjust any of the eight AUX sends by dragging the appropriate slider.

Hold the SHIFT button and press the HOME button under the LCD display to toggle a display of V-Track/Locator/Scene information, as shown in Figure 15.11. You may also toggle this information by clicking on the horizontal black arrow between the track display area and the V-Track area on the VGA.

Figure 15.11
The V-Track grid display.
Select the LOC/SCN
tab to view locator and
scene information.

❋ **HINT: V-Track Selection**

You can click on the small V-Track representation icons to select them with the mouse. After each selection, the VS-2480 displays a confirmation message. You cannot make any other changes while this message is displayed.

To speed selection of multiple V-Tracks, press the ENTER/YES button after making each selection to remove the V-Track confirmation message.

Mixer Views

You can choose to view the Input Mixer, Track Mixer, or current fader group on the VGA screen. Many of the visual representations of channel settings may be adjusted by clicking and dragging with the mouse. Access the mixer views via the MIXER menu or the function keys.

16 } Tracking

Tracking refers to the process of recording the original tracks for a song. The primary objective of tracking is to store a clean signal on the hard drive so you can process it later. Tracking sessions should be enjoyable, with a minimum of technical distractions for the performer.

Input Monitoring

When recording analog sources, properly setting the input level is the most important detail. We'll run through a quick sequence of events that you'll follow almost every time you plug in a mic.

Connect your inputs, and/or select them from the Routing screen if necessary. Remember to provide phantom power for any mic that requires it.

Provide a nominal signal at the source. Ask the performer to warm up or to play a bit in the anticipated style of the recording.

While viewing the Home screen, press F1 (on page 1/3) or click on the INPUT SELECT button with the mouse to display the input level monitors.

Traditionally, recording engineers have tried to get a "hot" level to tape. They did so primarily to overcome "tape hiss." Luckily for us, there is no tape hiss to overcome on the VS-2480, so you can afford to reduce your input levels a bit, thus providing a little extra "headroom" for the signal before clipping occurs. Strive for input levels predominately "in the yellow," meaning between –12dB and –4dB on the meters. A bit of red in your levels is OK, especially if the actual source of the signal is pretty loud itself, but by setting the preamp gain too high when recording a quiet vocal, a great take may be ruined by clipping when the expressive singer pumps up the volume a bit.

The input level is controlled before the signal hits any fader. It is a combination of how strong the signal is at the VS-2480's input jack and the settings of the SENS and PAD controls.

When adjusting your input source with the PAD and SENS controls, try to keep the SENS as low as possible. Start with the PAD out and the SENS control fully CCW. If the incoming signal is still too hot, press the PAD in and adjust the SENS accordingly.

The Input Clip section of the Home screen gives you a convenient way to keep tabs on the input levels while not actually monitoring the IN VU meters. The level at which these clip indicators illuminate may be set to 0dB, –3dB, or –6dB in the Global Parameters menu.

Remember, it is much easier to boost the volume of a track that was recorded slightly low than to mask the clipping of a track that was recorded too hot. When in doubt, shoot low!

Input Mixer Monitoring

Now that the actual input levels have been set, we need to set the level of the signal as it leaves the Input Mixer on its way to the recording track.

While viewing the Home screen, press F2 (on page 1/3) or click on the IN1-24 selector with the mouse to display the Input Mixer monitors. Press F6, or mouse-click on the PRE and POST selectors, to select whether the VU meters display the signals before (PRE) or after (POST) the Input Mixer faders.

Recording Dry

Again, due to the absence of tape hiss, recording your tracks dry, with no effects or compression of any kind, is a good, quick alternative to "getting it right going to tape." A performer may become frustrated if he has to keep warming up while the engineer fiddles with the settings. Recording dry keeps your tracking sessions moving quickly. You can always apply compression or effects later in your mix.

If the performer wants to hear some compression on his track as he is performing, apply the compression (or effects) in the Track Mixer, not the Input Mixer.

For any channel that is being recorded dry, you can set its Input Mixer fader to 0dB. Hold CLEAR and press the CH EDIT button above the desired channel to automatically move the fader to 0dB.

Recording with Effects

Sometimes, you just *know* what you want to do with a signal. If you have created a custom patch that always works with your bass, or you are playing thru a guitar amp simulator patch for a certain sound, go ahead and apply it to the signal as it is in the Input Mixer. This method is a good, economical use of effects, as it frees up effects for use later in the mixing process. As mentioned earlier, applying the HPFs in the Input Mixer is a quick way to prevent too much bass build-up in your mixes.

You may decide to raise the Input Mixer fader above 0dB if you take a lot out of your signal in the Input Mixer. If the signal is too hot with the Input Mixer fader at 0dB, there is probably something not quite adjusted properly in the Input Mixer.

Have It Both Ways

With some simple routing, you can simultaneously record two versions of the input signal: one straight and one processed. Here's how to set it up:

1. Connect your signal to Input 1.

2. In the patch bay area of the Routing screen, drag the connection from Input Mixer 3-4 to analog inputs 1-2, as shown in Figure 16.1. (Input Mixer source selection is by paired channels only.)

3. Set Input Mixer channel 1 control with no processing at all.

4. Set Input Mixer channel 3 with any dynamics, effects, and EQ desired.

5. Record both tracks 1 and 3, as shown in Figure 16.2.

6. After recording, you may choose to move track 3's data to another V-Track of channel 1. For example, your "flat" recording could be on V-Track 1.1, and your "processed" recording on V-Track 1.2, as shown in Figure 16.3.

7. Remember to reset the patch bay after use to avoid confusion later.

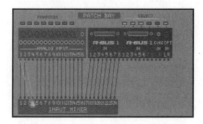

Figure 16.1
Connect two Input Mixer
channels to one input.

Figure 16.2
Record on both channels.

Figure 16.3
Move the second channel data to an open V-Track under the first channel's V-Track.

Recording FX Separately

Both loop and insert effects may be recorded at the same time as the input signal, if desired. In the case of a loop effect, the effects return may be routed to a recording channel, as shown in Figure 16.4.

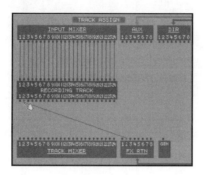

Figure 16.4
Routing the effects return to a recording track.

In the above example, the output of loop effect 2 will be recorded in mono on track 2.

In the case of an insert effect, apply the effect in the Track Mixer and route the output of the track to another recording channel. Loop effects may be routed to a linked pair of recording tracks to preserve the stereo image of the effect, or to a single channel for a mono effect.

In Figure 16.5, the output of track 1, including any insert effect, will be recorded on track 2. Both track 1 and track 2 must be armed to record.

Figure 16.5
Routing the output of one recording track to another.

Name Your Tracks

The VS-2480 automatically assigns the name of the recording track to the phrases it records on that track. If you take the time to name the tracks before recording, the name you enter for the track will be included in the name of any phrase that is recorded on that track. As shown in Figure 16.6, access to the Track Name function is via the Track menu.

Figure 16.6

Select the Track Name
menu item.

First select a track to name, then press F1 to invoke the Name Edit dialog box, as shown in
Figure 16.7.

Figure 16.7

The Name Edit dialog box.

You may use your mouse to select letters, type them on a connected PS2 keyboard, or use the
Time/Value dial to scroll through the characters. The F1-HIST (History) button will step backwards
through your last few entries, which you may then edit for your new track name. This is a very
convenient feature for multiple takes!

17 } Track Editing

Editing functions are those functions that rearrange the order in which the phrases are played within your project. The VS-2480 has a powerful set of editing features to help you craft your music, and luckily for us, it also has an UNDO button! Familiarize yourself with the process and results of the editing procedures, and if (or, more likely, when) something unexpected happens, just undo the edit and try again.

Phrases and Regions

Regions and phrases both refer to sections of audio, but there are differences between them.

Regions

A region may be made up of less than one complete phrase or encompass many phrases on multiple tracks. There may even be spaces between the phrases within a region. You set the beginning and ending points of a region via the IN and OUT buttons, respectively.

Phrases

A phrase is one continuous segment of audio. When you edit phrases, you affect the entire phrase. You can make it shorter (or sometimes longer!) with Trim In and Trim Out operations. You can move or copy phrases in their entirety. You can manually split phrases into smaller sections or let the VS-2480 automatically divide a long phrase into several shorter ones.

Only the phrases actually "touching" the current timeline are available for editing.

Phrase Parameter Editing

Each phrase has a name and can be programmed with its own playback level and fade in/out times, all independent of channel and fader settings.

The Phrase Parameter edit dialog is accessed from the Track menu, as shown in Figure 17.1.

Figure 17.1
Select Phrase Parameter
from the Track menu.

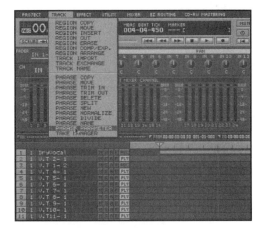

You can only edit one phrase at a time. Both halves of stereo phrases must be adjusted manually. Figure 17.2 shows only one phrase available for editing.

Figure 17.2
Select from the list of
available phrases.

The Phrase Parameter screen default settings, shown in Figure 17.3, may be customized to create a special effect or to correct a problem with the phrase. The parameters you set for a phrase will be passed along to any sub-phrases created from the phrase.

Figure 17.3
The Phrase Parameter
screen default settings.

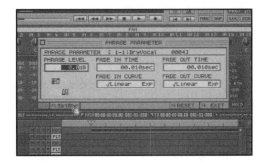

Take Manager

The Take Manager is a text list of all the takes currently associated with the project. A take is the complete phrase of audio that is stored just after recording. Smaller phrases culled from this take do not themselves become takes. So long as any phrase culled from a take is included in the project, the entire take remains in the project. Even phrases that have been removed from the project during a phrase or region erase operation do not actually disappear from the hard disk, but stay listed in the Take Manager and may be recovered for use by the project.

The Take Manager displays the name, start and end points, disk usage, and recording date of each take. The list may be sorted by name, history, or V-Track number.

Moving Regions and Phrases

One of the most common editing functions is the relocation of data in either regions or phrases. The VS-2480 has slightly different methods of moving or copying regions or phrases.

When you are editing phrases, as shown in Figure 17.4, only the phrases currently intersecting the timeline are available. The length of data copied or moved is determined by the phrases themselves; consequently, only the FROM and TO points need to be assigned when working with phrases. To help visualize it, think to yourself, "I'm copying this entire phrase (or these entire phrases) FROM here TO there."

Figure 17.4
Phrase selection.

After the phrase copy operation shown in Figure 17.5, the copied phrases are in the same positions relative to each other as the original phrases.

Figure 17.5

Result of phrase copy operation.

Regions must have both a start point (IN) and end point (OUT). The IN and OUT points do not have to be visible on the screen to be relocated. This time, think, "I'm copying the region that starts at IN and ends at OUT, and I'm copying it FROM here TO there." Figure 17.6 shows a marked region and the result of the region copy operation.

Choosing exactly how to move your data may depend on how the data was originally recorded. If your project was recorded to the VS-2480's internal metronome, the actual FROM and TO points can easily be set to exact measures, beats, and ticks. If your project was recorded from a drum machine that was not synchronized to the VS-2480, you may have to move data referenced from a kick drumbeat in measure 14 to a kick drumbeat in measure 38, for example. If you are replacing one bad bass note with a properly played one from somewhere else in the performance, you may move from the start of the "good" bass note to the start of the "bad" bass note.

Nondestructive Editing and Pointer-Based Playback

The VS-2480 remembers everything it records—well, technically, everything that has not been undone. For playback and editing, the VS-2480 "points" to different sections of the original audio track. For the sake of illustration, let's imagine that you've just recorded a guitar track, and

Figure 17.6
Result of region
copy operation.

everything was great except the second verse. You played to a click track, so both the first and the second verse are the same tempo. Why not copy the first verse to the second verse? When you copy the first verse guitar track to the second verse, you don't really move audio on the hard disk. For each track, the VS-2480 keeps a playlist of beginning and end points. In the example of copying the guitar verse, the playlist might be something like:

❋ Play from the start of the track to the start of the second verse.

❋ Play from the start of the first verse to the end of the first verse.

❋ Play from the end of the second verse to the end of the song.

After the edit, the original guitar track for the second verse remains on the hard drive and is available for use later on, just in case.

Phrase Trim Demo

OK, how about a quick demo of the power of nondestructive editing? We'll look at the Phrase Trim functions.

Hook up a mic and record a simple count—just "one, two, three, four" will be enough. For discussion, let's say we've recorded to V-Track 1.1. Select WAVE DISP so you can easily see to edit the phrase. Position the track so the timeline is before the word "three." Press the IN button. The FROM button will automatically be set to the same time. Now move the track forward so the timeline is past the word "three," as shown in Figure 17.7, and press the OUT button.

253
❋ ❋ ❋

Figure 17.7

IN/FROM and OUT lines before and after the word "three."

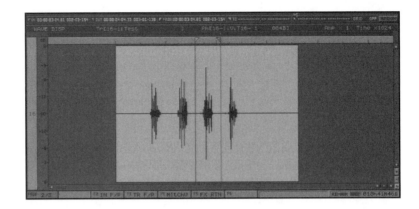

Now, move the timeline out several seconds past the original recorded phrase and press the TO button. Now select TRACK → REGION COPY from the menus, and select V-Track 1.1 as your source and destination. Go ahead and copy the region, as shown in Figure 17.8.

Figure 17.8

The phrase containing the word "three" has been copied.

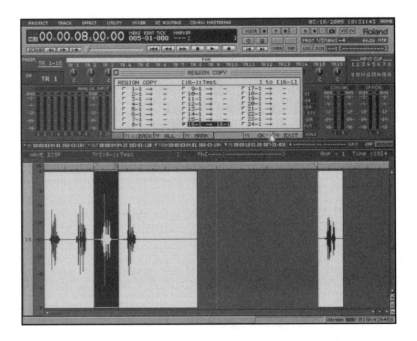

Now let's go look at the copied phrase. If you play that phrase, it is only the word "three." Now, make sure that you have Phrase Editing selected (as opposed to Region Editing), and move your mouse to the start point of the phrase. The mouse pointer becomes a square bracket, as shown in Figure 17.9. You can now drag the start point of the phrase either way, making the phrase longer or shorter.

Figure 17.9
A square bracket lets you know the VS-2480 is in Phrase Trim mode.

If you move it far enough to the left, you can uncover the words "one, two" from the copied phrase.

In Figure 17.10 above, the word "two" has already been recovered. To uncover the word "four," click on and adjust the end point of the phrase.

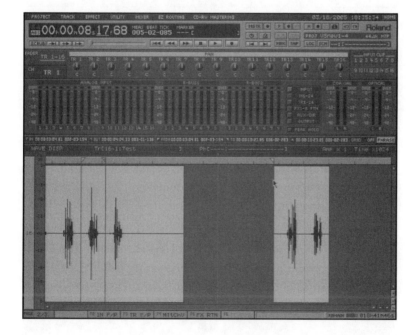

Figure 17.10
Phrase Trim In completed.

If you move the mouse past the end of the phrase, the display will indicate the actual length of the phrase. Figure 17.11 shows that the mouse has been dragged past the end of the phrase. Figure 17.12 shows the final result of the Phrase Trim Out procedure.

Figure 17.11
Phrase Trim Out function,
showing phrase length.

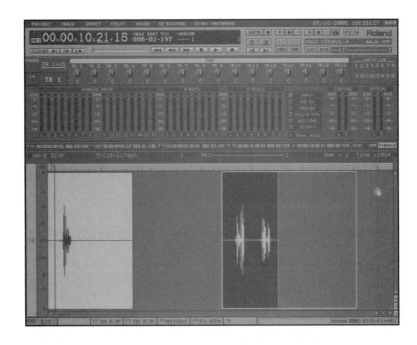

Figure 17.12
Phrase Trim Out result.

This same Phrase Trim adjusting theory also works when you are punching in during tracking or copying regions during editing. Understanding this concept lets you adjust edit points after the data has been edited.

> ❄ **WATCH THAT MOUSE POINTER**
>
> When using the Phrase Trim In or Phrase Trim Out function, keep an eye on your mouse pointer. It is a little tricky to grab just the edge of the phrase. Make sure you have a square bracket, not a hand, when you go to drag the edge, or you may mistakenly move the entire phrase instead of just adjusting the IN/OUT point. When (not if) this happens to you, don't panic. Simply undo the Phrase Move and try again.
>
> Also, if you are adjusting the point where two phrases meet, make sure you have the desired phrase selected, not the adjacent phrase.

Setting Edit Points

Accurately setting your IN, OUT, FROM, and TO points is essential to efficient editing. You can set these points by ear, by eye, or by beat.

The Preview Controls

The Preview controls all deal with a small area of data close to the timeline. Use these controls to set your edit points by ear.

The TO control plays from one second before the timeline up to the timeline. The FROM control plays from the timeline to one second after the timeline. The THRU control plays from one second before to one second after the timeline.

The TO, THRU, and FROM controls play all enabled tracks in the current mix.

The Scrub control continuously loops a small section of audio leading up to the timeline. The Scrub function only plays the currently selected track, not the entire mix.

You can adjust the length of time for the Preview functions in the Utility → Play/Record menu area.

.WAV View

In .WAV view, you can see a visual representation of one track's audio data. You can zoom out enough to identify view several measures of audio or zoom in tight for very precise edits. The vertical zoom controls allow you to magnify the visual representation of the audio to find quieter passages.

Use the .WAV view to set your IN, OUT, FROM, and TO edit points to reference the actual audio events themselves, as shown in Figure 17.13.

Figure 17.13

.WAV view of a kick drum
positioned to the timeline.

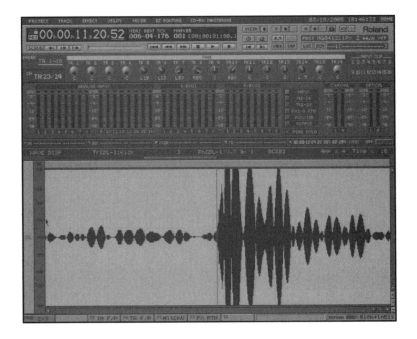

Use the cursor buttons to set the focus to the SubFrames value, and use the Time/Value dial to
precisely position an event in the .WAV display to the timeline.

> ❋ **Search and Destroy Audio Problems**
>
> Use the .WAV view to pinpoint problems and eliminate them. You can easily remove a "popped P" or
> a squeaky bass string by zooming in, selecting the problem with the mouse, and performing a region
> erase procedure on the problem audio.
>
> The smallest phrase the VS-2480 can play is one-half second long, but the VS-2480 can skip over very
> small sections of audio. The "hole" in the track most likely won't be heard in the context of a mix.

Working with Measures and the Grid

If you have recorded your project using the VS-2480's internal metronome, or if you used MIDI
to sync a drum machine to the VS-2480's internal tempo, you can use the VS-2480's measures
and beats counters to set your edit points. This makes it very easy to copy a well-played section
to another part of the song and have it remain in perfect time.

The grid may be displayed in various densities, from whole measures to 32nd notes. If the grid
is displayed, any edited data "snaps" to the closest grid when moved. The grid is especially

useful for editing loops and phrase sequences, but may get in the way when dealing with random-timed events.

After you move or copy data locked to measures and beats, there may be an audible edit—possibly a half of a breath—or any section of audible audio that gets cut into by the edit point. Remember, you can use the Phrase Trim functions to locate an acceptable transition point without disturbing the timing. This combination of using beats to determine the edit points and then adjusting the phrase edges makes for some very efficient editing.

18 } Mixes, Scenes, and Automix

Mixing refers to the process of balancing and combining the individual tracks. The VS-2480 has an extensive set of controls to help shape your tracks. Most of the settings may be automated and altered in real time by the VS-2480 during the final mix, or at any stage in between. You can quickly compare mixes and document custom patches by using scenes.

Record Monitor Selection

Very often there is some form of recording happening as part of the mix process. The VS-2480 has two methods of monitoring recording tracks, Auto and Source. This selection is made on page 1 of the UTILITY → PLAY/REC PARAMETER dialog box.

When the Record monitor is set to Auto, and the VS-2480 is placed into Play mode, the VS-2480 plays the audio, if any, that already exists on any track that is armed to record. When the VS-2480 switches from Play to Record, it automatically switches so you can you hear the audio being sent to the recording track. You can selectively monitor the source audio by pressing the TRACK STATUS button of the desired track, but this gets reset every time the VS-2480 goes back into Play mode. This mode is useful when a performer is punching in and wishes to hear what he has played up until the punch-in point.

When the Record monitor is set to Source, the VS-2480 always presents the audio being sent to the recording channel to the Mix bus. This mode is best for performing track bouncing or submixing operations. Track Mixer outputs that are routed to recording channels are not audible if the recording channel's track status is set to Play.

Submixes

Submixes, sometimes referred to a "stems," are useful for several different reasons. If you are running out of available tracks for your project, performing a submix of a group of similar tracks can create some breathing room for you. You might decide to mix the drums to a stereo pair, the rhythm guitars to a stereo pair, and the background vocals to a stereo pair, and then use these submixes to construct your final mix. Let's look at three ways to create a submix on the VS-2480.

Submixes on the AUX Busses

One very common way to create a submix is using an AUX bus. Every time you send more than one track to a loop effect, you are creating a submix on an AUX bus. The AUX busses may be routed to recording tracks for printing. Linked pairs of AUX busses can be used to create stereo submixes and can be routed to linked pairs of recording tracks.

You can set up the VS-2480 in such a way that you can create AUX mixes using the faders. This feature makes creating a mix on an AUX bus as intuitive as normal mixing, complete with flying faders.

The trick is the VS-2480's Knob/Fader Assign feature. When invoked, it allows either the Pan knobs or the track faders themselves to be used to control any of the eight AUX mixes or a single user-selected parameter across all tracks. I prefer to use the faders instead of the knobs, and I will refer to faders in the rest of this discussion. Make your selection in the UTILITY → GLOBAL PARAMETERS menu.

To invoke the Knob/Fader Assign mode, press the KNOB/FDR ASSIGN button, located along the right side of the Locator/Marker/Scene area. The button flashes to remind you that the faders no longer represent your current main mix. The numeric buttons now become AUX select buttons. Press numeric buttons 1–8 to access the corresponding AUX bus mixes. For each AUX bus mix, you can select any of the four input and track fader groups to view and adjust.

This can all get pretty confusing at first, but with a little practice, you can create and modify AUX mixes with ease.

Submixes via Routing

Using the Routing screen, you can create either a mono or a stereo submix. To create a stereo submix, the destination must be a linked pair of tracks. If you are creating a stereo submix, the standard channel Pan knobs on the individual source tracks will control their stereo placement within the submix.

In the Routing screen's Track Assign area, connect all the source tracks from the Track Mixer to the destination recording track (or track pair).

The Quick Routing feature of the VS-2480 can help you set up your routing in a hurry, using only the TRACK STATUS and CH EDIT buttons. Let's set up a submix using Quick Routing. For our example, we'll set up a mono submix on recording track 9.

Press and hold track 9's TRACK STATUS button. All the TRACK STATUS and CH EDIT buttons except track 9 will start blinking, and the Quick Routing screen, as shown in Figure 18.1, will be presented.

Figure 18.1
The Quick Routing screen.

In Quick Routing, the TRACK STATUS buttons represent the destination recording track, and the CH EDIT buttons represent the sources. The Fader Assign buttons also flash, indicating that you may select sources and destinations from all four fader groups.

Track 9's TRACK STATUS button is solid green, indicating that Track 9 is the destination track. Let's submix tracks 10–13 to track 9. Press each of these four tracks' CH EDIT buttons to select them. As you press each one, a line appears on the Quick Routing screen indicating a connection from the source track to the destination track. Figure 18.2 shows the Quick Routing screen after the four source tracks have been selected

Now that the submix is routed, you must arm the destination track to record in order to monitor the submix. The individual fader and channel strip settings of the source tracks will determine the actual content of the submix. The destination track's fader and channel strip settings will determine how the submix is presented to the Master bus. One advantage of setting up a submix via routing is that you can hear the submix within the context of the entire mix.

Submixes via Mastering

Submixes achieved via the mastering room are always stereo submixes. The process is quite simple. Set up a mix exactly the way you want your submix to sound, all by itself. Invoke the mastering room, but leave the CDR button off. This will create a stereo pair of tracks in the native recording mode of the project. After recording the submix, you may select the V-Tracks 23/24 that contain the submix and phrase move the submix to another set of linked tracks, if desired.

Figure 18.2

A mono submix routing.

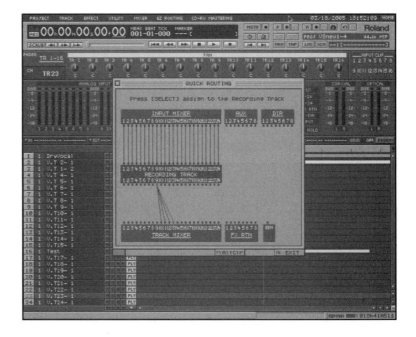

One advantage of creating submixes via the mastering room is the fact that the process is intuitive. What you hear is what you get, including any effects. The main disadvantage is that you cannot hear the rest of the mix. This may be viewed as a distraction by some, but it does allow you to fully concentrate on the submix itself, knowing that the submixed track may be further processed in the final mix.

Using Printed Effects

Printing effects allows you to incorporate more effects into your mix than you physically have. Even with eight possible simultaneous effects, there are times when you will want to print an effect. As mentioned in Chapter 16, "Tracking," both loop and insert effects may be printed.

One reason to print effects is to have more control over how the effect is presented to the mix. Printed effects may be compressed, EQed, and panned to create a more interesting mix. For instance, the width of a stereo effect may be reduced, allowing the effect to be more precisely placed in the stereo image.

Refer to the section on recording effects separately in Chapter 16 to review routing methods for printing effects.

Linked Track Tricks

Many audio sources—including synths, drum machines, microphones, effect units, and others—are recorded on linked pairs of tracks as a stereo signal. If each of your stereo sources simply remains a stereo source all the way to mix, individual sources may begin to be masked as all the stereo sources remain centered in your mix. There are a few adjustments you can make to help each of your stereo sources command its own place in your mix.

To access these parameters, call up the Channel view of a linked pair of tracks. In the lower right corner, under the faders, is a small box marked SUB DISP. In Normal mode, dragging either fader with the mouse automatically drags the other. When you click on the SUB DISP box, it turns red, and the faders and pan controls become individually adjustable. Figure 18.3 illustrates the differences between the Normal and SUB DISP views.

Figure 18.3
Normal and SUB DISP views of the fader section for a linked pair of tracks.

The individual fader controls allow you to compensate for a track that has been recorded with one side softer than the other. In the example above, the left channel has been reduced to compensate for a weak right channel. When in Normal view, the faders are displayed as equal, even if they are not equal in SUB DISP view.

Reducing the width of a stereo track concentrates its presence in the stereo image. The individual pan controls in SUB DISP view allow you to pan each track to exactly where you want it. After the individual controls have been set, you may pan the more concentrated image using the channel pair's master pan setting. The Pan knob icon's shape changes to reflect the new settings. Figure 18.4 show how the Normal full left and full right settings are displayed.

Figure 18.4
Default linked track pan
settings.

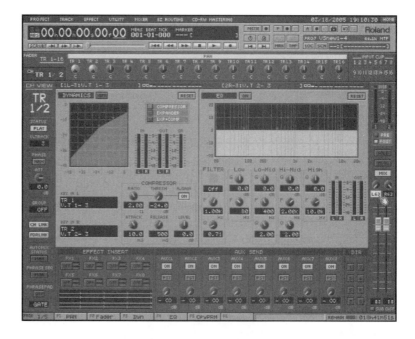

Figure 18.5 shows a linked pair whose individual track panning has been reduced to concentrate the image in the center.

Figure 18.5
Reduced width pan
settings.

Figure 18.6 shows the concentrated image panned left. This method allows the stereo instruments to retain their personality without overtaking the stereo image.

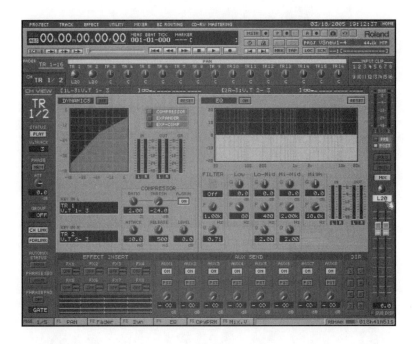

Figure 18.6
Reduced width image panned left.

To be sure, you may obtain the same results simply by panning both of the individual channels to the left and leaving the primary track pan control centered. But by concentrating the stereo track to the center first, you can quickly change the panning on the fly with the primary track Pan knobs.

Using Scenes

When the VS-2480 stores a scene, nearly every important aspect of your current mix is written to your project. Fader positions, EQ settings, pan, dynamics, effects settings, track status... the list of what is stored with each scene is long. Scenes can be used to store tracking setups, submixes, main mixes, or mastering setups for easy recall at a later time.

Similar to locators, there are 100 scenes available for any project. They are organized in 10 banks of 10 and are accessed in the same manner as the locators, with one major difference: The SCN button must be illuminated to store or recall scenes.

Scenes can be named in the Scene dialog box, accessible via the SCN button, as shown in Figure 18.7.

Figure 18.7

Accessing the Scene
dialog box.

The date and time are logged when a scene is stored, and that information is displayed along
with the scene name.

Figure 18.8

The Scene dialog box.

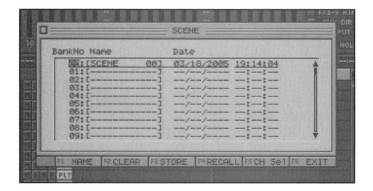

One very useful feature of scenes is the ability to select what channels will be included when a
scene is recalled. Press F5 from the Scene dialog box to access the Scene Active Channel Select
screen, as shown in Figure 18.9.

Figure 18.9

The Scene Active Channel
Select dialog box.

In the above example, tracks 21–24 are set to ignore scene changes. This feature allows you to
combine the best features of several different scenes. By carefully selecting which track, AUX,
and effects setting will be recalled and saving your steps in between, you can share selected
elements of one mix with another.

Let's walk through an example. Let's take a bass track setting from scene 3 and incorporate it into an existing scene 5, saving it as a new scene 6. Here are the steps to take.

1. Verify that all the boxes are filled in on the Scene Active Channel Select screen.

2. Recall scene 5. You may wish to immediately store scene 6, just to mark your intentions.

3. Let's assume your bass is on track 16. In the Scene Active Channel Select screen, click on everything except Track Mixer 16, setting them all to Ignore status. The only box left filled in black should be Track Mixer 16. If the bass mix utilized any effects, you may want to recall that effects setting as well, but be aware of the potential for a change if scene 5 used the effects for something else.

4. Recall scene 3. Track16 should be the only track whose settings were changed.

5. Save the new mix to scene 6.

Scenes are a powerful tool for archiving your progress. Liberal use of scenes will allow you to re-create and modify key elements of your mix.

HINT: WATCH THOSE BUTTONS

Be sure the SCN button is illuminated when selecting or clearing scenes, and the LOC button is illuminated when selecting or clearing locators. It is easy to forget to check this, and the results can be frustrating.

Automix

The VS-2480's Automix feature allows you to automate most of your mix's parameters. Faders, EQ settings, panning, and more may all be put under the precise control of the VS-2480.

Automix data is represented as a list of events that occur at specific times throughout the project. Even gradual fadeouts are represented as a series of discrete points and values.

Automix Controls and Setup

To place the VS-2480 in Automix mode, you may press the AUTOMIX button on either the VS-2480 or the VGA screen. Figure 18.10 show the Automix controls on the VGA screen.

Figure 18.10
The Automix controls.

From left to right are the Automix On/Off, Record/Play, Undo/Redo, and Snapshot controls. When the VS-2480 is in Automix mode, the AUTOMIX button is illuminated, and the CH EDIT buttons represent Automix status, as follows:

Table 18.1   Automix Status Button Colors

Color	Status	Notes
Yellow	MANUAL	The channel will ignore all Automix information.
Red	WRITE	Changes made to the channel settings while in Automix Record mode will be written to the Automix list.
Green	READ	The channel will respond to events in its Automix list.

Even though many of a track's parameters may be Automixed, the VS-2480 lets you decide what will and won't be included. To access the Automix Setup screen, shown in Figure 18.11, you may either hold SHIFT while pressing AUTOMIX or select Automix Setup from the Utility menu.

Figure 18.11
The Automix Setup screen.

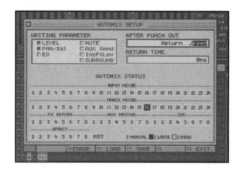

In the above example, while the VS-2480 is in Automix Record mode, changes made to Track Mixer 16's fader level or pan settings will be written to the Automix list.

The After Punch Out selection, when set to Return, will automatically add events to the Automix list that return the parameters to what they were before the control was moved. The Return Time parameter can smooth this out by inserting a series of events over the specified time.

In general, I find it useful to set the After Punch Out parameter to Keep during the initial Automix of any given track and set it to Return while performing corrective or special Automix operations.

Viewing Automix Data

You may view a visual representation of the Automix list data by selecting the UTILITY → AUTOMIX EDIT menu item. The Automix Edit screen resembles the Home view, and the zoom controls work the same way in both views. Automix data is displayed as a series of discrete points, depending on the zoom level. Figure 18.12 shows two tracks in a moderate zoom resolution.

Figure 18.12
The Automix Edit screen, showing Automix data on track 16.

Interestingly enough, Automix data does indeed scroll in real time at all zoom resolutions.

Automix Record Mode

Automix Record mode may be activated either by clicking on the icon on the VGA screen or by holding AUTOMIX and pressing the REC button. The AUTOMIX button flashes and the words Automix Rec flash at the bottom of the VGA display while the VS-2480 is in Automix Record mode. The VS-2480 will stay in Automix Record mode until the STOP button is pressed or until a Stop operation is executed by a loop or preview operation.

Any Automix-enabled control whose value is actually changed while in Automix Record mode will add data to the Automix list.

Automix data is not updated to the Automix Edit display until the VS-2480 exits Automix Record mode.

Automix Snapshots

In addition to writing items to the Automix list by actually adjusting channel parameters, you may take an Automix Snapshot of data. Since a snapshot writes data to the Automix list, the VS-2480 must be in Automix Record mode, and individual channels and features must be enabled.

Figure 18.13 shows the same two tracks, with the addition of an Automix Snapshot taken of both tracks.

Figure 18.13
The Automix Snapshot data appears as a single event.

It is a good idea to take an Automix Snapshot just before the start of a song. The snapshot should represent the nominal, or average, fader settings to be used for your mix. This will ensure that the faders are in the proper positions to begin the song.

Automix After Punch Out Operation

Figure 18.14 show the result of an After Punch Out Return operation. I punched in, brought track 16's fader down to infinity, and punched out. The timeline shows where the punch-out occurred. The VS-2480 added the data required to return the fader to its previous position over 400ms, my selected time value.

Figure 18.14
Automix After Punch
Out data.

If the After Punch Out setting had been set to Keep, the data would not have been added.

Automix Editing

Automix data is not edited along with the track data. That is to say, if you have Automix data associated with an audio track, and you edit the audio track, then the Automix data must be edited separately.

The time-based Automix edit operations are very similar to the corresponding region operations. You may move, copy, erase, cut, and insert data in the same way, using the IN, OUT, FROM, and TO buttons or the mouse.

Automix editing also provides a few ways to edit the Automix data. Gradation will create a series of steps between two values over a length of time. Compress/Expand will either lessen or increase the change to a setting within a selected time period. The SHIFT button will increase or decrease each event by the same amount. Let's see an example of each.

Automix Gradation Demo

Figure 18.15 shows track16 set up for a fade out via the Gradation operation. The IN point is where the fade out will start. I located to that point, pressed IN, and took a snapshot of track 16 to create an Automix list event there. I next located to the end of the audio phrase on track 16, pressed OUT, and took another Automix Snapshot. I next pressed F3 to mark the region between IN and OUT. I could have set my IN and OUT points and marked the region with the mouse, then located to the IN and OUT points to take snapshots. The important thing is to have a region with snapshots at both the IN and OUT points. The region may include any number of tracks.

Figure 18.15

Track16 setup for Automix Gradation.

Now that the region is marked, pressing the Gradation control on the VS-2480 displays the Gradation dialog box, shown in Figure 18.16.

Figure 18.16

Automix Gradation dialog box.

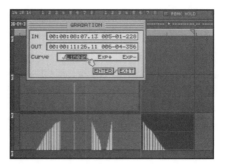

The IN and OUT points are displayed, and you may select from three curve settings. Linear creates a straight line ramp. Exp+ creates an exponential curve whose values change the most at the start of the operation, and Exp– creates an exponential curve that starts gradually and ends quickly. Figure 18.17 shows the result of a Linear Gradation operation.

Figure 18.17
Results of Automix Linear Gradation operation.

Automix COMP/EXP/SHIFT Demo

Figure 18.18 shows track 16 set up for a COMP/EXP/SHIFT operation. I set my IN and OUT points and marked the region with the mouse.

Figure 18.18

Track 16 set up for Automix Comp/Exp/Shift.

Now that the region is marked, pressing the COMP/EXP button on the VS-2480 displays the COMP/EXP dialog box, shown in Figure 18.19.

Figure 18.19

Automix COMP/EXP dialog box.

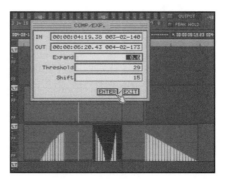

The IN and OUT points are displayed, along with settings for Expand, Threshold, and Shift. Expand is a value by which each existing point will be multiplied. Values of less than 1 reduce the range of the existing data, and values of greater than 1 increase the range of values. Threshold is the base value for the computations. Values will be changed based on their original relation to the Threshold value. The Shift setting is a value that will be applied equally to the results of the multiplication operations. Figure 18.20 shows the result of this operation.

Figure 18.20
Results of Automix COMP/
EXP operation.

Automix Edit Target Section

The Automix Edit Target setting defines what parameters the visible Automix data represents. It can be as specific as the LoMidEQ Gain or as broad as All Track Parameters. Located just above the channel status area of the VGA are the AUTOMIX SECT (Section) and PRM (Parameter) display and selection areas. Figure 18.21 shows the pop-up list of section choices.

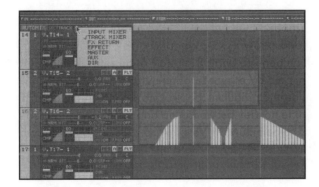

Figure 18.21
Automix Edit Target section
choices.

Depending upon which section is selected, the parameters list may be quite extensive. Figure 18.22 shows the choices for the Track Mixer parameters.

Figure 18.22

Automix Target Track Mixer parameter choices.

Automix Pattern Save and Load

The VS-2480 can store nine separate Automix patterns per project. Access the Automix Pattern Save (or Load) dialog box via the Automix Edit dialog box. As shown in Figure 18.23, Automixes may be named when stored.

You cannot erase stored Automix patterns, but you may save a new pattern over an existing one. Once your Automix pattern has been stored, you may or may not decide to erase the existing Automix data from the current project. The Automix Erase function is accessed via the Automix Setup screen.

Automix Micro Edit

In Micro Edit mode, edits are made to the Automix list directly. Refer to Figure 18.24 for a representation of the Automix Micro Edit screen.

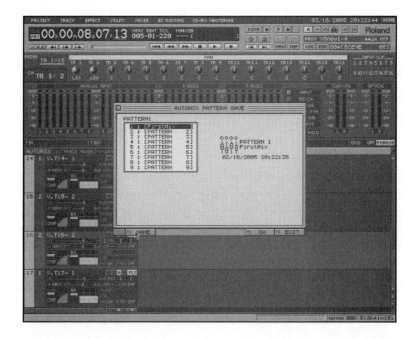

Figure 18.23
Automix Pattern Save dialog box.

Figure 18.24
Automix Micro Edit dialog box.

At the top of the dialog box is a fixed-resolution graphical display of each data event. Below this is a list of Automix events. Each event is displayed on its own line. Time, target parameter, and value information is displayed. You can change the time or the value of a list item, but you cannot change the target parameter. You may delete and create events in the Automix list.

The Micro Edit screen provides a very detailed view, and it provides very precise editing capabilities. It is not, however, particularly user friendly. Proceed slowly when in Automix Micro Edit mode.

Using Scenes and Automix Together

Combining the use of scenes and Automix can really speed up your editing process. I prefer using scenes to store static data—that is, data that does not change for the duration of the song. Scenes hold more data than Automix can alter. For that reason, I like to have a scene that represents the nominal position of all controls for the song being mixed.

I prefer to limit Automix data to parameters that actually need to change during a mix. If a track does not pan, adding pan information to the Automix list only makes edits more difficult. I prefer Automixing a single element—like level, pan, or EQ—at a time.

Individual Track Adjustments

We looked at the channel strips in some depth earlier. It is your starting point in any mix. If you have recorded your tracks "flat," now is the time to get some life into those nice, clean tracks. Here is where you can choose to let you imagination soar or try your best to re-create an authentic reproduction of an intimate live recording. Mixing is an art that is heavily influenced by personal opinion, with very few hard and fast rules, but there are common scenarios that occur when mixing any type of music. Let's look at how to approach some of them on the VS-2480.

EQ Before Dynamics

Recall from our discussion on the VS-2480 channel strips that signals hit the Dynamics processor before they hit the EQ section. Often this is not a problem, but here's an example of how it can be an issue. Let's think of a track—maybe an acoustic guitar—that has too much bass in its track. As we send the signal through the Dynamics processor, the compressor detects the loud bass notes and reduces the overall level accordingly. So we can think of the signal now "pumping" to the over-abundant bass. Now the signal hits the EQ, and we decide to roll off some of that bass. The bass is still there in the Dynamics processor, and the Dynamics processor is still pumping to the bass, but we can't hear the bass. The resulting signal can be a bit unnatural sounding, as it pumps to a component of the sound that we cannot hear. Even if we want to use one of our effects card compressors as an insert, the effects insert is still before the EQ.

One workaround for this would be to print the EQed version of the track to another track, then use the Dynamics processor or an effects insert on the printed track. That's an acceptable solution, but some folks might want to play with the EQ and the dynamics settings to see how one affects the other, and you can't do that with a pre-printed EQ track.

My preferred solution is to route the signal to a second track and route the second track to a third track. Let's assume our bass-heavy guitar track is on track 1, and there are V-Tracks available on track 2 and track 3. Figure 18.25 illustrates the routing required.

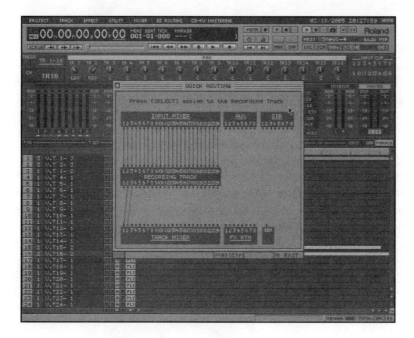

Figure 18.25
Routing for EQ before dynamics recording.

In this example, the EQ will be applied to track 1 and sent to recording track 2. The Dynamics processor on track 2 can now respond to the signal from the EQed guitar track, and the final result will be printed on track 3, as illustrated in Figure 18.26.

Both track 2 and track 3 must be armed to record. The EQed guitar will be printed to track 2, but this track will only consume disk space and may be safely deleted. Remember to store this setup—with routing, EQ, and dynamics settings intact—as a scene in case you wish to repeat the process with modified parameters.

Figure 18.26
Signal flow for EQ before dynamics recording.

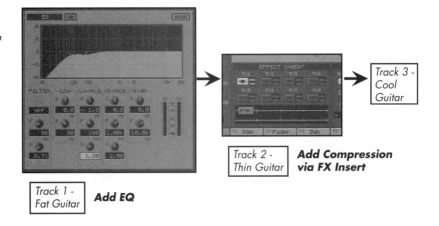

Track 1 - Fat Guitar | **Add EQ**

Track 2 - Thin Guitar | **Add Compression via FX Insert**

Track 3 - Cool Guitar

Kicking a Hole in the Bass

Very often the bass guitar and the bass drum compete to rule the low end of the mix. Trying to resolve this delicate balance without making the tracks sound wimpy or having a lot of overs on the Mix bus can be an exercise in frustration. However, what if you could automatically reduce the bass guitar track each time the bass drum kicks? The Key In feature of the VS-2480's Dynamics processor lets you do exactly that. Refer to Figure 18.27 for an overview of the setup.

Figure 18.27
Using the Key In feature on the bass track.

Track 16 - Bass Guitar

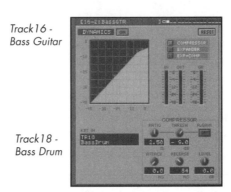

Track 18 - Bass Drum

In this example, the bass on track 16 has been printed as desired, with all the EQ and compression it needs as a bass track. It is important that the hole-in-the-bass trick is applied to the track as the very last process, often as the final mix is happening. The key in has been set to track 18, the bass drum. This means that the Dynamics processor on track 16 will actually respond to the audio on track 18. Set the attack to 0.0ms so the response is immediate, and set the release to a fairly fast rate, or your bass track may seem to drop out longer that needed. Set the threshold according to the strength of the bass drum signal and the ratio for the amount of gain reduction desired.

Another use for this method is to punch holes in overhead drum tracks to bring out the cymbals. You can create a submix of snare, rack, and floor toms, print this to a track, and use the resultant track as a key in source for the overhead tracks. The difference here is that this "hole-in-the-mix" process should be performed and printed before being dynamically processed for the final mix. This will allow your final Dynamics processor to respond to the cymbals, not the snare and toms.

Adding External Sources at Mix Time

Remember, the Input Mixer is also available at mix time! If you have external effects or MIDI-sequenced sound modules you may choose to simply add these sounds to your mix in real time rather than use tracks for them.

Recall from our discussion of the channel strip that the Input Mixer and Track Mixer are virtually identical in layout and operation. Also recall the dynamics limitation: If any Track Mixer channel requires both compression and expansion, no dynamics will be available for the Input Mixer.

Input Mixer parameters may be Automixed just like Track Mixer parameters.

19 Tempo Map, Metronome, Sync, and MIDI

The VS-2480's Tempo Map allows you to create an outline of the basic rhythmic structure in your project. Using MIDI messages, Tempo Map information can be shared with other MIDI devices that will allow them to synchronize to the VS-2480. Many drum machines and synthesizers have the ability to replay sequenced performances under the command of the VS-2480. It is possible to add these live sound sources to the mix via the Input Mixer, freeing up additional recording tracks.

> ❋ **PLAN AHEAD!**
>
> Recordings that are synchronized to the VS-2480's Tempo Map are easier to edit because the VS-2480 can locate to precise measures and beats. You can easily take exactly one measure and copy it to cover a mistake in a corresponding measure somewhere else in the project. If the edit is not clean after the copy, you can quickly switch to .WAV view, observe the edit points, and use the Phrase Trim functions to adjust the edit points without changing the timing.

Metronome

Discussions and experiments with tempo will be easier if we can actually hear the tempo, so let's take a look at the metronome first. The VS-2480's metronome can provide three different types of click sounds or—my favorite when working with songs in their earliest stages—a little beat box of drum sounds. Access the metronome via the Utility menu. The metronome setup screen is shown in Figure 19.1.

The Metronome Out choices are OFF, INT (Internal), or MIDI. If INT is selected, the INT LEVEL setting controls the volume of the metronome. If MIDI is selected, MIDI messages are sent from the VS-2480 to trigger external sound sources. For our discussion, we'll select INT and leave the LEVEL at 0.0dB.

Figure 19.1

The metronome setup screen.

The metronome only sounds while the VS-2480's transport is moving, but it may be further limited to only sound while recording. The mode choices of Rec Only or Rec&Play determine when the metronome will be heard. Another option is printing the metronome to a track, turning the metronome off entirely, and performing to the printed copy instead. Let's set the mode to Rec&Play. After making the setting, you should be able to press the PLAY button on the VS-2480 and hear the metronome. Press the STOP button to silence the metronome. If you press PLAY again, the metronome will continue from where it was stopped. You may press the ZERO button to force the metronome to start on a downbeat.

The Tone Type selections provide access to a traditional click track (CLICK1), a beeping type of click track (CLICK2), a click track where you can customize the notes (CLICK2(Note)), and the drums. When using either of the first two click settings, the first beat of the measure is accented. When using the CLICK2(Note) setting, you can customize the accent and normal notes and their velocities in the MIDI settings area of the Metronome screen. These adjustments also control any externally connected MIDI sound generator if the metronome is set for MIDI output.

When the drums are selected, a Pattern Edit screen is available. Figure 19.2 shows the default 4/4 drum pattern.

In the upper right of the Pattern Edit screen are controls to adjust the tempo and time signature. The Percussion selection in the upper left lets you add handclaps, cowbell, or maracas to the hi hat, snare drum, and bass drum. The number of beats enabled for editing depends on the selected

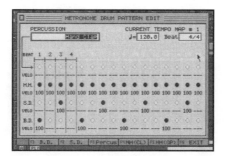

Figure 19.2
The Pattern Edit screen.

time signature. Under each beat, you may select which of the four available sounds will be played on that beat. You can also adjust the velocity of each sound played. With a little experimentation, surprisingly complex patterns can be created.

For percussion, snare drum, and bass drum, a grey circle indicates a rest, and a black ball in the grid represents a note played. For the hi hat, a grey circle indicates a rest, a black ball indicates a closed hi hat sound, and a black circle indicates an open hi hat sound. Velocity of each note played is adjustable from 0 to 127. Figure 19.3 illustrates the use of these features in a simple 6/8 pattern.

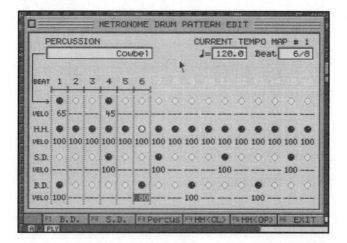

Figure 19.3
A simple pattern in 6/8 time.

You can spend a lot of time playing with the pattern editor, but, unfortunately, the internal drum sounds themselves leave a bit to be desired and, in most cases, won't be heard on a final project. They are useful, however, for providing a hint of a rhythmic feel early on in a project's development. Since the metronome is tied to the VS-2480's Tempo Map, the metronome can easily be replaced by a sequenced drum track later on.

Printing the Metronome

Another option is to print the metronome to a track and then turn the metronome off entirely and perform to the printed copy of it instead. This makes it easy and convenient to control the level of the click track while performers are tracking. The metronome is available as one of the source options of the GEN/OSC. To print the metronome, first select it in the GEN/OSC screen and then route the output of the GEN/OSC to a recording track.

Tempo Map

The Tempo Map is the heart of the VS-2480's timekeeping abilities. You can create a song that has a constant tempo, insert the odd measure of an alternate time signature, and even program gradual tempo changes via the Tempo Map. A sync track is similar to the Tempo Map, but you cannot edit a sync track. Access the Tempo Map screen via the Utility menu or by holding SHIFT and pressing TAP.

In the VS-2480 manual, the term Tempo Map is used in two ways. It defines a single Tempo Map as the combination of a specific time signature and a specific tempo, starting at a specific measure number. The collection of these individual Tempo Maps is also referred to as the Tempo Map of the project. For convenience, I'll refer to a project's Tempo Map as having individual zones. Any new song has only one zone, with one tempo and one time signature, and that time signature starts at measure 1. Figure 19.4 shows the initial configuration of the Tempo Map screen.

Figure 19.4
The initial Tempo Map screen.

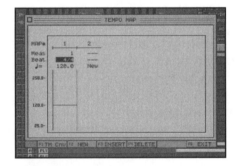

At the top of the screen we see map 1, below which we see the measure at which this map starts (1), the time signature of this map (4/4), and the tempo of the map. The horizontal line across the bottom two-thirds of the screen also indicates BPM. Let's add a new zone and discuss the settings.

First, press or click F2(NEW). A new Tempo Map zone is created with the same time signature and tempo as its predecessor. Let's pick up the tempo from 120 to 160BPM at the ninth measure. Highlight the BPM and Measure fields to adjust their settings. Figure 19.5 shows the newly created and edited Tempo Map.

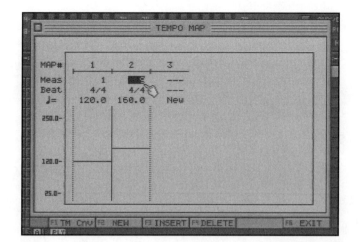

Figure 19.5
A Tempo Map with two individual maps.

Let's go ahead and add two more new maps, keeping the same tempo but changing to 6/4 at measure 17, then back to 4/4 at measure 18. Figure 19.6 illustrates these edits.

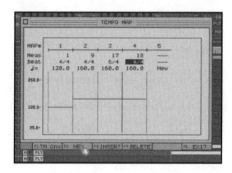

Figure 19.6
A more complex Tempo Map.

The VS-2480 places measure markers in the grey bar just above the playlist area. Each black vertical line represents the first beat of a measure. If you choose to adjust the MEAS (measure) counter in the Time Transport display, you can use the Time/Value dial or the mouse to position your timeline precisely to the start of any measure. In Figure 19.7, we have selected measure 17, and we can see the timeline positioned directly under a measure marker.

Recall from our Tempo Map that measure 17 was in 6/4, and notice the difference in distance among the measure markers indicating the 4/4 measures surrounding measure 17. The measure markers give you a rough visual indication of the project's tempo.

Figure 19.7

Measure markers at measure 17.

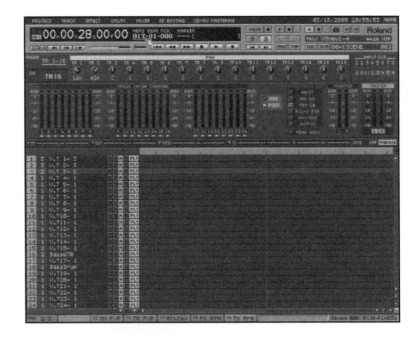

Implementing Gradual Tempo Changes

Remember, the Tempo Map is limited to working with whole measures. However, with clever programming, you can have very exact control over gradual changes in a project's tempo. The trick lies in the VS-2480's ability to create arbitrary time signatures with 16th-note resolution.

Let's imagine a song in 4/4 time with an eight-measure intro at 120BPM, accelerating to 200BPM during the last two measures of the intro. First we'll set up two zones and set the second zone to the desired 200BPM at measure 9, as shown in Figure 19.8.

Figure 19.8

A sudden jump in tempo.

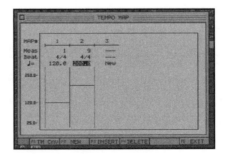

With MAP (zone) 2 selected, press or click F3 (INSERT) two times to insert two single-measure zones into the Tempo Map, as shown in Figure 19.9.

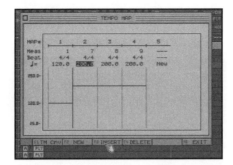

Figure 19.9
Two zones inserted.

You may set the tempo of the zones with the Time/Value dial or by dragging the zone's horizontal tempo indicator line with the mouse. The idea is to create a series of steps from one tempo to another. Figure 19.10 illustrates the results.

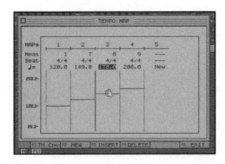

Figure 19.10
Accelerating by
whole measures.

OK, that's great... or at least it's better than one sudden jump. Let's make it smoother by doubling the number of steps.

Recall that the Temp Map only works with whole measures, so if we wish to have the tempo change within a measure, we must create smaller measures. Four measures of 2/4 time take the same amount of time as two measures of 4/4 time, but the former allows us to create four steps of tempo change instead of only two. Figure 19.11 shows the result of this change to the Tempo Map.

As the sharp-eyed reader may have noticed, this solution introduces a problem—the Tempo Map measure count no longer matches the actual measure count of the score. The 200BPM tempo desired at measure 9 now occurs at measure 11, but there is the same number of beats. Furthermore, any sequenced devices that respond to MIDI song pointer messages will need to be programmed in the same way—four measures of 2/4 instead of two measures of 4/4—to allow them to locate correctly in response to MIDI messages sent from the VS-2480.

Figure 19.11
Fooling the Tempo
Map with smaller-
sized measures.

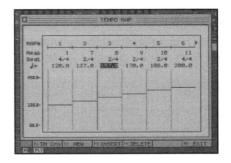

The expressive power of this programming cannot be denied, however, and are generally worth the concessions. Tempo Map zones as small as a sixteenth note may be created for very precise control. As the tempo of a project decreases, the ability to control the tempo in smaller increments becomes more important.

Synchronization

Keeping multiple devices "locked" as they play, record, or locate is called "synchronization." In synchronization schemes, there is one master and one or more slaves. The VS-2480 may be synchronized to incoming professional SMPTE or MIDI Time Code (MTC) signals. Another form of synchronization, MIDI Clock, is used to control some MIDI devices, but it is not precise enough to control the VS-2480. The VS-2480 may, however, use received MIDI Clock messages to construct a sync track. The sync track MIDI Clock data may then be broadcast by the VS-2480 for other units to follow. The VS-2480 may also be set up to broadcast MIDI Time Code derived from its internal Tempo Map.

To access the VS-2480's Sync Parameter screen, as illustrated in Figure 19.12, hold SHIFT and press the EXT SYNC button, or use the Utilities menu.

Figure 19.12
The Sync Parameter
screen.

In any synchronization scheme, there can be only one master controller but any number of slave devices. Setting the Sync mode to INT (Internal) will put the VS-2480 in Master mode, and setting it to EXT (External) will put the VS-2480 in Slave mode.

The external sync source allows the VS-2480 to receive MTC via the MIDI IN jack or either R-BUS connector, or to receive SMPTE from the SMPTE IN jack. The Sync with Gap setting determines what the VS-2480 will do if the sync signal is interrupted. If set to OFF, the VS-2480 will stop when the sync signal is interrupted. If set to ON, the VS-2480 will continue to play for a while in anticipation of receiving another sync command soon. The error level determines how tightly the VS-2480 anticipates sync commands. Lower error level settings result in tight synchronization at the risk of increased dropouts.

The selection of frame rate, expressed in fps (frames per second), must match the application at hand. 30fps is standard for audio work. Other rates are primarily used for synchronization with video equipment, and the frame rate setting will be dictated by the video equipment.

The sync offset time may be adjusted to compensate for differences in project start times between the VS-2480 and an external device.

The three sync generator control boxes determine what sync signals, if any, will be transmitted by the VS-2480. The MIDI OUT may send MTC, MIDI Clock, or sync track events. R-BUS devices only sync via MTC.

Recording a Sync Track from an External Source

The VS-2480 has the ability to record a sync track from the MIDI Clock and song pointer information received from an external MIDI device. The VS-2480 can then construct a Tempo Map from the recorded sync track. After the VS-2480 has the sync track information, the external device(s) may be set to synchronize to the VS-2480's commands.

To record the sync track, the MIDI OUT of the external device must be connected to the MIDI IN of the VS-2480. Call up the Sync Parameter screen. Verify that the Sync mode is set to internal and select F1 STrRec. The message Waiting for Start Command will be displayed, as shown in Figure 19.13.

Figure 19.13
Ready to record a
sync track.

When the external device begins to send sync data, the VS-2480 displays a running count of measures and beats, as shown in Figure 19.14.

Figure 19.14

Recording a sync track.

The VS-2480 does not play any tracks while recording a sync track, nor does its time display increment. The only indication of progress is the running counter in the dialog box. When the sequence ends, the VS-2480 automatically exits Sync Track Record mode.

To convert the sync track to a Tempo Map, call up the Tempo Map screen and select F1 TM Cnv. Select Sync Track to Tempo Map conversion and the time signature of the sync track. Unfortunately, this conversion is limited to a single time signature, even if the original performance included alternate time signatures.

Creating a Sync Track from Time Points

If you know the exact starting and ending points of a song, you know the number of measures in the song, and the song is in a constant tempo, the VS-2480 can build a Tempo Map for you. One side effect of this is that the sync track will start measure 1 of the Tempo Map at the point specified, even if that point is not at zero. The VS-2480's metronome will not play until the VS-2480 reaches the beginning of the sync track. Figure 19.15 shows the Tempo Map Convert dialog box, set for 18 measures of 4/4 in exactly 20 seconds.

Figure 19.15

The Tempo Map Convert
dialog box.

In theory, this feature should allow you to import a song that is constant in tempo, pick two points that are exactly 32 measures apart (downbeat to downbeat), and create a Tempo Map for the song. I have had mixed results using this method. Perhaps the initial timing generator of my source tracks was slightly erratic.

This method works great for creating commercial spots, however. Just dial in 20 seconds (or however long the project will be) and select the number of measures to create, and you'll have a perfectly timed project.

Creating a Tempo Map from Tap Points

If your project is in a constant time signature, you can place tap points at each beat or downbeat, and the VS-2480 will create a Tempo Map for you. All you need to set are the time signature and the number of taps you placed per measure. Once again, this process is not perfect, but it can get you in the ballpark.

MIDI

There are several other MIDI parameters that determine how your VS-2480 behaves in a MIDI environment. You can save and restore scenes, user routings, and user effect patches via MIDI. Access the MIDI Parameter screen, shown in Figure 19.16, from the Utility menu.

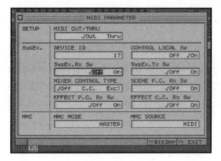

Figure 19.16
The MIDI Parameter
screen.

There are three main sections of the MIDI Parameter screen.

SETUP

The MIDI OUT jack may be switched from MIDI OUT operation to a MIDI THRU function. This may be useful in situations where the VS-2480 is a slave and another slave unit requires the MIDI signal. Setting the MIDI OUT to the THRU mode allows daisy-chaining of MIDI devices, as the VS-2480 will simply repeat any MIDI messages it receives and add no MIDI information of its own.

SysEx. (System Exclusive)

SysEx. is a standard MIDI abbreviation of system exclusive and refers to MIDI messages that are solely intended for specific device control. The settings you choose in this section determine the behavior of advanced features in the VS-2480's interface.

The Device ID refers to the VS-2480's own MIDI IN. The Control Local switch determines if the faders will "fly"—that is, respond to bank selection, scene, and Automix data. When set to OFF, the VS-2480 continues to regulate the mix as it normally would, executing Automix fader commands internally, but the faders themselves do not physically move.

The SysEx.Rx and SysEx.Tx switches determine if the VS-2480 will receive (Rx) and/or transmit (Tx) system exclusive messages. The VS-2480 can transmit or respond to MIDI SysEx messages that represent fader, EQ, dynamics, scenes, and effects parameters. This data stream can be recorded on an external MIDI sequencer, if desired, and then played back into the VS-2480, which will adjust its controls in response to the received messages. The Mixer Control Type setting, when set to EXCL (Exclusive), exposes almost every variable of every Input and Track Channel, even more than what is included in the Automix list. When the Mixer Control Type setting is set to C.C. (Control Change), the VS-2480 may receive scene program change messages, effects program change messages, and effects control change messages. Reception of these three types of messages may be selectively enabled by the three off/on boxes.

MMC (MIDI Machine Code)

MIDI Machine Code messages include those that control the transport or place the machine in Record mode. The VS-2480 may be either the MMC master (transmits MMC messages) or it may be an MMC slave (responds to MMC messages). MMC messages may be received from the MIDI IN jack or from either R-BUS port.

BlkDmp (Bulk Dump)

The Bulk Dump feature is used to share VS-2480 data via a MIDI SysEx dump of data. This data can be received and saved as a file on a PC with a MIDI interface or a MIDI sequencer. The data may then be reloaded into the VS-2480 at a later time. This feature is useful for those times when you must update the OS and for sharing scene data between projects. Figure 19.17 shows the Bulk Dump dialog box.

The Bulk Dump dialog box is divided into three sections. Multiple sections may be enabled simultaneously. In the example above, scene 1 and all user effects patches will be transmitted. Refer to Figure 19.18 for a representation of a Bulk Dump Transmit progress screen.

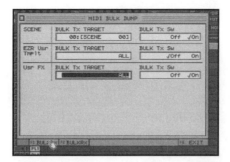

Figure 19.17
The MIDI Bulk Dump
dialog box.

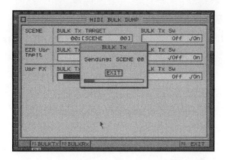

Figure 19.18
A MIDI bulk dump transmit
in progress.

To receive bulk data, press F2(BULKRx), and a waiting message will appear. Once the MIDI data begins to arrive, the VS-2480 displays what is being downloaded, as shown in Figure 19.19.

Figure 19.19
A MIDI bulk dump recep-
tion in progress.

After all the data has been sent, you must press or click EXIT to let the VS-2480 know there is no more data. The VS-2480 will present a data confirmation screen, as shown in Figure 19.20.

This semi-cryptic message is a verification that you do indeed wish to replace the current VS-2480 data with the data that was just received via the bulk dump. Press or click YES to apply the received data to the VS-2480's memory.

Figure 19.20

The MIDI data verification
dialog box.

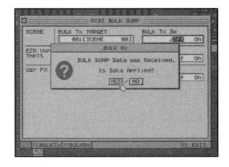

During the bulk dump process, the VS-2480 will remind you that you need to enable SysEx. if
you have forgotten. If no data has arrived when a bulk reception is terminated by pressing Enter,
the VS-2480 notifies the user of this fact.

Appendix

The VS-2000CD Workstation

The VS-2000CD workstation is the latest Roland V-Studio. The VS-2000CD, shown in Figure A.1, provides 20 tracks, eight XLR inputs, and support for third-party plug-ins using the optional VS8F-3 Effect Expansion Board. Connecting a mouse and keyboard is possible by using the optional VS20-VGA Output Board.

The VS-2000CD includes the following features:

❋ A 20-track digital studio with 40GB hard drive, CD-RW drive, and plug-in support

❋ Eighteen playback tracks, 320 V-Tracks, and stereo mastering track

❋ Support for 24-bit and 16-bit recording at 44.1kHz

❋ Eight balanced XLR/TRS inputs with phantom power

❋ A 40-channel digital mixer with channel dynamics and 4-band EQ, onboard effects, and mastering tools

❋ New Harmony Sequence function adds realistic harmonies to vocals

❋ Third-party plug-in support with optional VS8F-3 Effect Expansion Boards

❋ Tracks 17–18 double as stereo rhythm track with onboard drum sounds

❋ Support for mouse-based editing using optional VS20-VGA and monitor

❋ USB 2.0 for hi-speed data transfer, .WAV/AIFF import, and .WAV export

❋ V-LINK video control support*

Note: *V-LINK requires Edirol DV-7PR with software version 1.50 or higher (sold separately).

Figure A.1
Roland VS-2000CD Digital
Studio Workstation.

The VS-2000CD offers CD-quality recording at a choice of 16 or 24 bits. With the high-quality 24-bit mode, you get up to eight tracks of simultaneous recording and 12-track playback. An internal 40GB hard drive provides hours of reliable multitrack recording, while 320 V-Tracks give you all the room you'll need to be creative and "comp" the perfect take.

Whether you want to mic up a drum set or record multiple vocalists, you'll appreciate the VS-2000CD's eight XLR/TRS inputs with phantom power. Want to record a guitar? There's a HI-Z input as well, plus an S/PDIF digital input. The VS-2000CD's 40-channel digital mixer makes mixing inputs, tracks, and effect returns a snap, thanks to 17 faders and dedicated channel edit knobs. In addition, there are four knobs for controlling the dynamics and 4-band EQ for any input or track.

Right out of the box, the VS-2000CD comes with onboard effects that include essentials like reverb, delay, and chorus, plus Dynamics processors, EQ, and more. You also get access to Roland's coveted COSM effects like guitar amp and mic modeling. When you're ready to master, select the Mastering Tool Kit with multiband compression and burn a CD via the internal CD-RW drive.

By installing an optional VS8F-3 Effect Expansion Board (the VS-2000CD has room for two), you can bring the exciting world of plug-ins right to your V-Studio. Every VS8F-3 includes a selection of high-quality Roland plug-ins to get you started, and with optional plug-ins available from a growing list of third-party developers—including Antares, IK Multimedia, Massenburg, and Universal Audio—it's an exciting time to own a V-Studio.

The VS-2000CD comes with several new tools designed to help you make better recordings—and better music. Using the new Harmony Sequence function, vocalists can add instant harmonies to their performance. You can even program drums on tracks 17-18 using the new Rhythm Track feature. With lots of preset drum sounds included, it's like having a built-in drum machine! A handy chromatic tuner is also included so guitarists can tune up before recording.

By adding the optional VS20-VGA Output Board (with Version 2.0 software), users gain full mouse and monitor support, making working with the VS-2000CD feel more like using software. Simply connect your VGA monitor and mouse, and you can perform drag-and-drop editing and mix your tracks using a sleek software interface. With a mouse and monitor, you get the best of both worlds: reliable Roland hardware with the speed and flexibility of software.

With USB 2.0, you can transfer data between the VS-2000CD and a computer quickly and easily. This new generation of USB offers more than twice the bandwidth of the previous USB standard, making it faster than ever to load audio to and from your V-Studio. Using the bundled conversion software for Mac and PC, you can transfer V-Studio files to your computer desktop, where they can be converted to .WAV or AIFF format. Or simply use the built-in CD-RW drive to load and convert .WAV/AIFF files, or convert V-Studio files to .WAV format for export.

Thanks to Roland's V-LINK technology, you can easily integrate video material with your music. Just connect an optional Edirol video editor, and you can trigger clips or create effects like transitions and dissolves using the VS-2000CD's faders.

Last Minute Tips for Getting the Best out of Your VS Workstation

No matter which VS workstation you have, there are things you can do to keep your machine running in tip-top condition. By adhering to the following tips, you should be able to get the most out of your VS workstation and enjoy its performance for many years to come.

Use Undo Often

Your VS workstation records to a hard drive just like you find on a regular computer. The more you understand how a computer hard drive works, the more you will be able to understand how to maintain your VS hard drive.

When you overdub or punch in repeatedly, the older data remains on the drive. This is how your VS workstation is able to have 999 levels of undo. In most cases, this extra data is not needed and is only taking up valuable recording space on your hard drive.

If you are pretty sure you will not need the current take, use the UNDO button to delete it, instead of recording over it, before proceeding to the next take. This is a good habit to develop and will help keep your hard drive running smoothly.

Optimize at the End

Another way to rid your hard drive of all those unwanted takes is by using the Song Optimize function. This function deletes all the Undo levels stored in the song's memory. When you are finished with your song, and you are sure that you will not need to recall any previous takes (not V-Tracks), use Song Optimize and then save your song to the hard drive. Song Optimize also frees up additional space that can be used for recording other songs.

Save Your Work

If you have worked on any computer before, you probably realize the frustration of losing your work due to a power failure or freeze-up. If you are working on a song and the power source is interrupted, everything you have done after your last save will be lost. If you haven't saved your song at all, then the entire song will be lost. There is no magic button on the VS that will recover this data.

The only way to prevent such a nightmare from happening is by saving your work often. There is a shortcut for saving your work quickly, so remember it and perform it often. Hold SHIFT and press ←← (STORE). Then press YES.

Pressing the Transport Control Buttons

Most lock-ups and failures are caused by incorrectly pressing the transport buttons. On most VS workstations, you have ZERO, REWIND, FAST FORWARD, STOP, PLAY, and RECORD buttons. The button that gets overlooked the most is STOP.

If you are in Play mode, try to make it a habit to use STOP before pressing the other transport buttons. This gives your VS a chance to stop what it is doing and prepare for the next command. Pressing too many transport buttons at a time or pressing them too fast can cause your VS workstation to lock up or freeze. Many times, the only way to unlock the VS is by turning off the power. Unfortunately, you will lose any unsaved data by doing so.

Sometimes, if you press the transport buttons too fast, you may notice the VS will get caught in Play mode and won't stop playing no matter what buttons you push. If this happens to you, press the STOP button one time and let the VS play as long as it can until it stops on its own. If it gets to the end of the song and keeps playing even after you pressed STOP, you may have to restart the machine and lose your data.

There are some transport functions you can use without pressing STOP. For example, while the VS is in Play mode, you can press any marker or locator to move around. You can also press the REW and FF buttons while in Play mode, but don't press them too many times in rapid succession. If you need to move around faster, press STOP and then press the appropriate transport buttons as fast as you like.

Drive Busy

The dreaded "drive busy" message occurs when your hard drive is too busy to perform what you just asked of it. This is the hard drive's way of telling you that it has not yet finished performing the last function and it cannot proceed with the new function until it's done.

The best way to avoid the drive busy message is by following the advice under "Pressing the Transport Control Buttons."

Some other common causes of drive busy messages are:

* ❅   An overly fragmented hard drive
* ❅   A hard drive that does not have enough space left to smoothly perform the operation

An overly fragmented hard drive can be fixed by performing a drive initialization, as described in the section "Defragging," later in this appendix.

You can recover hard drive space by performing Song Optimize on songs where the Undo history is no longer needed. If you have an external CD-RW burner, you can back up your songs to CD-R and then initialize the hard drive.

INITIALIZING THE HARD DRIVE

Initializing the hard drive will erase all songs currently on the hard drive on all partitions. Always back up any songs you want to keep before performing this function.

Once the drive initialization is complete, load the song you were working on back into your VS. Now you should be able to continue working on the song without drive busy messages.

Shutting Down

When you shut down your PC, you have to press START → Turn Off Computer → Turn Off. Since your VS workstation also uses a computer hard drive, there is a specific procedure for shutting it down, too. Always perform this procedure when you are ready to turn off your VS workstation. This will also help in preventing the hard drive from becoming overly fragmented.

Hold SHIFT and press STOP (Shut/Eject). Then press YES. It will ask you if you want to save the current song. Press YES if you need to save it or press NO if you don't.

Leaving the VS Workstation Turned On

This topic has been debated in the computer world for years. Some computer users leave their computers turned on at all times. Some turn their computers off when they are done using them. Which answer is right for your VS workstation?

The right answer is there is no right answer. This will be a personal choice of yours, depending on which philosophy you subscribe to. I personally turn my VS off when I am done using it for that day, but I have read about others who never turn it off and have never had any problems.

Defragging

Fragmented files are files that have holes or spaces between them. A computer hard drive will become fragmented from the inevitable process of adding and deleting data. In a Windows operating system, you can go to your System Tools and defrag your hard drive, but how can you defrag your VS workstation?

Your VS workstation does not have a defragging option, so you will need to use other methods. There are several ways to maintain an unfragmented and healthy hard drive.

The best method is by using the UNDO button frequently and optimizing your songs when completed. After years of use, it is still possible that your hard drive can become fragmented. In that case, the best method for defragging your hard drive is backing up all your songs and then initializing the hard drive with physical format turned on. When you initialize the hard drive, all audio files are deleted with the low-level format. The recovery process puts all the files together and removes any spaces or gaps that are between them. The files are now contiguous files (files with no spaces between them). Contiguous files are easier to manage, and they allow your hard drive to operate smoother.

If you don't have an optional CD-RW burner connected to your VS workstation, here is another way to defrag the space on your hard drive:

※ Use Song Copy Playable to copy all the songs from your current partition to an empty partition.

※ Delete all the songs from the original partition. The original partition is now defragged. You can start a new song or copy another song to that partition to work on.

The reason this works is because all the files have been deleted off the current partition. Since there are no files left on the partition, there are no files, holes, or spaces to "jump over" to access data. Thus, you will be working with only contiguous files.

Muting Inputs

Always mute any inputs you are not using while recording tracks. This will prevent unnecessary noise from being accidentally recorded to your song.

Tilting a VS Workstation

Is it okay to tilt your VS workstation? This question gets asked a lot. The answer is yes. There are stands you can sit the VS on that allow it to sit at an angle. This provides for easier viewing of the LCD, buttons, and controls.

Using the Monitor Knob as a Pan Knob

Some VS workstations have dedicated Pan knobs. Others, such as the VS-1680, do not. You can use the Monitor knob as a Pan knob for any track or channel you want by doing the following:

1. Press the CHANNEL EDIT button for the track or channel you want to adjust pan settings for.

2. While holding the CHANNEL EDIT button, turn the Monitor knob and you will see the pan display move on the screen. You will also hear the pan move in your speakers.

❋ **BE CAREFUL**

If you use this method to adjust the pan to the far right, remember to return the Monitor knob back to your original position when done or you can end up with your monitor volume being turned up too loud, which can cause possible damage to your monitors.

This will only be a concern if your monitors are physically connected to the monitor out jacks and not the master out jacks. I connect my monitors to my master out jacks to avoid this problem.

Releasing Insert Effects

So many times, new VS workstation users wonder why they are not able to select a loop effect after using an insert effect. The reason is because the insert effect is tying up the effects card so that it can't be used for other effects.

The best tip I can give you for using insert effects is to un-insert them after you are done using them. This will always ensure that your effects cards are ready to be used for any effect you want.

Keeping the Dust Out

Dust is a major enemy to the VS workstation. It can creep inside your VS and cause unwanted static noise when you move your faders. Once the dust gets inside your VS, it's very hard to get it out, short of opening the VS and using a light vacuum or duster. This would be a very last resort, and I don't recommend it—you could potentially damage something inside your machine and even void your warranty, depending on what damage you cause.

The best way to keep dust out of your VS workstation is by covering it up when not in use. They have specially made VS dust covers that you can purchase, or you can use any piece of cloth that is big enough to cover it. I have been using a bathroom towel to cover mine for several years. It works great.

Online Forums and Support

VS-Planet: http://www.vsplanet.com

VS-Planet is an international online community dedicated to helping its members learn and master Roland's VS line of digital audio workstations. Now into its sixth year with over 13,000 registered members, VS-Planet is the world's largest online VS user group. The community's goal is to provide a one-stop resource for VS musicians and home recordists to learn and get help with their recording problems. This forum-based site hopes to flatten the learning curve by providing numerous resources for VS users to collaborate and exchange ideas with other VS users from around the world!

In addition to being a technical resource, another goal of VS-Planet is to foster artist development and provide an avenue for artists to get their music into the hands and ears of the public. To that end, VS-Planet Radio (VSPR) is an online radio station that features the music of the independent artists of VS-Planet. In addition, VS-Planet provides full-service artist benefits, such as publishing and distribution. The VS-Planet Music Center is an online music store, featuring the best deals on pro audio gear, including Roland VS workstations, third-party plug-ins, accessories, and more.

VS-Planet International is a wholly owned subsidiary and registered trademark of Virtual Studio Systems, Inc. (VSS), a privately held corporation founded in September 1999 and a member of NAMM since November 2000. The company's goal is to promote musical creativity and deliver the finest online solutions to problems encountered by musicians, songwriters, and home and project studio engineers. For more information about VSS and VS-Planet, contact information@virtualstudiosystems.com, visit their Web sites at http://www.virtualstudiosystems.com (VSS) and http://www.vsplanet.com (VS-Planet), or call (888) 732-1176.

Roland US: http://www.rolandus.com

Roland US provides information and support for a number of products, including the VS workstations. You can download product manuals and operating system upgrades and view the schedule of upcoming events and clinics around the country. You can also view interactive product demos and videos of various VS workstations and third-party plug-ins.

The Track Talk Recording Community (http://www.rolandus.com/tracktalk) is dedicated to educating VS and BR buffs, entertaining Roland and BOSS recording newbies, and just plain cutting through the geek speak so anyone can understand digital audio workstations.

}Index

Numerics

2-band EQ, 52

3-band EQ, 52

4-Band EQ, 229

24 bit internal AD converters, 138

A

After Punch-Out operation, Automix function,
    272–273

algorithms and effect blocks, 32

amplifier simulator effects, 33

analog connections, 18

analog inputs

    VS-880 and VS-890 series, 39

    VS-1680 workstation, 133

    VS-2480 workstation, 211–213

analog outputs, VS-880 and VS-890 series, 39

analog transfers, 122–123

arming tracks, 62

ATT track parameter, 87

attenuation settings, 180

Auto Punch recording, 63–64, 152–153

Automix function

    After Punch-Out operation, 272–273

    best use of, 95–96

    COMP/EXP/SHIFT operation, 275–276

    controls and setup, 269–270

    data, viewing, 270–271

    discussed, 35, 89

    display, adjusting, 191–192

    Edit Target section, 277–278

    enabling, 91

    Gradation, 94, 195–197, 273–274

    Micro Edit mode, 278–280

    patterns, 278

    Realtime Automix records, 91–92, 192–193

    Record mode, 271

    scenes with, 92

    Snapshot Automix, 93–94, 193–195, 271–272

    VS-880/890 compatibility, 90

AUX buses, 181–182, 262

AUX MSTR channels, 215

AUX Sends, 229

B

backing up

    discussed, 50

    projects, 233–234

    songs to CDs, 118–120

backup vocal tracks, recording techniques, 67

Band Eliminate Filter (BEF), 228

Band Pass Filter (BPF), 228

bar display, VS-880 front panel layout, 48

bar/measure display, VS-1680 workstation, 127

Bass-Cut Filter (BC) effect block, MTK, 112, 204

beat, editing functions, 76

BEF (Band Eliminate Filter), 228
BlkDmp (Bulk Dmp), 296–298
bouncing tracks, 153–154
  drum tracks, 107
  with external effects, 105–106
  with Insert effects, 102–103
  mono and stereo bouncing, 96–97
  performing, 99–101
  rhythm tracks, 107–108
  routings, creating, 97
  send/return effects, 103–105
  Track Mixer mode, 27
  using internal effects, 101–105
BPF (Band Pass Filter), 228
Bulk Dump (BlkDmp), 296–298
burning songs
  to CDs, 114–118
  DAO (Disc-At-Once) option, 115–116
  SCSI CD burner limitations, 114–115
  TAO (Track-At-Once) option, 115
buzzing noises, 225

C
CD Capture function, VS-1824 workstation, 139
CD/RW MASTERING button, VS-1880 workstation, 138
CD/RW writer, VS-1824 workstation, 139
CDR markers, 237
CDR mode option, VS-1880 workstation, 139
CDR recording mode, 23
CDs
  backing up songs to, 118–120
  burning songs to, 114–118
  recovering songs from, 120–121
channel faders, VS-2480 workstation, 214–215
channel strips
  components of, 19
  Expander effect, 225
  phantom power, 223
  Phase switch, 223
  Phrase Pad mode, 224
  selections, 221–222
  track selection and control, 222–224
channels, linked
  panning adjustment, 179–180

  unlinking, 177
  volume level adjustment, 178
chorus
  chorus effects, 32
  marking beginning, 74
CMP (Compressor) effect block, MTK, 112, 205
combining songs, 171–172
COMP/EXP/SHIFT operation, Automix function, 275–276
Composite Object Sound Modeling (COSM), 21
compression
  compressed recording mode, 23–24
  compressing tracks while recording, 146–147
  compression effects
    discussed, 33
    Track Expansion/Compression function, 83
    while recording, 71
  Track Compression/Exchange function, 160
  VS-2480 workstation, 224
Compression/Expansion function, 32
Compressor (CMP) effect block, MTK, 112, 205
connections
  analog, 18
  cursor button, 219
  digital, 18
  mouse, 218–219
  peripheral, 19
  Quick Routing screen, 219
  RBus, 212
  SPDIF, 213
converters, 24 bit AD, 138
copying
  audio, 31
  projects, 233
  Track Copy function, 78–79, 160, 163–165
COSM (Composite Object Sound Modeling), 21
current conditions, VS-880 front panel layout, 44–45
current marker condition, VS-880 front panel layout, 45
current measure and beat, VS-880 front panel layout, 45–46
current scene number, VS-880 front panel layout, 46
current time, VS-880 front panel layout, 47
cursor buttons

connections, 219

project management, 234–235

VS-880 front panel layout, 44

cutting

audio, 31

Track Cut function, 82, 160

D

DAO (Disc-At-Once), 115–116

data sharing, project management, 234

default sample rates, 51

defragmentation, 304

delay effects, 32

deleting

mixer scenes, 188

scenes, 88

dialog boxes

Project List, 231

Scene, 267–268

digital connections, 18

digital inputs

recording from, 71, 148–149

VS-880 and VS-890 series, 40

VS-1680 workstation, 133

VS-2480 workstation, 212–213

digital outputs, VS-880 and VS-890 series, 40

digital transfers, 122–123

DIR Sends, 229

Direct Out assignments, external mixers, 198

Disc-At-Once (DAO), 115–116

disk partitioning, hard disk recorder, 22–23

display screen, mixing console, 20

display section, VS-880 front panel layout,
44–48

drive busy message, 303

Drive Check utility, 124

drum tracks

bouncing tracks, 107

recording, 155–156

dry recording, 66–67, 244

dual-mono effects, 33

dust covers, 306

dynamic processors, 205–206

E

echo effects, 32

edit condition button, VS-880 workstation series, 43

edit points, setting, 162, 257

Edit Target section, Automix function, 277–278

editing functions

beat, 76

Compression/Expansion, 32

Copy function, 31

Cut function, 31

edit points, setting, 162, 257

effects, 101–102

Erase function, 31

Insert function, 32

location points, setting, 76

measures and grids, 258–259

Micro Edit function, 197

Move function, 31

non-destructive editing, 31, 252–257

IN and OUT points, 31

phrase editing, 159–160, 165–166, 249–250

Phrase Trim functions, 253–257

pointer-based playback, 252–257

FROM and TO points, 31

preview options, 76–77, 257

regions, beginning and end points, 249

regions, moving, 251–252

Scrub function, 77

Song Arrange function, 167–169

Song Combine function, 171–172

Song Optimize function, 84, 302

Song Split function, 169–170

START and END points, 31

starting and ending points, 31

Take Manager, 251

Track Compression/Expansion function, 160

Track Copy function, 78–79, 160, 163–165

Track Cut function, 82, 160

TRACK Edit Condition options, 75

Track Editing feature, 161

track editing *versus* phrase editing, 159–160

Track Erase function, 82, 160, 162–163

Track Exchange function, 80, 160

Track Expansion/Compression, 83
Track Import function, 160
Track Insert function, 81–82, 160
Track Move function, 80, 160
Track Name function, 160
undo/redo operations, 83–84
V-Tracks, selecting to edit, 77–78
.WAV view, 257–258
effect cards, VS-1680 workstation, 133–134
effects
  adding to tracks, 147–148
  algorithms and effect blocks, 32
  amplifier simulator, 33
  chorus, 32
  compression, 33
  delay, 32
  dual-mono, 33
  echo, 32
  EQ, 32–33, 186–187
  external, bouncing tracks with, 105–106
  guidelines for, 186
  insert, 33–34, 183–184
    bouncing tracks with, 102–103
    Insert-L, 33–34
    Insert-R, 33–34
    Insert-S, 34
    un-inserting, 305
  internal
    bouncing effects using, 101–105
    mastering songs, 111
  loop, 183, 218
  microphone, 33
  printed, 264
  reverb, 32
  selecting and editing, 101–102
  send/return, 32–33, 103–105
  simulators, 33
  stereo effects processor, 20–22
  user effects, 185
Effects bus, 181
Effects Return Mixer mode, 27–28
Enhancer (ENH) effect block, MTK, 112, 205
EQ (equalization), 32
  2-band EQ, 52
  3-band EQ, 52

4-Band, 229
EQ effect block, MTK, 112
EQ effects, 186–187
EQ Switch track parameter, 87
Four-Band, 204
microphone effects, 33
erasing
  audio, 31
  Track Erase function, 82, 160, 162–163
Expander (EXP) effect block, MTK, 112, 205, 225
expansion, Track Expansion/Compression function, 83
external effects, bouncing tracks with, 105–106
external mixers, 198
external preamps, 144
external sources, mixing to, 113
EZ routing, 28, 69–70

F
FADER/PAN display, VS-880 series front panel layout, 48
faders
  grouped, 181
  stereo linked faders, 137
  VS-1824 workstation, 139
filters
  BEF (Band Eliminate Filter), 228
  BPF (Band Pass Filter), 228
  HPF (High Pass Filter), 227
  LPF (Low Pass Filter), 228
flashing play button, VS-880 front panel layout, 46
footswitch punch-in recording, 63
forums and support, 306–307
Four-Band EQ tone-shaping processor, 204
fragmented files, 304
FROM and TO points, editing functions, 31
front panel layout, VS-880 workstation series
  bar display, 48
  current conditions, 44–45
  current marker condition, 45
  current measure and beat, 45–46
  current scene number, 46
  current time, 47
  cursor buttons, 44

display section, 44–48

edit condition buttons, 43

FADER/PAN display, 48

flashing play button, 46

locator buttons, 43

mixer section, 42

overview, 41

parameter buttons, 44

PLAY button, 42

PLAY LIST display, 48

POST LEVEL display, 48

PRE LEVEL display, 48

preview buttons, 43

recorder section, 42–44

remaining recording time, 46

SHIFT button, 42

sync mode, 46

transport controls, 43

FX RTN channels, 215

G

Gradation, Automix functions, 35, 94, 195–197, 273–274

gradual tempo changes, 290–292

grids, editing functions, 258–259

grouped faders, 181

H

hard disk recorder

disk partitioning, 22–23

recording modes, 23–24

recording time, 23

sample rates, 25

hard drives

initialization, 303

re-initializing, 49

Hi-Z input, 212

High Pass Filter (HPF), 227

Home screen view, viewing projects, 238–241

I

importing, Track Import function, 160

IN and OUT points, editing functions, 31

IN (Input) effect block, MTK, 112

initialization, hard drives, 303

input channels, VS-2480 workstation, 215

Input (IN) effect block, MTK, 112

input levels, recording techniques, 62

Input Mixer mode

discussed, 26–27

routing techniques, 53–54

VS-1680 workstation, 130

input monitoring, 243–244

inputs

analog, 39

VS-1680 workstation, 133

VS-2480 workstation, 211–212

digital, 40

recording from, 71, 148–149

VS-1680 workstation, 133

VS-2480 workstation, 212–213

Hi-Z, 212

muting, 305

insert effects, 33–34, 183–184

bouncing tracks with, 102–103

Insert-L, 33–34

Insert-R, 33–34

Insert-S, 34

Track Insert function, 81–82

un-inserting, 305

inserting

blank space, 32

Track Insert function, 160

internal effects

bouncing tracks using, 101–105

mastering songs, 111

J

jogwheel, 143

K

keyboard sequencers, 157

KFey options, VS-2480 workstation, 218

L

L1V recording mode, 24

Limiter (LMT) effect block, MTK, 112, 206

linear recording mode, 23

linked channels
    panning adjustment, 179–180
    unlinking, 177
    volume level adjustment, 178
linked faders, stereo, 137
linked tracks, 265–267
LMT (Limiter) effect block, MTK, 112, 206
locator buttons, VS-880 front panel layout, 43
locators
    auto punch-in recording, 63
    location points, setting, 76
    naming, 237
    project management, 236–237
    recalling, 73
    setting, 73
    switching between, 73
    undefining, 236
    uses for, 34
    verses and choruses, marking beginning, 74
    VS-1680 workstation, 134–135
loop effects, 183, 218
loop playback, auto punch recording with, 64
loops, seamless, 163–165
Low Pass Filter (LPF), 228
LV2 recording mode, 24

M

M16 recording mode, 24
M24 recording mode, 23
manual punch recording
    discussed, 63
    with footswitch, 151–152
    by hand, 150
markers, 34–35
    auto punch-in recording, 64
    CDR, 237
    clearing, 75
    dropping, 237
    navigating to previous or next, 75
    placing new before existing, 74–75
    project management, 237
    removing, 237
    settings, 74
    VS-1680 workstation, 134–135

Master Block settings
    recording basics, 53
    VS-1680 workstation, 131–133
Master Clock settings, 149, 213
master tracks
    mixing down to, 202–203
    playing back, 203
mastering
    mastering room, VS-1680 workstation, 136–137
    Mastering Room feature, 27, 202
    Mastering Tool Kit (MTK), 112–113
        effects processors, 204
        patches, 208–209
        presets, 208–209
        submixes via, 263–264
        using internal effects, 111
measures, editing functions, 258–259
merging songs, 49–50
metronome choices, 285–288
Micro Edit function, 197, 278–280
microphone connections, VS-880 and VS-890
    series, 39
MIDI
    connections, VS-880 and VS-890 series, 41
    drum tracks, recording, 155–156
    MIDI OUT operation, 295
    MIDI THRU operation, 295
    recording with, 154–156
    SysEx. (System Exclusive), 296
MIDI Machine Code (MMC), 214, 296
Mix bus, 181
MIX button, 230
MIX (Mixer) effect block, MTK, 112
MIX track parameter, 87
mixer scenes
    deleting, 188
    recalling, 188
    saving, 188
    updating, 188–189
mixer section, VS-880 series front panel layout, 42
mixing
    Automix function, 35
        best use of, 95–96
        discussed, 89

enabling, 91

gradation, 94

Realtime Automix records, 91–92

scenes with, 92

Snapshot Automix, 93–94

VS-880/890 compatibility, 90

Effects Return Mixer mode, 27–28

external mixers, adding, 198

to external sources, 113–114

initialization, 199

Input Mixer mode, 26–27

mixer modes, toggling between, 25, 49

mixing console layout, 19–20

Track Mixer mode, 27

MMC (MIDI Machine Code), 214, 296

Monitor knob, 305

monitoring input, 243–244

mono tracks, bouncing, 96–97

mouse connections, 218–219

moving

audio, 31

regions, 251–252

Track Move function, 80, 160

MT1 recording mode, 24

MT2 recording mode, 24

MTK (Mastering Tool Kit), 112–113

effects processors, 204

patches, 208–209

presets, 208–209

MTP (Multi-Track Pro), 128

muting

inputs, 305

MUTE button, 230

Mute mode, 125

N

naming

locators, 237

songs, 52

tracks, 160, 247–248

user effects, 185

noises, buzzing, 225

non-destructive editing, 31, 252–257

O

Ofs Bal track parameter, 87

Ofs Level track parameter, 87

online forums and support, 306–307

operating systems

upgrades, 121–122

VS-880/890 series, 121

optimization, Song Optimize function, 84, 302

OUT (Output) effect block, MTK, 113

outputs

analog, 39

digital, 40

TRS, 212

overdubbing tracks, 62–63

P

panning

of linked channels, adjusting, 179–180

Pan track parameter, 87

parameters

parameter buttons, VS-880 front panel layout, 44

tracks, 87–88

partitioning

hard disk recorder, 22–23

hard drives, re-initializing, 49

patch bay section, VS-2480 workstation, 215–216

patches, MTK, 208–209

patterns, Automix function, 278

PCs, shutting down, 303–304

peak indicator lights, recording techniques, 62

peripheral connections, 19

phantom power

channel strips, 223

VS-1680 workstation, 134

VS-2480 workstation, 216

Phase settings, 180–181

Phase switch, channel strips, 223

Phase track parameter, 87

phrase editing, 249–250

phrase selection, 165–166

track editing *versus,* 159–160

Phrase Pad mode, 224

INDEX }

Phrase Trim functions, 253–257
pin assignment, 180
pitch, VariPitch function, 189
PLAY button, VS-880 front panel layout, 42
PLAY LIST display, VS-880 series front panel
    layout, 48
playback
    adding effects to tracks during, 147–148
    loop playback, auto punch-in recording with, 64
    master tracks, 203
    pointer-based, 252–257
pointer-based playback, 252–257
POST LEVEL display, VS-880 front panel layout,
    48
PRE LEVEL display, VS-880 front panel layout, 48
PRE/POST sends, 229
preamps, vocal track recordings, 144
presets, MTK, 208–209
preview buttons, VS-880 front panel layout, 43
Preview controls, 257
preview options, track editing functions, 76–77
printed effects, 264
processors
    dynamic, 205–206
    tone-shaping, 204–205
Project List dialog box, 231
projects
    copying and backing up, 233–234
    cursor buttons, 234–235
    data sharing, 234
    locators, 236–237
    markers, 237
    moving forward/backward, 236
    moving to edge of phrase, 236
    naming, 232
    new project creation, 232
    parameters, copying, 232
    Project List dialog box, 231
    project type information, 232
    saving and protecting, 233, 302
    Time/Value dial, 234–235
    viewing
      Home screen view, 238–241
      mixer views, 241
      zooming options, 240

punch-in recording, 63–64, 150–153
punch-out recording, 150–153

Q
Quick Routing screen, 219, 262–263

R
R-DAC compression technique, 24
RBus connectors, 212
Realtime Automix records, 91–92, 192–193
recalling
    locators, 73
    mixer scenes, 188
Record mode, Automix function, 271
Record monitor selection, 261
recorder section, VS-880 front panel layout, 42–44
recording
    arming tracks, 62
    Auto Punch, 152–153
    backup vocal tracks, 67
    compressing tracks while, 146–147
    compression effect while, 71
    from digital inputs, 71, 148–149
    drum tracks, 155–156
    dry, 66–67, 244
    input levels, setting, 62
    levels, setting, 142–144
    Master Block settings, 53
    with MIDI, 154–156
    multiple takes, V-Tracks, 30
    naming songs, 51
    new song creation, 51
    overdubbing, 62–63
    peak indicator lights, 62
    punch-in, 63–64, 150–153
    punch-out, 150–153
    recording modes
      hard disk recorder, 23–24
      VS-1680 workstation, 128–129
    recording time, hard disk recorder, 23
    routing
      clearing all, 58
      concept of, 54
      EZ, 69–70

Input Mixer techniques, 53–54
routing display, 54–56
setup techniques, 57–58
stereo tracks, 58–61
with sequencers, 156–157
song template options, 69, 157–158
STATUS button indicators, 70
track sheets, 65
tracks, setting up, 142
V-Tracks, 65–66
vocal tracks, 144–145
wet, 68
Recording bus, 181
redo operation, 301–302
track editing functions, 83–84
VS-1680 workstation, 135–136
regions
beginning and end points, 249
moving, 251–252
remaining recording time, VS-880 front panel layout,
46
reverb effects, 32
rhythm tracks, bouncing tracks, 107–108
Roland US Web site, 307
routing
clearing all, 58
concept of, 54
creating, 97
EZ, 28, 69–70
Input Mixer techniques, 53–54
routing display, 54–56
setup techniques, 57–58
source signals, 28
stereo tracks, 58–61
submixes via, 262–263

S

sample rates
default, 51
track minutes, 25
saving
mixer scenes, 188
projects, 233, 302
save options, 50

user effects, 185
scenes
accessing, 88
Automix function and, 92
date and time of, 268
deleting, 88
mixer scenes
deleting, 188
recalling, 188
saving, 188
updating, 188–189
Scene Active Channel Select screen, 268
Scene dialog box, 267–268
uses for, 34, 89
Scrub function, track editing functions, 77
SCSI CD burner limitations, 114–115
SCSI ports, VS-880 and VS-890 series, 40–41
SCSI transfers, 123–124
seamless loops, 163–165
send/return effects
bouncing tracks with, 103–105
chorus, 32
delay, 32
echo, 32
Effects Return Mixer mode, 27–28
reverb, 32
sequencers
keyboard, 157
recording with, 156–157
software computer, 156
stand-alone hardware, 156
syncing, 157
sharing projects, 234
SHIFT button, VS-880 front panel layout, 42
shrinking audio, 32
shutting down PCs, 303–304
signal buses, 181–182
signal processing changes, 27
simulator effects, 33
sites, online forums and support, 306
Snapshot Automix function, 35, 93–94, 193–195,
271–272
Soft Clip processor, 206
software computer sequencers, 156

software upgrades
    VS-880 workstation, 2–3
    VS-880EX workstation, 5
    VS-890 workstation, 9
    VS-1680 workstation, 4
    VS-1824CD workstation, 11
    VS-1880 workstation, 7
    VS-2000CD workstation, 15
    VS-2400CD workstation, 13
    VS-2480 workstation, 10
    VS-2480CD workstation, 11–12
    VS-2480DVD workstation, 15
    VSR-880 workstation, 6
SOLO button, 125, 230
Song Arrange function, 167–169
Song Optimize function, 84
song templates, recording techniques, 69, 157–158
songs
    backing up to CDs, 118–120
    burning
        to CDs, 114–118
        DAO (Disc-At-Once) option, 115–116
        SCSI CD burner limitations, 114–115
        TAO (Track-At-Once) option, 115
    creating new, 51, 141–142
    default sample rates, 51
    editing
        Song Arrange function, 167–169
        Song Combine function, 171–172
        Song Split function, 169–170
    mastering
        Mastering Tool Kit (MTK), 112–113
        using internal effects, 111
    merging, 49–50
    naming, 52
    recovering from CDs, 120–121
    Song Optimize function, 302
    splitting, 49–50
source signals, routing capabilities, 28
SPDIF connectors, 213
splitting songs, 49–50, 169–170
stand-alone hardware sequencers, 156
starting and ending points, editing functions, 31
STATUS button indicators, recording techniques, 69
stereo effects processor, 20–22

stereo linked faders, 137
stereo tracks
    bouncing, 96–97
    routing, 58–61
stretching audio, 32
submixes
    on AUX buses, 262
    discussed, 261
    via mastering, 263–264
    via routing, 262–263
support, 306–307
synchronization
    multiple workstations, 124
    recording from external sources, 293–294
    sequencers, 157
    sync mode, VS-880 workstation front panel
        layout, 46
    Sync Parameter screen, 292–293
    time points, creating sync tracks from, 294–295
SysEx. (System Exclusive), 296

T

Take Manager function, 251
TAO (Track-At-Once), 115
tap points, 295
tempo
    tempo changes, gradual, 290–292
    Tempo map options, 288–292
tilting workstations, 305
time indicator, VS-1680 workstation, 127
time points, creating sync tracks from, 294–295
time-shrinking audio, 32
time-stretching audio, 32
Time/Value dial
    discussed, 219
    mixing console, 20
    project management, 234–235
toggling, between mixer modes, 49
tone-shaping processors, 204–205
Tone Type selections, metronome, 286
Track-At-Once (TAO), 115
track channels, VS-2480 workstation, 215
Track Copy function, 78–79, 160, 163–165
Track Cut function, 160

Track Erase function, 82, 160, 162–163
Track Exchange function, 30, 80, 160
Track Expansion/Compression function, 83
Track Insert function, 160
track minutes, sample rates, 25
Track Mixer mode, 27, 130–131
Track Move function, 80, 160
track sheets, recording techniques, 65
Track Talk Recording Community, 307
tracking
    dry recording, 244
    input monitoring, 243–244
    tracks, naming, 247–248
tracks
    arming, 62
    bouncing, 27, 153–154
      drum tracks, 107
      with external effects, 105–106
      with Insert effects, 102–103
      mono and stereo bouncing, 96–97
      performing, 99–101
      rhythm tracks, 107–108
      routings, creating, 97
      send/return effects, 103–105
      Track Mixer mode, 27
      using internal effects, 101–105
    compressing, while recording, 146–147
    editing functions
      beat, 76
      edit points, setting, 162, 257
      location points, setting, 76
      measures and grids, 258–259
      non-destructive editing, 252–257
      phrase editing, 165–166, 249–250
      Phrase Trim function, 253–257
      pointer-based playback, 252–257
      Preview controls, 257
      preview options, 76–77
      regions, 249, 251–252
      Scrub function, 77
      Song Optimize function, 84
      Take Manager function, 251
      Track Compression/Expansion function, 160
      Track Copy function, 78–79, 160, 163–165
      Track Cut function, 82, 160

TRACK Edit Condition options, 75
Track Editing feature, 161
track editing *versus* phrase editing, 159–160
Track Erase function, 82, 160, 162–163
Track Exchange function, 80, 160
Track Expansion/Compression, 83
Track Import function, 160
Track Insert function, 81–82, 160
Track Move function, 80, 160
Track Name function, 160
undo/redo operations, 83–84
V-Tracks, selecting to edit, 77–78
.WAV view, 257–258
    effects, adding, 147–148
    linked, 265–267
    master
      mixing down to, 202–203
      playing back, 203
    naming, 247–248
    overdubbing, 62–63
    parameters, 87–88
    transferring individual, 50
    V-Tracks, 29–30
      recording techniques, 65–66
      selecting to edit, 77–78
    vocal, recording, 144–145
transfers
    analog, 122–123
    digital, 122–123
    SCSI, 123–124
transport control buttons, 302–303
    button types, 19
    VS-880 front panel layout, 43
trimming, Phrase Trim functions, 253–257
TRS output, 212

U

undo/redo operations, 301–302
    track editing functions, 83–84
    VS-1680 workstation, 135–136
updating mixer scenes, 188–189
upgrades
    operating systems, 121–122
    VS-880 workstation, 2–3

VS-880EX workstation, 5
VS-890 workstation, 9
VS-1680 workstation, 4
VS-1824 workstation, 139–140
VS-1824CD workstation, 11
VS-1880 workstation, 7, 137–139
VS-2000CD workstation, 15
VS-2400CD workstation, 13
VS-2480 workstation, 10
VS-2480CD workstation, 11–12
VS-2480DVD workstation, 15
VSR-880 workstation, 6
user effects, 185

V

V-Tracks (virtual tracks), 29–30, 148
    recording techniques, 65–66
    selecting to edit, 77–78
V-Xpanded units, 2–3
VariPitch function, 125, 189
verses, marking beginning, 74
viewing projects
    Home screen view, 238–241
    mixer views, 241
    zooming options, 240
Virtual Studio Systems (VSS), 306
vocal tracks, recording, 144–145
volume levels, adjusting, 178
VS-880 workstation
    analog inputs, 39
    analog outputs, 39
    digital inputs, 40
    digital outputs, 40
    front panel layout
      bar display, 48
      current conditions, 44–45
      current marker condition, 45
      current measure and beat, 45, 56
      current scene number, 46
      current time, 47
      cursor buttons, 44
      display section, 44–48
      edit condition buttons, 43
      FADER/PAN display, 48
      flashing play button, 46

      locator buttons, 43
      mixer section, 42
      overview, 41
      parameter buttons, 44
      PLAY button, 42
      PLAY LIST display, 48
      POST LEVEL display, 48
      PRE LEVEL display, 48
      preview buttons, 43
      recorder section, 42–44
      remaining recording time, 46
      SHIFT button, 42
      sync mode, 46
      transport controls, 43
    highlights of, 1
    history of, 1–3
    MIDI connections, 41
    models, 2
    operating systems for, 121
    SCSI ports, 40–41
    series differences, 37–38
    software upgrades, 2–3
    V-Xpanded units, 2–3
VS-880EX workstation
    highlights of, 5
    history of, 4–5
    operating systems for, 121
    software upgrades, 5
VS-890 workstation
    analog inputs, 39
    analog outputs, 39
    digital inputs, 40
    digital outputs, 40
    highlights of, 8–9
    MIDI connections, 41
    operating systems for, 121
    SCSI ports, 40–41
    series differences, 37–38
    software upgrades, 9
VS-1680 workstation
    analog input connections, 133
    bar/measure display, 127
    digital input connections, 133
    effect cards, 133–134
    highlights of, 3–4

Input Mixer, 130
locators, 134–135
markers, 134–135
Master Block, 131–133
mastering room, 136–137
phantom power, 134
recording modes, 128–129
software upgrades, 4
time indicator, 127
Track Mixer, 130–131
undo/redo operations, 135–136
VS-1824 workstation
CD Capture function, 139
CD/RW writer, 139
faders, 139
upgrades, 139–140
VS-1824CD workstation
highlights of, 10
software upgrades, 11
VS-1880 workstation
CD/RW MASTERING button, 138
CDR mode option, 139
highlights of, 7
software upgrades, 7
upgrades, 137–139
VS-2000CD workstation
features of, 299
highlights of, 14
history of, 13–15
onboard effects, 300
software upgrades, 15
VS-2400CD workstation
highlights of, 12–13
software upgrades, 13
VS-2480 workstation
analog inputs, 211–212
AUX MSTR channels, 215
channel faders, 214–215
compression dynamics, 224
digital inputs, 212–213
FKey options, 218
FX RTN channels, 215
highlights of, 10
history of, 9–10
input channels, 215

loop effects, 218
output assignment, 217–218
patch bay section, 215–216
phantom power, 216
software upgrades, 10
track assignment routing, 216–217
track channels, 215
VS-2480CD workstation
highlights of, 11
software upgrades, 11–12
VS-2480DVD workstation
highlights of, 15
software upgrades, 15
VS-Planet Web site, 306
VS workstations
analog connections, 18
digital connections, 18
input/output, 17–19
mixing console layout, 19–20
peripheral connections, 19
synchronizing, 124
tilting, 305
VSR-880 workstation
highlights, 6
operating systems for, 121
software upgrades, 6
VSS (Virtual Studio Systems), 306

W

.WAV view, editing functions, 257–258
Web sites, online forums and support, 306
wet recording, 68
workstations
analog connections, 18
digital connections, 18
input/output, 17–19
mixing console layout, 19–20
peripheral connections, 19
synchronizing, 124
tilting, 305

Z

zooming options, viewing projects, 240